AN ANTHOLOGY
OF REVOLUTION
ARY POETRY

Compiled and Edited by MARCUS GRAHAM

With an Introduction by RALPH CHEYNEY & LUCIA TRENT

First Limited Edition 1929

PRINTED IN THE UNITED STATES
THE ACTIVE PRESS, INC.
NEW YORK, N. Y.

Printing Statement:

Due to the very old age and scarcity of this book, many of the pages may be hard to read due to the blurring of the original text, possible missing pages, missing text and other issues beyond our control.

Because this is such an important and rare work, we believe it is best to reproduce this book regardless of its original condition.

Thank you for your understanding.

Let liars fear, let cowards shrink,
Let traitors turn away,
Whatever we have dared to think
That dare we also say.

JAMES RUSSELL LOWELL

★

We are the Spirit of Those piteous ones,
The Wronged, the Oppressed, the Robbed,
And we bid You open Your warm heart—
Your Light-Lit Soul to Us!

FRANCIS W. L. ADAMS

PREFACE

*W*HEN the thinkers of ancient Greece had thoughts worthy of being imparted to their fellowmen, they carved them on rocks or made written copies on parchment paper. The printed word was as yet an unknown thing to man.

Since those days the world has made eventful strides. One of the first innovations in the new era of the machine age has been the printed word. It rapidly supplanted the old ways of conveying thought.

Nowadays printing presses are kept running almost without a stop. Millions of copies of newspapers, weeklies and monthlies are issued every day in the year. Hundreds of thousands of books make their simultaneous appearance. The printed word is literally flooding, or rather overflooding, the world!

An array of numberless little minds are constantly at work supplying "copy" to the ever-grinding presses; and their "activity" consists in transmitting in an automatic, clock-like manner biased as well as invented news and stories of every description. The skilfulness with which this systematized dulling and poisoning of the people's minds is being perpetrated has already aroused many thinkers to a realization of the menace that the printed word has brought with it. The danger lies not alone in the fact that it has long since lost that respected hearing that was once the proud joy of the ancient thinkers. The far more serious menace is its having been turned into a weapon for covering every kind of wrongdoing and injustice that man inflicts upon man.

What is even worse, is that the fraudulent employment of the printed word has been carried into every form of literature. Poetry, being one of the most expressive forms of man's emotions, was bound to suffer most.

A glimpse at the numerous poetry anthologies that are being heaped upon the book markets will reveal the glaring fact that none of these relates to the social question of our times. Every sort of subject imaginable is being sung about but the one of social justice. True, here and there can be found a poem chanting of freedom. But is this Freedom being sung about, a word with a genuine, sincere meaning? Is it applicable to the greater part of the human race? Let the inquirer turn to the pages of history. They will give the answer. The creators of these vain-meaning poems stand revealed—as they were justly termed by the very ones who employed them—as "court-jesters." For a pot of gold they turned into clown-like, docile servants of whatever monarchical or republican régime was in power.

There were and are, however, in the world's literature, other poets also. The great poets of humanity, who refused to barter their minds and souls in praise of injustice, or of any earthly or imaginary power, the existence of which was commonly assumed. For the first time in the history of the English language the work of these poets has been compiled in one volume.

These justice-loving poets of the past and present century (and in a few instances quite a few centuries back) are voicing eloquently man's innermost sorrows and pains. They are pouring condemnation upon the causes that have brought suffering and want to human beings. They go even farther, daring to question the total worth of the past and present centuries of "civilization" and "progress."

Poets who represent twenty countries and sixteen languages, encircling almost the entire globe, have woven out, thread by thread, the great prophetic dream of the ages, the dream of a new DAWN that will liberate man from all the shackles that keep him enthralled. It is this dream that will be found re-echoing through every poem of this anthology.

Two-score years have already elapsed since "Songs of Freedom," a collection of original English poems compiled and edited by Henry S. Salt, appeared in England. It is the only collection that comes close to being an anthology of the nature of the present volume. "The Cry for Justice" edited by Upton Sinclair contains some revolutionary poems. As a whole, though, it is more an anthology of prose than of poetry. That this Anthology of Revolutionary Poetry should

6

prove to fill a long-felt want in the struggle for emancipation is the hope of the compiler. It certainly should compare favorably with any single book of prose dealing with the social phase of life.

As to the question whether this initial attempt is complete, I hasten to state that it is not. Despite the closest search in newspapers, magazines and books that I thought would yield something of value to the Anthology, it is inevitable that some material has escaped notice. A perusal of the list of publications and the acknowledgments, the sources from which the material for the Anthology has been gathered, will show that this was not done intentionally. For any suggestion of additional material and data for future editions, the compiler will be most grateful.

There are a few poems that require an explanation, more for the future student of the labor movement than for those of today. Among them are the poems dedicated to the memory of the five Chicago Anarchists: Engels, Fischer, Lingg, Parsons and Spies. These were the first sacrificial offerings of the labor movement in its struggle for the eight-hour day in America. Their judicial murder by the state of Illinois on November 11, 1887, has long since been proved to be such by the most impartial historians.

Forty years later history repeats itself, with a more abominable brutality. In the annals of man's struggles there is scarcely anything to compare with those tragic days that preceded the black night of August 22, 1927, in the Charlestown prison of Massachusetts. From one end of the globe to the other every human being who could think or feel petitioned, begged and implored its own self-created monster—the State —to desist from perpetrating the "legal" assassination of two innocent men for the "crime" of being Anarchists. But the beast in sheep's hide, the Government, remained defiant and adamant to the cry of humanity, whose "servant" it pretends to be. Armed with machine guns and every other conceivable implement of destruction at its command, it carried out the cowardly murder of Nicola Sacco and Bartolomeo Vanzetti.

It is to the memory of these two courageous newly added victims in the struggle for liberty, that Ralph Cheyney and Lucia Trent have placed a great and fitting monument: "America Arraigned"—a protesting outcry from sixty of America's best-known rebel-spirited poets. It is with a sad but nevertheless proud feeling that I include a few poems dedicated to these two victims.

Another group of poems is related to the still prevalent brutality now devastating civilization: the bloody carnage of *war*. It is ever the down-trodden who bear the brunt of every war that is foisted upon the people.

Some poems bear on prisons—the shameful hell-holes that the despoilers of mankind have so cunningly contrived. What an incredible and yet most tragic jest! Having the masses themselves build the very prisons into which they alone will repeatedly be thrown whenever they dare to rebel against their despoilers!

Other poems portray the deception carried on for ages by self-appointed "representatives" of an imaginary "almighty" up in the skies.

Welcome for inclusion were poems dealing with the ever-constant attempts of the oppressed to revolt—via the General Strike.

Most welcome also were those poems expressing the poet's response to the greatest upheaval since the French Revolution —the Revolution in Russia.

Man has yet to learn to be as just to the defenseless animal as he desires his fellow-man to be just to him. The day will surely dawn when man shall return to the wise and healthy ways of ancient times, replacing his present disease-causing carnivorous diets by nature's unadulterated foods. Hence the inclusion of the pro-vegetarian poem: "Homo Rapiens."

Between the lines of the poems of irony and satire will be found a deeply felt serious protest against the evils that tend to uphold everything unjust.

In the compilation and revisions made, the chief aim has been to include every poem that was thought to contribute something towards the soul-structure of the work as a whole. No poem was too revolutionary, if it only possessed poetic value as well. Only one exception was made, relative the songs of the various revolutionary movements throughout the

8

world. These were included for historical rather than for literary merit.

Many poems by living authors appear in a revised form, these revisions having been done by the authors or translators themselves.

A few poems are original, making here their first appearance in print or translation form. These are "Third Degree," by Marcus Graham; "Rhapsody," by Nicholas Moskowitz; "Vision," by V. Eichenbaum; "Workers," by Nahum Yood; and "The Anarchist March," Anonymous.

As regards the various languages represented by translations, it is only regrettable that, compared with the original English poems, there are only a meager number available as yet. It is in this great loss to literature (and even more so as a leading source of political and economic misunderstandings utilized to this end by the rulers of the world) that the need and justification for one universal language becomes fully apparent. Man thinks, acts, struggles, suffers, hopes and dreams alike the world over.

Not all the historical data about authors, the forerunners in particular, could be obtained. As to those poems lacking even an initial, the publication from which the poem was taken is named. There is also a possibility that some of the poems among the Forerunners are by authors still alive, but of whom no data were available. The second part is exclusively a section representing living poets. By dividing the original group of English poems into two parts, instead of giving them, as also others, in chronological order, I had in mind the inception of the revolutionary movement and its development to date. For each poet is not only a spokesman of the spirit of his day but the prophet of its dreams and aims as well. It should though be borne in mind that all deceased modern authors are also placed among the forerunners.

Society destroys the bodies and souls of men whenever attempts at expressing their true reactions towards life are made. No stronger illustration can be given than by citing two occurrences during this century. The first is that of Basil Dahl (Joseph Bovshover). Unable to bear the strain of the economic burdens, he turned insane, wasting the greater part of his youthful life in an asylum, until death finally brought an end to his long sufferings. The second one is that of Francis W. L. Adams, who was forced by the cruelties of life, which he could no longer endure, to commit suicide just after reaching three-score years! Let their poems speak of what the world lost in their premature and unnatural death. And these are but two instances that have become known.

Many of the poets, forerunners and moderns as well, have been hounded, tortured, imprisoned and persecuted by the various Governments of the world. A number of poems have been written in jails. One of the writers of the introduction to this book, Ralph Cheyney, has been in jail, as has also been the compiler of this anthology. Very likely it is the only poetry anthology ever published that dares to give with pride rather than shame such a "pedigree" of its contributors and editor.

No little surprise will be evoked by the revelation that many men famous in other branches of literature have also wielded their pens in the poetic form of expression.

Every human being is a world unto himself. This explains why one finds such a variance of tastes, dislikes and reactions towards everything one faces in life, including, of course, literature. For the very same reasons one could hardly find two compilers choosing identical selections for any anthology of poetry.

Some of the poems will appear as too gloomy and embittered. Let the reader then bear in mind what Ernest Crosby so truthfully expressed:

> It is not I that have written;
>   It is not I that have sung.
> I'm the chord that Another has smitten,
>   The chime that Another has rung.
>
> I give but the things that I am given;
>   I show but the things that I see;
> I draw, but my pencil is driven
>   By a Force that is master of me.

Yet above the poets' re-echoing sounds of the masses' woes the spirit of optimism predominates. Poets singing of misery, yet never forgetting to raise the dream of beauty. Singing of bitter despair, but not forgetting to paint also the coming day of Liberation. Fiercely denouncing slavery, and at the same time calling to Rebellion. Heart throbs that express feelings of kindred love and sympathy not only towards their fellow-sufferers but even to those who are the causers of all the man-created misery. Dreamers of a society that is to come, while being surrounded and dwelling in the midst of so much misery and want. Dreaming while at work, dreaming while rebelling, dreaming while in jail, dreaming before being executed, dreaming in defeat, dreaming—forever dreaming!

Most encouraging of all is the spirit prevailing uppermost in the very outcry against the new Frankenstein creation of the present: the machine—monster that is annihilating bit by bit everything that is human within man. It is the spirit giving expression to man's longing to return to the bosom of mother-nature, whereon earth's children may weave dreams and attempt to carry them through; where life can cease to be a drudgery of suffering, pain and want; where life may once again become natural, human and beautiful; where life shall at last begin to signify what the word actually implies —*Life*.

It is with deep regret that I am parting with what has become to me the most interesting labor I have ever undertaken. Scanning every page of so many newspapers, periodicals and books was indeed a strenuous task. Recompense was ever found, though, in the discovery of some worthy poem that in all probability might have remained a treasure lost to future generations. The only consolation at parting is the knowledge of having made accessible this collection to all who are willing to lend a hearing to the trumpeting chords of hope and joy that the pages of this Anthology hold forth for the man that is to be—the *Free Man* in a *Free Society*.

The preface would be incomplete were I to forget to mention the part played by comrades and personal friends who helped to bring this anthology to completion.

The members of the Publication Committee, whose names

11

follow here, have been a great aid in obtaining whatever moral support has been given by the press and private individuals towards the appearance of the anthology. These are:

WITTER BYNNER	ANGELA MORGAN
RALPH CHAPLIN	NICHOLAS MOSKOWITZ
RALPH CHEYNEY	BENJAMIN MUSSER
STANTON A. COBLENTZ	NORMAN MACLEOD
COUNTEE CULLEN	GRACE FALLOW NORTON
JOSEPH DEAN	WILLIAM C. OWEN
JAMES DICK	HENRY REICH, JR.
MARGARETTE BALL DICKSON	LOLA RIDGE
MIRIAM ALLEN DE FORD	E. MERRILL ROOT
JOSEPH FREEMAN	MARY SIEGRIST
LOUIS GINSBERG	ROSE PASTOR STOKES
COVINGTON HALL	LUCIA TRENT
ERNEST HARTSOCK	ROBERT WHITAKER
HIPPOLYTE HAVEL	ROBERT WOLF
ALFRED KREYMBORG	ADOLF WOLFF
LOUISE B. LAIDLAW	C. ERSKINE SCOTT WOOD
ISOBEL LUKE	CLEMENT WOOD
JEANNETTE MARKS	GREMIN ZORN

Of the individuals, first and foremost are Ralph Cheyney and Lucia Trent—two poets ever ready to lend their energetic spirits to any righteous cause. Their reading of the manuscript and proofs, their advice and encouragement, have been a constant source of inspiration in the preparation of the work.

Benjamin Musser, owner and co-editor with Ralph Cheyney and Lucia Trent of "Contemporary Verse," was not only the first to lend the aid of a poetry *magazine* towards making known the publication of the anthology, but has aided financially as well. Norman Macleod, editor of "Palo Verde"; Ernest Hartsock, editor of "Bozart"; Clara Catherine Prince, editor of "The American Poetry Magazine"; C. B. McAllister, editor of "The Lantern"; Carl Haessler, editor of "The Federated Press"; Hippolyte Havel, editor of "The Road to Freedom"; Sh. Niger, literary editor of "The Day," have all helped splendidly.

The "Monitor" of Newark, "Oklahoma Leader," "The New Leader," "The New Masses," "The Daily Worker," and many other poetry and radical publications here and abroad —too numerous to mention—each and all have given most magnificent aid without any remuneration.

Henry Reich, Jr., chairman of the Publication Committee, and Nicholas Moskowitz, treasurer, have aided in reading of proofs and many other ways. Mr. James F. Morton and Mr. Joseph T. Shipley have aided by reading the page proofs. William Rose Benèt, Alice Stone Blackwell, Martin Feinstein, Louise B. Laidlaw, Isobel Luke, Percy MacKaye, Jeannette Marks, Wade Oliver and A. D. Ficke have given moral and financial aid. Last but not least I express appreciation to William C. Owen and Max Spiegel. The former, although living in England, has aided immensely, offering his long years of experience as an editor and proofreader by going through all the proofs. The latter is responsible for the advice and aid given in making the Anthology possess whatever merits of typography and format one may find in it.

I am also particularly indebted to the publishing firms of Henry Holt & Co. and Harcourt, Brace & Co., who were generous enough to grant me permission to reprint any poems of Carl Sandburg, the first from "Chicago Poems," and the second, from "Smoke and Steel."

To each and all of the individuals and publications I have mentioned I express my deepest appreciation. Their aid and co-operation will always remain to me a treasure of delightful memory.

The difficulties entailed in making possible the appearance of the Anthology were not in the financial burden only; that I, a worker, had (and shall have for a long time) to bear. Obtaining permission for the inclusion of copyrighted poems threatened at first to prove an almost hopeless task. After much persuasion, I succeeded in obtaining permission from most of the publishers, but that is to apply only to this first limited edition. For all future editions a fee will have to be paid for the copyrighted poems. It was also at the request of the publishers, who wished to have their copyrights protected, that I had to copyright the Anthology. Publications are quite welcome, however, to reprint any poems that are not copyrighted, giving credit to the Anthology.

As a final word I shall add: The inspiration that led me to embark upon the venturesome plan of making this dream of the anthology come true I owe to the ideal that has aided me to gain whatever understanding of life my mind now embraces. This ideal, most misunderstood and misrepresented, most distorted and maligned of all the ideals laid bare before humanity—the ideal that signalizes man's complete liberation from every form of economic, political, physical and spiritual bondage—Anarchism. It is to this Ideal that I dedicate An Anthology of Revolutionary Poetry.

MARCUS GRAHAM.
(Sh. Marcus)

New York, 1929.

ACKNOWLEDGMENTS

The following poems are reprinted by special arrangement with and permission granted by the publishers who hold the full copyright to them. Most sincere thanks are hereby expressed to all the publishers, editors, and authors. Without their aid this first limited edition would have been an impossibility.

THE AMERICAN FEDERATIONIST:
"Ninety-Nine in the Shade," by Ernest Crosby.

AMERICAN POETRY MAGAZINE:
"Freedom," by Isobel Luke.

RICHARD G. BADGER:
"In the Factory," from *Songs of Labor and Other Poems* of Morris Rosenfeld, translated by Rose Pastor Stokes.

BEHRMAN'S JEWISH BOOKSHOP:
"Revel, Revel, Angry Tempests," of Abraham Raisen; "The Prophet," of Yeoash, from *Modern Jewish Poetry*, edited by P. M. Raskin.

JETHRO BITHELL:
"The Song of the Forges," of Ivan Gilkin; "Burning Glass," of Maurice Maeterlinck; "The Butcher's Stall," of Émile Verhaeren; "Blacksmith Pain," of Otto Julius Bierbaum, translated by Jethro Bithell.

THE BOOKMAN:
"Sentimentality," by Maxwell Bodenheim.

BOZART:
"Portrait of a Politician," by Robert Cary.

BRENTANO'S:
"I Sing the Battle," from *The Cry of Youth*, by Harry Kemp.

JONATHAN CAPE, LTD. (England):
"Lion and Gnat," from *Fables of Ivan Krylov*, translated and edited by Bernard Pares.

UNIVERSITY OF CHICAGO PRESS:
"Poverty," from *The Panchatantra*, translated by Arthur W. Ryder.

W. B. CONKEY CO.:
"The Disappointed," from *Picked Poems*, by Ella Wheeler Wilcox.

CONTEMPORARY VERSE:
Poems by Maxwell Anderson, Helene Claiborne, Rex G. Fuller, Ernest Hartsock, Josephine Johnson, Percy MacKaye, Lucia Trent and Blanche Shoemaker Wagstaff.

COWARD-McCANN:
"Advertisement," from *Less Lonely*, by Alfred Kreymborg.

DEAN & CO.:
"Justice Is Dead," by Harold D. Carew; "Red Flag," by Ralph Cheyney; "Prayer in Massachusetts," by Arthur Davison Ficke, from *America Arraigned*, edited by Ralph Cheyney and Lucia Trent; "The Queen's Coronation Robe," from *Poetic Pennings*, edited by Joseph Dean.

J. M. DENT & SONS, LTD. (London):
"Ye Songs of Mine," of N. A. Nekrassov, from *Songs of Ukrainia* and *Ruthenian Poems*, by F. Randall Livesay.

THE DIAL:
"The Hollow Men," by T. S. Eliot.

DOUBLEDAY, DORAN & CO.:
"Roofs" and "The Apartment Houses," from *Poems, Essays and Letters*, of Joyce Kilmer, edited by R. C. Holiday George; "Unrest," from *The Awakening and Other Poems*, by Don Marquis.

LAURENCE J. GOMME:
"The Rebel," from *Verses*, by Hilaire Belloc.

FREE VERSE:
"I Am," by Albert Edward Clements.

FREUND (Friend):
"Workers," of Nahum Yood, translated by Marcus Graham.

HARCOURT, BRACE & CO.:
"Leisure," from *Selected Poems*, by William H. Davies; "The Workingman," from *Contemporary German Poetry*, edited and translated by Babette Deutsch and Avrahm Yarmolinsky; "If We Must Die," from *Harlem Shadows*, by Claude McKay; "The Liars" and "Smoke and Steel," from *Smoke and Steel*, by Carl Sandburg; "Caliban in the Coal Mines," and "Sunday," from *Challenge* by Louis Untermeyer; "The Beggars," from *Factories*, by Margaret Widdemer.

16

17

THE LOTHIAN BOOKSHOP (Australia):
"The Crazy World," by William Gay; "Proletaria," by Bernard O'Dowd from *Australian Verse*, edited by Walter Murdock.

HORACE LIVERIGHT & CO.:
"He Whom A Dream Hath Possessed," and "Women with Shawls," from *Jealous of Dead Leaves*, by Shaemas O'Sheel; "To a Harnessed Thoroughbred," from *After Disillusion*, by Robert Wolf; "Revolution," from *For Eager Lovers*, by Genevieve Taggard.

MITCHEL KENNERLY:
"The Rough Rider," from *Poems*, by Bliss Carman; "The Cry of the People," from *Poems*, by John G. Neihardt; "Diogenes," from *Child of the Amazons and Other Poems*, by Max Eastman.

ALFRED A. KNOPF:
"The Day," from *A Chanticle of Pan and Other Poems*, by Witter Bynner; "The Slave," from *The Sea*, by James Oppenheim.

THE MACMILLAN CO.:
"The Man He Killed," from *Collected Poems*, by Thomas Hardy; "The Leaden-Eyed," from *Collected Poems*, by Vachel Lindsay; "The Road," from *Songs of the Clay*, by James Stephens; "A Consecration," from *Collected Poems*, by John Masefield; "I Shall Shout That Day," from *Children of the Sun*, by James Rorty; "To a Friend Whose Work Has Come to Nothing," from *Collected Poems*, by William Butler Yeats.

EDWIN MARKHAM:
"Armageddon," 'The Peril of Ease," and 'The Man with the Hoe," from *The Collected Works*, by Edwin Markham.

DAVID McKAY:
"Europe, 1848," and "The Song of the Open Road," from *Leaves of Grass*, by Walt Whitman.

THE MERCURY (London):
"The Cage," by Martin Armstrong; "Going and Staying," by Thomas Hardy; "Hobo," by Robert Nichols; "The Man in the Settlement," by Frank Prewett; "Anarchy," by J. C. Squire.

MRS. JOAQUIN MILLER:
"Riel: The Rebel," from *The Poetical Works*, by Joaquin Miller.

THE MOODY PUBLISHING CO.:
"Factory Children," from *The Younger Choir*, by Richard Burton.

THE NEW MASSES:
"Message to Siberia," of A. S. Pushkin, translated by Max Eastman;
"The Day Must Come," by Martin Russak; "Billiard Academy," by
Herman Spector.

THE NATION:
"Sacco and Vanzetti," by Kathleen Millay.

OPPORTUNITY:
"Silhouettes," by Langston Hughes.

THE ORACLE:
"Contrasts in Futility," by William Kenneth Moyer.

SUSAN OWEN:
"The Miners," from *Poems*, by Wilfred Owen.

ROBERT PACKARD & CO:.
"Is Freedom But a Name?" from *Flames and Fireflies*, by Walter
Hendricks.

PALO VERDE:
"The Song of Rebellion," by Benjamin Musser.

POETRY:
Poems by George Cosbuc, Florence Kiper Frank, Stanley Kimmel,
Valencia Guillorme, Jim Waters, and Sergey Yesenin.

POETRY OF TODAY (England):
"A Change of View," by S. Marguerite Goode.

POETRY REVIEW (England):
"From the Brothels," by Paolo Buzzi.

A. M. ROBERTSON:
"In the Market Place," and "The Goddess of Liberty," from *Poems*,
by George Sterling.

THE NEW REPUBLIC:
"Children of Darkness," by Robert Graves.

SCANDINAVIAN REVIEW:
"The Miner," by Hendrik Ibsen.

CHARLES SCRIBNER'S SONS:
"La Dame Revolution," from *Path Flower*, by Olive Tilford Dargan;
"Invictus," from *New Poems and Various Readings*, by William
Ernest Henley; "Courage," from Poems, by John Galsworthy;
"Had I the Power That Have the Will," from *Verses,
New and Old*, by Robert Louis Stevenson.

SIDWICK & JACKSON, LTD. (England):
"The City of Sleep," from *Selected Poems*, by Laurence Housman.

FREDERICK A. STOKES CO.:
"Peace" (Dedication to The Wine Press), from *Collected Works*, by Alfred Noyes.

THE STRATFORD CO.:
"Resist All Evil," from *Vanitas*, by Paul Eldridge.

THE CHICAGO TRIBUNE:
"Have You Paid the Boy?" by W. D. N.

THE NEW YORK TIMES:
Workers, by Elizabeth Newport Hepburn.

THE NEW YORK TRIBUNE:
"Against Destruction," by Stanley J. Kunitz, and "That Would—" by Rosa Zagnoni Marinoni.

UNICORN PUBLISHING CO.:
"Flames," from *Lost Eden*, by E. Merrill Root.

VANITY FAIR:
"Geddo Street" and "The Factory," by Theodore Dreiser.

THE VIKING PRESS, INC.:
"Inscription for a City's Gate of Warriors," by Henri de Règnier, from *Poets of Modern France*, by Ludwig Lewisohn; "The Prophet," from *The Lynching Bee and Other Poems*, by William Ellery Leonard; "Reveille," from *Sun Up*, by Lola Ridge; "Clay Hills," from *Growing Pains*, by Jean Starr Untermeyer.

HAROLD VINAL, LTD.:
"This I Shall Hold," from *You That Come After*, by Mary Siegrist.

A. P. WATT & SON (England):
"What Will There Be to Remember," from *The March of the Black Mountain*, by Gilbert K. Chesterton.

JAMES T. WHITE:
"Factory Smoke," from *The Thinker and Other Poems*, by Stanton A. Coblentz.

WILMRATH & CO.:
"The Question," from *Life Sings a Song*, by Samuel Hoffenstein.

THE WORLD TOMORROW:
"Nationalism," by Rabindranath Tagore.

THE DAILY WORKER:
Poems by Vera Bush, Oskar Kanehl, Aron Kurtz, H. Leivick, A. B. Magil and John Ramburg.

YALE UNIVERSITY PRESS:
"The Comrade," from *The Middle Miles and Other Poems*, by Lee Wilson Dodd; "Poor Girl," from *The Falconer God and Other Poems*, by William Rose Benét.

THE YEAR BOOK PRESS, LTD.:
"Serfs," from *Songs of the Dead End*, by Patrick MacGill.

POETS
who were kind enough to give their own permission for inclusion of their works:
Maxwell Anderson, Charles Ashleigh, Joseph Auslander, Hilaire Belloc, William Rose Benét, Berton Braley, Vera Bush, Witter Bynner, Ralph Chaplin, Ralph Cheyney, Helene Claiborne, Sarah N. Cleghorn, Stanton A. Coblentz, Julia Walcott Cockcroft, Countee Cullen, Miles Menander Dawson, Miriam Allen de Ford, Babette Deutsch, Margarette Ball Dickson, Lee Wilson Dodd, Theodore Dreiser, John Drinkwater, Max Eastman, Paul Eldridge, W. N. Ewer, Arthur Davison Ficke, Sara Bard Field, John Gould Fletcher, Florence Kiper Frank, Joseph Freeman, Charlotte Perkins Gilman, Louis Ginsberg, Arturo Giovannitti, Michael Gold, Arthur Guiterman, Bolton Hall, Covington Hall, Ernest Hartsock, Walter Hendricks, Laurence Housman, Langston Hughes, Harold Roland Johnson, James Weldon Johnson, Josephine Johnson, Harry Kemp, Alfred Kreymborg, Aron Kurtz, Joseph A. Labadie, Louise Burton Laidlaw, Richard Le Gallienne, W. E. Leonard, J. William Lloyd, Isobel Luke, Percy MacKaye, Norman Macleod, A. B. Magil, Edward Markham, Jeanette Marks, Rosa Zagnoni Marinoni, Don Marquis, Edgar Lee Masters, Mildred Plew Merryman, Edna St. Vincent Millay, Kathleen Millay, Lydia Gibson, Harold Monro, Angela Morgan, H. S. Morris, James F. Morton, Nicholas Moskowitz, William Kenneth Moyer, Benjamin Musser, Grace Fallow Norton, Alfred Noyes, Wade Oliver, Shaemas O'Sheel, William C. Owen, John Ramburg, Henry Reich, Jr., Lola Ridge, E. Merrill Root, James Rorty, Carl Sandburg, Joseph T. Shipley, Mary Siegrist, Herman Spector, J. C. Squire, Rose Pastor Stokes, Genevieve Taggard, Charles Hanson Towne, Lucia Trent, Jean Starr Untermeyer, Louis Untermeyer, George Sylvester Viereck, Elizabeth Waddell, Blanche Shoemaker Wagstaff, Jim Waters, Henry George Weiss, Robert Whitaker, Margaret Widdemer, Robert Wolf, Adolf Wolff, Clement Wood, Charles Erskine Scott Wood, and Gremin Zorn.

21

DEFUNCT PUBLICATIONS
(Where many of the poems included among the Forerunners,
appeared originally.)

Advance, The
Alarm, The
Anarchist, The (London)
Anarchist, The Walshall (England)
Appeal to Reason
Arizona Socialist
Blast, The
British Socialist, The
Brotherhood (England)
Class Struggle, The
Coming Nation, The
Commonweal, The (England)
Comrade, The
Conservator, The
Contemporary Review
Democrat
Demonstrator
Denver Labor Enquirer, The
Everyman
Fair Play
Freedom (England)
Free Russia (England)
Firebrand
Herald of Anarchy (Glasgow)
Humanity
Industry
Intercollegiate Socialist
International Socialist Review
Justice (Sydney, Australia)
Labor
Labour Herald (London)
Labour Leader, The (England)
Liberator
Liberator (Chicago)
Liberty
Link, The (England)
Lucifer
Masses
Measure, The
Minaret, The
Mother Earth

National Rip-Saw, The
New Hobo
New Justice
New National Era, The
New Palladium, The
New Review, The
New Time
New York Call
Palladium of Labor
Public, The
Public Ownership
Rebel, The
Revolt
Revolutionary Review
Single Taxer, The
Social Democrat
Social War, The
Socialist Review
Solidarity (Chicago)
Solidarity (New Castle)
Solidarity (New York)
Spur, The (England)
Sun-Democrat
Sunday Republican
Sydney Bulletin (Australia)
Tailor, The
Twentieth Century
Today (England)
United States Journal
Voice of Industry, The
Voice of Labour (England)
Western Comrade
Woman and Labor
Why
Wilshire's
Wilshire's Magazine
Worker, The (Melbourne, Au

Worker, The
Working Bee, The
Worker's Dreadnought, The

CONTENTS

Shakespeare, William
   History
   To the Poor
Shelley, Percy Bysshe
   The Royal Masque
   To the Men of England
   The Trinity (From
      "Prometheus Unbound")
Sherwood, Gen. Isaac R.
   Pursery Rhyme
Sterling, George
   In the Market-Place
   To the Goddess of Liberty
Stevenson, Robert Louis
   Had I the Power That
      Have the Will
Swift, H. Gordon
   The Faith-Fiend
Swift, Jonathan
   On an Ill-Managed House
Swinburne, Algernon Charles
   A Marching Song
Symonds, John Addington
   These Things Shall Be
Synge, J. M.
   Prelude

Taber, Stewart Stanton
   The Unemployed
Tennyson, Alfred
   Why Not?
Thomas, A. W.
   Democracy
Thomson, Philips
   The Power of Thought
Thoreau, David Henry
   True Freedom
Tichenor, Henry M.
   I Look Far Down the
      Reddened Road
Traubel, Horace
   Labor

Ullad, Bert
   For Those Who Give
      Thanks

Valter, John Francis
   The Genius of Revolution

Weeks, Ida Ahlborn
   A Song of Academic
      Freedom
Whitehead, Celie Baldwin
   Fight, What For?
Whitman, Walt
   Europe (1848-1849)
   Song of the Open Road
Whittier, John Greenleaf
   Stanzas for the Times
Wilcox, Ella Wheeler
   The Disappointed
Wilde, Oscar
   After a Hanging (From
      the "Ballad of Reading
      Gaol")
Willis, N. P.
   Why Is This?

THE MODERNS

Aber, Loureine A.
   Cut Loose
Aldington, Richard
   Vicarious Atonement
Allman, James
   The Queen's Coronation
      Robe
Anderson, Maxwell
   A Slave Prays to the Wind
Armstrong, Martin
   The Cage
Ashleigh, Charles
   Everett, November Fifth
Ashley, Kenneth H.
   Out of Work
Auslander, Joseph
   The Riveter

Bacon, Ralph
   Evidence
Barnard, William Francis
   The Gods
Bell, Ralcey Husted
   The Reapers
Belloc, Hilaire
   The Rebel
Benét, William Rose
   "Poor Girl"

25

Binyon, Laurence
  The Builders
Bland, E. (Nesbit)
  A Great Industrial Centre
Bodenheim, Maxwell
  Sentimentality
Boone, Stanley
  The County Jail
Bowen, Sterling
  Cages
Boyesen, Bayard
  Declaration
Braley, Berton
  Labor
Burgess, Haldane
  The Harp Note
Burnet, Dana
  A Ballad of Dead Girls
Burton, Richard
  Factory Children
Bush, Vera
  Looping Silk Stockings
Bynner, Witter
  The Day
Carew, Harold D.
  Justice Is Dead
Carman, Bliss
  The Rough Rider
Carpenter, Edward
  The City of the Sun
Cary, Robert
  Portrait of a Paltry
  Politician
Chaplin, Ralph
  The Warrior-Wind
Chesterton, Gilbert K.
  What Will There Be to
  Remember?
Cheyney, Ralph
  Red Flag
Claiborne, Helene
  Pardoned
Cleghorn, Sarah N.
  Golf Links
Clements, Albert Edward
  I Am
Coblentz, Stanton A.
  Factory Smoke

Cockcroft, Julia Walcott
  Employment
Colum, Padraic
  The Fire-Bringer
Cullen, Countee
  From the Dark Tower
Cummings, E. E.
  Impressions

Dargan, Olive Tilford
  La Dame Revolution
Davies, Mary Carolyn
  The Dead Make Rules
Davies, William H.
  Leisure
Dawson, Miles Menander
  Solidarity
De Ford, Miriam Allen
  Russia (1917)
De Witt, S. A.
  Hurricane
Deutsch, Babette
  Ironic
Dickson, Margarette Ball
  White Hyacinths
Dobson, David Irving
  My Words
Dodd, Lee Wilson
  The Comrade
Dreiser, Theodore
  Geddo Street
  The Factory
Drinkwater, John
  Holiness
Dunsany, Lord
  Why?

Eastman, Max
  Diogenes
Einsein, Isaac
  Hands Wanted
Eldridge, Paul
  Resist All Evil
Eliot, T. S.
  The Hollow Men
Ellis, Havelock
  Onward, Brothers
England, George Allen
  My Heroines

28

Oppenheim, James
  The Slave
O'Sheel, Shaemas
  Women with Shawls
  He Whom a Dream Hath
    Possessed
Owen, William C.
  My Lady

Pinchon, Edgcomb
  The Lost Strike
Pound, Ezra
  Commission
Prewett, Frank
  The Red Man in the
    Settlements

Ramburg, John
  Subway
Redbeard, Ragnar
  A Christmas Carol
Reich, Jr., Henry
  Skyscrapers
Ridge, Lola
  Reveille
Rittenhouse, Jessie B.
  Vision
Robbins, Matilda
  The Buried Gold Diggers
Robinson, Edwin Arlington
  Because
Root, E. Merrill
  Flames
Rorty, James
  I Shall Shout That Day
Rosenthal, David
  Warning
Russak, Martin
  The Day Must Come

Salt, Henry S.
  Homo Rapiens
Sandburg, Carl
  I Am The People, The Mob
  Skyscraper
  Government
  Smoke and Steel
  The Liars
Sassoon, Siegfried
  Fight to a Finish

Shipley, Joseph T.
  Truth
Siegrist, Mary
  "This I Shall Hold"
Sitwell, Osbert
  The Blind Pedlar
Sorenson, Alice T.
  Carnegie's Libraries
Spector, Herman
  Billiard Academy
Squire, J. C.
  Anarchy
Stephens, James
  The Road
Stokes, Rose Pastor
  The Alarm Clock
Strong, Anna Louise
  City Comradeship
Strong, L. A. G.
  "Safe for Democracy"
  In a War Museum

Taggard, Genevieve
  Revolution
Thomas, Elizabeth
  Labor
Thorland, Richard
  Government — The Living
    God
Torrence, Ridgley
  The Singers in a Cloud
Towne, Charles Hanson
  The Time-Clock
Trent, Lucia
  Breed, Women, Breed!
Tucker, Irwin St. John
  The Sacrifice
Stuckey, Norman
Turner, Lizinka Campbell
  Distinguo

Untermeyer, Jean Starr
  Clay Hills
Untermeyer, Louis
  Caliban in the Coal Mines
  Sunday

Viereck, George Sylvester
  The Winners

Jean, Theodore
  One Flag
Potter, Eugene
  The International

GERMAN
Barthel, Max
  The Locomotive
Bierbaum, Otto Julius
  Blacksmith Pain
Dehmel, Richard
  The Workingman
Freiligrath, Ferdinand
  Revolution
Goethe, Johann Wolfgang von
  Begin—Anew (From
    "Faust")
Heine, Heinrich
  The Weavers
Herwegh, George
  The Comrade's Song
Kanehl, Oskar
  Challenge to Strike
Lilencron, Detlev von
  In a Large City
Mackay, John Henry
  World Citizenship
Nietzsche, Friedrich
  Among Enemies
Schiller, Johann Christoph Fried-
  rich von
    Hope
Toller, Ernest
  From the Imprisoned
Anonymous
  People—Whose Fault?

GREEK
Euripides
  Captive Good Attending
    Captain Ill

HUNGARIAN
Ady, Andrew
  The Song of the Street
Petöfi, Alexander
  War and Peace

INDIAN
Naidu, Serajini
  Dawn
Tagore, Rabindranath
  Nationalism

ITALIAN
Bruno, Giordano
  The Philosophic Flight
Buzzi, Paolo
  From the Brothels
Carducci, Giosuè
  Freedom's Dead

JAPANESE
Anonymous
  The Beggar's Complaint

JEWISH
Dahl, Basil (Joseph Bovshover)
  Revolution
Edelstadt, David
  A Summons
Frug, Sh.
  The Banner
Herbert, M. L.
  Wall Street at Night
Leivick, H.
  Prison Poems
Raisen, Abraham
  Revel, Revel, Angry Tem-
    pests
Rosenfeld, Morris
  In the Factory
Yeoash (Solomon Bloomgarden)
  The Prophet
Yood, Nahum
  Workers

NORWEGIAN
Ibsen, Henrik
  The Miner

ROUMANIAN
Cosbuc, George
  We Want Land

RUSSIAN

Blok, Alexander
  The Twelve
Bryusov, Valery
  The City
Eichenbaum, V.
  Vision
Gorky, Maxim
  The Song of the Storm-
  Finch
Krylov, Ivan
  Lion and Gnat
Lermontov, Mikhail Yuryevich
  A Thought
Lunacharsky, A. V.
  Song of "Old Rebble"
Marienhoff, Anatoly
  October
Mayakovsky, Vladimir
  Our March
Nadson, Semion Yakovlevitch
  In the Crowd
  Forward
Nekrasov, N. A.
  Ye Songs of Mine
Polivanov, P.
  In Alexis Ravelin
Pushkin, Alexander Sergeyevitch
  Message to Siberia

Turgeniev, Ivan
  The Revolutionist
Tyutchev, Fyodor
  As Ocean's Stream
Yesenin, Sergey
  Transfiguration
Anonymous
  The Anarchist March

SANSKRIT

Panchatranta
  Poverty

SPANISH

Giraldo, Alberto
  My Clarion Call
Guillorme, Valencia
  From "Anarchs"
Magón, Ricardo Flores
  Farewell
Miron, Salvador Diaz
  The Cloud
Zepedo, Alfonso
  My Shield

UKRAINIAN

Shewchenko, Taras
  The Haidamaky—"Knights
  of Vengeance"
Tarnowsky, Nicholas
  To The Poets

INTRODUCTION

*S*IRENS *scream. Weary men, women and children drag their ill-nourished bodies into the narrow mouths of factories. Rifles spit. Strikers and their wives and children wheel, totter and sink on the ground, which slowly crimsons. Mounted police and troopers charge frothing horses on peaceful crowds and lean from their saddles to crash skulls. Printing presses rumble, ravaging forests to spread lies. Riveters resound. But above the raucous rumble and roar there rise and flutter in the minds and hearts of an ever-growing multitude of workers shouts of defiance toward those who enslave them and vows of loyalty to the Movement which will lead the oppressed and despoiled from earthly hell to earthly heaven. Mingled with oaths of revolt are songs—songs of destiny and deliverance. For the makers of history today and the recorders of history tomorrow, many of these songs have been gathered in the book now before you.*

The hewers of wood and drawers of water in tawny-throated, sunburnt Egypt whispered to themselves long before Cleopatra helped brew spiritual poison for Rome that some day they would seize the lash from their overseers. The helots and slaves upon whose bleeding backs was mortared "the glory that was Greece and the grandeur that was Rome" swelled the whisper to a cry.

The Communards lifted the cry into a song which they sang as they stormed the Bastille and erected barricades— a song which set tyrants all around the world trembling on their luxury-rotted thrones.

Americans heard historic songs of revolt, sung by the men of the I.W.W. and radicals of all shades sentenced again and again to many years of imprisonment for the one crime which the master class will never forgive: working, however peacefully, for the rise of a sun which will see no longer the masses condemned to life-terms of suffering and slavery.

*Russia resounded with songs that bear the same burden
and the same promise of freedom from unjust burdens when
soldiers, workers and peasants joined hands to overthrow
Tzarism and win Bread and Land.*

*Now the ancient whisper has grown to a demand which
thunders around the globe, and will thunder ever louder until
there are no rich and no poor but only happy, free men and
women working together and enjoying the fruits of their
labors in peace and comradeship.*

*Songs which echo and swell this thunder throb between
the covers of this book. Listen and you will hear an indictment "terrible as an army with banners" and a prophecy nur-
tured by the well of truth and spring of beauty, sweeter
than any other known to much-enduring man.*

II

*The world is tumbling about our ears. The old order
has collapsed. "The World War brought to an end the
illusionment of bourgeois idealism." We stand among falling
débris. America is becoming or has become industrialized.
Individualism of the pioneers has fallen away before standardization. The trust has risen and capitalism expanded.
Youth is more aware and articulate. Women are less willing
to be dominated by men.*

*Labor is slowly but unmistakably reaching the realization
that to it belong all things and the resolve that it shall
possess them. No economic, industrial, social and cultural
system can endure long which is based on the fact now true
of the United States: that two per cent of the population,
conservatively speaking, own seventy-one per cent of the
wealth, while more than sixty per cent of the people own
but twenty per cent of this world's goods. No system can go
on long which denies a job to one out of every nine working
men. Five million unemployed is a host which may light
the spark of revolution.*

*The creation of some valid order of values is the most
fascinating and imperative task the intellect faces today. The
creation of values in the emotional realm is the primary func-
tion of poetry. Chaos gives birth to a dancing star only if
we breathe into it that visible, audible fragrance of passion*

34

which is poetry. The world will be new-born only with the spread of that consciousness which is creation, and poets are the pioneers of consciousness. They, therefore, are naturally among the leaders in the development of class-consciousness. Life is faith. Without faith there can be no poetry, and without poetry no civilization. But intelligent faith can come only after complete, hard-boiled disillusionment with the supernatural and with bourgeois idealism.

Poetry and propaganda are two sides of the same shield. Without passion there can be no poetry, and all who feel strongly burn with a zeal to have others share their feeling. True poets are also propagandists, even though their propaganda may be simply for the love of life and the life of love.

A poem is a rune, spell, incantation, evocation. Poetry throws open mental windows and doors, pushes back horizons, reveals a new heaven and leads us back to Mother Earth with a fresh vision of how to regain Eden. What we see often, we do not see at all, a fact which blinds us to the evils of the present industrial and social system. The statement of Simonides, "Literature is spoken painting," should stand beside Madame De Stael's "Architecture is frozen music." Poets clear our eyes and sharpen our ears. Poetry serves civilization and helps usher in a happier world as no other human activity can. For the very essence of poetry is SYMPATHY.

There is no other art which can emphasize more concretely and more beautifully the spiritual values of human life. "We can not live by bread alone" is a trite phrase, but one which contains a generous measure of truth. Too many today lack bread itself. Savages and civilized men are alike in their blind groping for an explanation of the hidden sources of the universe. Authentic poetry gives utterance to the eternal adventuring in search of spiritual truths and the Promised Land, long prophesied but to be realized only through the uprising of united workers.

The poets who rebel against the smug, superficial materialism of the age in this imperialistic nation and contribute thought as well as words are in the main pessimistic. Their poems are question-marks. They face frustration and see the hole in the universe. Not seeing the hope of a new, true civilization that is rising in the East, notably Russia and India, their eyes are fixed on the downfall of the Western World and they despair. Their world is staggering like a drunken man, toppling like a shot deer. For most of them are of the bourgeoisie, and they feel, even if they do not see, that their class is decaying and disappearing. The collapse of a class is foretold in the disruption of its ideals and arts, though their echoes may ring through the ages. Much that is gracious and lovely endures from the times of feudalism, but aristocracy succumbed to plutocracy and the middle class came into power. Now the days of the middle class are numbered—and their end is to be seen by the disillusionment among bourgeois poets and other artists, by the prevalence of spiritless manufactured-by-formulae imitations of art and by the new interest in primitive and folk contributions to the arts.

Is there not some fair and fertile virgin soil beyond the wasteland, some faith on which poets may seize?

"Yes," the answer must be, if poetry is to survive. For, as Emerson said, "Poetry is faith." Where can the poets of today find a living faith, how can they make their work a force in the life of today? To our mind, there can be but one answer: The poets can find faith only where it is found by the workers: in the movements dedicated to ushering in the Co-operative Commonwealth.

Honor to the poet who can find poetry in stunted city trees and the parched flowers in a tenement window, who sings the humdrum life of a factory hand or an office clerk! Honor to the poet who shouts against the infamy of lynchings and prisons and the red-eyed monster of war! Such poets are working with the mortar which will build a more enduring social structure. They are the standard-bearers of a new emancipated humanity. These are the poets whom the present may crucify, but whom the future will honor.

III

In this book are sung the real modern wonders of the world. What are the modern seven wonders of the world?

We suggest as the seven modern wonders: the increasing recognition that equal, unrestricted opportunity belongs to all individuals of all races and creeds or lack of creed; the

36

labor movement; the rising opposition to violence and mur-
der, whether they be expressed in lynching, capital punish-
ment, or war; the emancipation of women; modern psychology
and the extensions of consciousness; birth control; and the
development of machinery to lessen labor and increase pro-
duction. The poet who cannot find inspiration in these won-
ders is no seer, no humanist, no prophet, no voice of the
spirit crying aloud in the wilderness—in short, no true poet.

In a land where rich men and athletes are adored and
poets scorned, a land whose appropriate symbols are the
cash register and the time-clock, sensitive souls are crucified.
If not on the electric chair like Sacco and Vanzetti, they
nevertheless are seared. In the standardization of a machine
age there is tragic need but scant room for the nonconformist.
Our wings are clipped from birth, our souls mangled by
wheels. Most of us, even we poets, are willing to let our
souls sicken and succumb or to keep them like canaries
trilling monotonously in a small gilt cage. Some few there
are, however, who struggle for the integrity of their spirits
and mint from the consequent agony dynamic song.

The poet has a real task in the work of the world. He is
filling a needed rôle. There are two main types of poetry—
that of escape from the world around us and that of accept-
ance of it and affirmation of the beauty in it; the first seda-
tive, the second stimulant. If poetry is to be only a soothing
syrup for the comfortable classes who have time to kill and
are ready to stamp out the springs of all nobler poetry,
we are tempted to recommend that both poets and poetry be
poisoned.

Modern psychologists are maintaining with increasing em-
phasis that people are influenced not by purely logical and
intellectual processes alone, but also by their emotional im-
pulses. A pamphlet giving statistics of a coal strike, stating
the issues at stake, the number of evictions, the number of
homeless miners and their families, is not as likely to rouse
the liberal public to indignation or to generous donations
as a stirring poem describing in graphic and harrowing de-
tail the plight of the strikers, telling how mothers are feeding
dry cracker crumbs to their babies and how their little chil-
dren are dying from cold and exposure.

If there be any among the radical movement who ignore the poet as a practical factor in the fight for freedom, let such recall the lives of Milton, Byron and Shelley, not to mention the successful influences of Thomas Hood and George Crabbe in mitigating the cruel laws of Great Britain.

Although, as the Frenchman said, "All generalizations are false, including this one," it is fairly safe to say that the greatest poets of the past have been the rebel and humanist singers who have shaken the thrones of tyrants with their rebellious music and risen to the defense of the martyred Saccos and Vanzettis of their own generations.

Every age has its poets, but this dark age of electricity, this mechanistic era, blackened by the monster shadows of giant machines, is essentially a harrowing age for poets. For the poetic mind lays emphasis on the human values of life rather than on those upheld by a standardized and crudely materialistic civilization. Therefore, the poet is stifled to-day perhaps more than he has ever been in the past, and if the radicals will not listen to him, will not welcome him, who will?

IV

Anthologies of poems of national patriotism abound. Here is an anthology of WORLD *patriotism. Poets have too long tooted and touted the merits—chiefly imaginary—of single nations. They have lent their voices too readily to the aid of recruiting sergeants. Like the weavers in Hans Christian Andersen's fairy tale, they have spun out of nothing bright robes for tyrants to wear. They have lied in their throats and in their hearts. True! But there have been others who sang the truth blithely at whatever cost. Sir Walter Raleigh, before his head was severed on the chopping-block in the old days of cruel Queen Bess, and Frank Little of the I.W.W. before he was tortured to death by American business-men thugs a few years ago, are brothers in this tradition, as are Ernest Toller, who wrote in a German jail, and Arturo Giovan-nitti in an American. In this book you will find poems by and about these bold men and many other whole-hearted spirits who fearlessly sounded defiance. True poets have ever been quick to answer such a summons as Clifford Gessler's call: "Set your lips to the bright horn of challenge and let its wild* notes ring clear and undaunted above the dark drums of fear."

Versifiers have not been lacking to earn immediate glory and future shame by paying homage to war and the greed out of which war springs. But poets have been present who saw war for the murder it is and who perceived that the real victims of war are the soldiers on both sides. Circe changed men to swine. War changes men to apes, wolves and snakes. Any work of art that glorifies war is surrender of Beauty to the Beast. Militarism breeds war. Literature that extols militarism is feeding the mouth that bites it.

Suffering due to economic and military causes accounts for only a part of the salt sea of human sorrow. Responsible also are our rabbit-warren morality, our attitude toward mates as personal private property, our life-denying inhibitions and tangled sex taboos.

V

A proletarian as well as a revolutionary venture, this book is stained with the very sweat and blood of labor. It should strengthen class-consciousness and inspire class-pride. It is a workers' monument to the working class.

The workers are capable of developing their own culture. They can toil for beauty as well as wages—"bread and roses." They can achieve art as well as feed and clothe and house the world. Competition is not needed for craftsmanship; and if there be competition, it need not be concerned with pay envelopes. Rich proof of these facts is offered by this anthology.

Few professional poets live in these days. By no means the lightest indictment of capitalism is its indifference to the poet and its glorification of the man of business, its hostility to the dreamer and its friendliness to the schemer, its penalizing of craftsmen and rewarding of the crafty. Most poets must earn their livelihood by denying their life for the best hours of each day. Many of the poems in this book were written with calloused hands but feeling hearts—different from so many anthologies written with manicured hands but callous hearts and callow minds.

Nearly all of the poems in this book flow straight from hearts which throbbed in unison with the working class.

Moreover, many of the poets were and are actually members of the working class. If there were further biographical details, we should almost undoubtedly cross out "many" and write "most." We do know that many poems were written in tenements in the shadow of factories and close to the mouths of mines and that some were pencilled in the narrow cells of jails. What heights poets may attain and help mankind reach when they enjoy freedom and greater leisure can only be dreamed.

When the workers are free, and only then, can we have real culture and real civilization. In the meantime all cultures are but night-blooming flowers, hidden from most men, women and children by smoke and steam, grime and soot, the fog and poisonous fumes loosed by capitalist-controlled schools and newspapers, churches and theatres—hidden also by the darkness of ignorance and fear. When the red day breaks and reveals the free society, these night-blooming flowers will droop. But in their place will gleam in the sun and dance in the breeze the true flowers of labor and dream.

The dark rivers of tears and blood that swell this sea rush chiefly from hearts, bodies and spirits crushed by the mills of the over-lords—which, unlike those of the gods, grind fast but exceedingly sure. Foully feeding every other misery stand overwork and law-protected robbery: underplay and underpay. Wage slavery is little better than chattel slavery. Without industrial and social democracy political democracy is a tragic farce. An unacknowledged caste system which can be broken in a few instances by grasping or lucky individuals is crueler in its hypocrisy and tantalizing, unkept promises than a frank caste system. "Plutocracy" is named more aptly than most realize, for Pluto was Lord of Hell.

Many poets forget that the Tower of Ivory is built of ivory-white bones and is shadowed by the Tower of Babel! But the wiser and greater poets know that none is safe when pestilence tramples the earth, be it the fever of disease that ravages the body or the fever of Capitalism which ravages bodies and all else human and humane. They know that we are "members one of another" and that it takes the joy of all to make the joy of one.

You will find their poems in this book. Some attack war, prostitution, child labor, the deadening effects of too long a

workday, unemployment and the other evil effects of Capital-
ism and exploitation. Others attack the present evil system
in its entirety. Some voice the protest of the Child. Others
sing the Women's Revolt. Most acclaim the Labor Move-
ment, which includes the revolt of women and children. Still
others prophesy of the Golden Age they see AHEAD *when the*
reign of gold shall be ended.

A large proportion of children are poets until our stand-
ardized educational systems and soul-stifling economic system
exert their stranglehold. Who can tell how many poets will
enrich the world with song when the dispossessed come into
their own?

Capitalism cuts its own throat by enslaving men to ma-
chines, the many to the few, creation to commerce. That
which offends against the creative spirit cannot endure.
Death wins partial victories. But life is the great victor in
every conflict. Every culture rooted in the mangled bodies
and souls of slaves has died or else even now is filling the
air with the stench of its decay. Just as surely, every system
manured by war, prostitution, and exploitation is doomed.

This anthology is a prophecy of the destruction of the old
"culture" and "civilization" based on slavery and of the birth
of the new humanism which surely will blossom from free-
dom. It is a death-knell and a cry out of the pangs of birth.
As such, look herein for strength rather than smoothness,
meaning rather than melody. See in it the picture of an
age of cruel lies and shameful shams, painted chiefly by
hands used to tools and machines, scythes and hammers.

The poems which constitute this anthology have been
selected with an eye alert to their revolutionary significance
and an ear attuned to their poetic merit. Some of the poets
represented are proletarian by right of sympathy rather than
accident of circumstance. But the compiler himself is a
worker. He has earned his bread by the sweat of his brow
since he was fourteen. He has proved his revolutionary in-
tegrity by his life as a revolutionist as well as by his activities
for a period of eight years in harvesting this treasury of the
poetry of revolt. Surely all who write or speak in the cause
of a free humanity owe gratitude to that class-conscious
worker and uncompromising rebel, Marcus Graham.

41

VI

The revolutionary value of this anthology as an arsenal of ideas and source of inspiration, especially for those active in propaganda, rests four-square upon the devotion and vision, knowledge and experience of the man who saw the need for it and devoted his leisure for eight long years to changing his dream into the fact you now hold in your hands. What sort of a man is this Marcus Graham?

An ascetic, spare and thin, with the eyes of a dreamer, the smile of a friend to all men, the jaw of a fighter and the hands of a worker, gentle in his manners but burning fiercely in his resolves, Marcus Graham belies in his person as do the contributors to this volume in their work the usual misconception of the revolutionist.

Yet his deeds as well as his words prove him a true-red revolutionist. For twenty of his thirty-five years he has lived in the United States. For nineteen of them he has been interested in the social question. For but one year less he has worked with the written and spoken word to give the workers' answer to this question. Born in Canada, he has achieved a world-view and deep fellow-feeling with all the workers of all the world.

The passage of the compulsory conscription law in the United States and Canada found him actively combating this act of tyranny in the center of the chief anti-conscription focus in Canada, Montreal. Under the name "Robert Parsons" he urged at innumerable meetings that bankers, editors and other "paytriots" form a battalion which would march at the head of the fighting army, instead of staying home and minting gold from blood in the foul alchemy of commerce. A year later he edited an underground Anarchist paper in Toronto, "Der Einziger." The next year he edited another underground journal, "The Anarchist Soviet Bulletin," this time in the United States. This activity led to his arrest. He was taken to Ellis Island, held two weeks, then released on bail. It was at this time that he conceived the idea of this anthology of revolutionary poetry. In other words, this book was born out of the storm and stress of revolt.

With the coming to the front of the "Council of Action" in England, he went to London in 1920, where in the British

Museum Library he started work on this compilation. He then returned to Canada, where he launched "The Awakener," and a little later to the United States, where he resumed the editorship of "The Anarchist Soviet Bulletin," the name of which was soon changed to "Free Society." Again he was arrested and subjected to that hangover from the Dark Ages, the THIRD DEGREE, *an experience described in his own poem in this collection. Instead of quenching his ardor, the brutal treatment he received fanned it to fiercer flame.*

He was held on Ellis Island for six months, but the case was finally dropped and the bail returned. It was on Ellis Island that he corrected (secretly) the proofs of his pamphlet, "Anarchism and the World Revolution," issued under the signature of Fred S. Graham.

There is no need to enter further into his history, to tell all of his many labors on behalf of a free society or of his toil by day and night in the libraries of Detroit, Cleveland, Chicago, Boston, Pittsburgh, Los Angeles, San Francisco, Ithaca, New Haven, Rochester, Buffalo, New York, Montreal, Toronto, Winnipeg, and—where he found the largest collections of radical periodicals—the Labadie collection in the University at Ann Arbor, Mich., and in the University at Madison, Wis. But it should be recorded that never once has he accepted a single penny of compensation for any speech or article he has contributed to the Cause!

That Marcus Graham is an Anarchist should occasion no surprise—for among Anarchists has ever thrilled a warm response to the best creative works. For his loyalty to his principles which led to his arrests there can be only admiration.

As to Marcus Graham's taste in poetry—as to anybody's taste in any of the arts—there can be and should be a question. Art is necessarily Anarchistic. That is, art knows no laws. It is a free expression of the free spirit. You have as much right to your tastes as we have to ours. You are free in art to do as you will as long as you do not hinder others from doing as they please. Above every birthplace of art is chiselled—no less clearly because invisibly—the rule of the Abbey of Theleme in the masterpiece of Rabelais, "Do What Thou Wilt." When comradeship is made an art, we

43

assuredly shall have Anarchism; and the handclasp shall replace the policeman's "billy" and the soldier's bayonet.

No two people would select exactly the same poems for an anthology as extensive and inclusive as this. But Marcus Graham has travelled far across the map in his search for the best revolutionary poems. And we, for two, are stirred to profound enthusiasm by the treasures he has brought back and now offers for your encouragement and inspiration.

LUCIA TRENT,
RALPH CHEYNEY.

DEDICATION

I Am The People, The Mob

I am the people—the mob—the crowd—the mass.

*Do you know that all the great work of the world is
done through me?*

*I am the workingman, the inventor, the maker of
the world's food and clothes.*

*I am the audience that witnesses history. The
Napoleons come from me and the Lincolns. They
die. And then I send forth more Napoleons and
Lincolns.*

*I am the seed ground. I am a prairie that will stand
for much plowing. Terrible storms pass over me.
I forget. The best of me is sucked out and
wasted. Everything but Death comes to me and
makes me work and give up what I have. And I
forget.*

*Sometimes I growl, shake myself and spatter a few
red drops for history to remember. Then—I
forget.*

*When I, the People, learn to remember, when I, the
People, use the lessons of yesterday and no longer
forget who robbed me last year, who played me
for a fool—then there will be no speaker in all the
world say the name: "The People," with any fleck
of a sneer in his voice or any far-off smile of
derision.*

The mob—the crowd—the mass—will arrive then.

CARL SANDBURG.

THE FORERUNNERS

THE ARMY OF THE NIGHT

In the black night, along the mud-deep roads,
  Amid the threatening boughs and ghastly streams,
Hark! sounds that gird the darknesses like goads,
  Murmurs and rumors and reverberant dreams,
Trampling, breaths, movements, and a little light.—
The marching of the Army of the Night!

The stricken men, the mad brute-beasts are keeping
  No more their places in the ditches or holes,
But rise, and join us, and the women, weeping
  Beside the roadways, rise like demon-souls.
Fill up the ranks! What shimmers there so bright?
The bayonets of the Army of the Night!

Fill up the ranks! We march in steadfast column,
  In wavering lines yet forming more and more;
Men, women, children, sombre, silent, solemn,
  Rank follows rank like billows to the shore.
Dawnwards we tramp, towards the hills and light.
On, on and up, the Army of the Night!

Francis William Lauderdale Adams
(1862-1893)

THE PROPHECY OF EARTH

Ye winds that blow the clouds across the sky
  And search among the trees for music sweet,
Ye leaves that fall to the river and float by
  The light that dances with mysterious feet
Among the grey-green willow's trembling shower,
Ye seem to me to weave the coming hour.

Billows that rush from the waste Ocean vast,
  Lightnings that cross great waters all alone,
With solitary mountains that o'ercast
  The peopled vale with shadows; have ye known
And seen what web the bright ascending sun
Spins with his beams for mortals? Is there none

Of the all-hallowing and enchanting stars,
  That hourly make new patterns in the night,
Can prophesy the ceasing of our wars
  And point the tomb of never pitying-might?
Have they not gold in all their twinkling shower,
Men's lives to free from Usury's purchased power?

The plunging waters answer from the deep,
  The prairies whisper through their distances,
The rivers murmur peacefully and creep
  Through banks whose lisp'd reed conferences
Utter the word we seek in cryptic speech,
And the stars hear it. Ah! Could they but teach!

There is a voice in all their ways for man,
  To lead him back through calm to his own heart;
There is a pinnacle whence he may scan
  The rolling clouds beneath him and apart;
There is a tongue in all the waves of sea
That, having neither fear nor hope, are free.

He that hath wandered in the woods of Spring
  With moss and lustrous violets carpeted,
Passing in that cool shade from everything
  That in the last word is disquieted,
He can regain the greatness of his kind,
Which most have never known—a gentle mind.

The music that is in the lonely caves,
  Where hunted patriots have harked by night,
Hath consolation. And the desolate graves
  Of nations that have disappeared from sight,
Under the changing forces of the sky,
To vanquish death for man, though he must die.

Oh! for a race of men to rise at length
  Who all to all these ways can enter free,
Who shall not speak of death, to image strength,
  But find all power in man's own constancy,
Who, in the sweet face of the summer fields,
Shames to be lord who rules or slave that yields.

H. P. Adams

THE DAY OF REBELLION

In the night of oppression and anguish
  When the hosts of tyrants rule wide,
And the people but shudder and languish,
  As they crouch from the furies of pride,
Comes a word of Revolt whispered grimly,
  Through the chaos of discord and fear,
Till the slaves and despots feel dimly,
  That the Day of Rebellion is near.

They know not the day nor the year,
  Yet soon shall its standards appear,
With defiance to rules and to rulers,
  The Day of Rebellion is near.

It will come as the lightning from heaven,
  As the wrath of the skies it will fall,
It will shatter, like bolt of the levin,
  Harsh monopoly's fortified wall;
It will dash down to dust and perdition,
  With a crash that shall echo through time,
The twin Monsters of rule and submission,
  That have fastened the world in their slime.

The Day of Rebellion is near,
  With omens for tyrants to fear,
And defiance to rules and to rulers,
  Wherever its standards appear.

J. A. Andrews

A SONG OF SLAVES

O Slave of the Wheel and Thread!
  O Slave of the Sewing Machine!
Your crust of bread you earn with dread
  Lest hunger lurk between!

O Slave of the Factory and Loom!
  O Slave of the Mill and Mine!
Ye weave your doom, ye dig your tomb,
  For toil alone is thine.

O Slave of the Spade and Hoe!
  O Slave of the Harrow and Plough!
The seed ye sow, the grain ye grow,
  Another reaps than thou.

O Slave of the Steam-breathing Steel!
  O Slave of the Truck and Engine!
The demons' speed ye needs must feed,
  Tho' hungry ye remain.

O Slaves of the Bellows and Fire!
  O Slaves of the Furnace and Flue!
Your limbs perspire, your muscles tire,
  Ye forge your chains anew.

O Slaves, is it not more than time
   That your servile chains ye broke?
Your brother calls from every clime!
   Arise, and add your stroke!
                Thomas C. Auld

LONDON

I WANDER through each chartered street,
   Near where the chartered Thames does flow;
A mark in every face I meet,
   Marks of weakness, marks of woe.

In every cry of every man,
   In every infant's cry of fear,
In every voice, in every ban,
   The mind-forged manacles I hear:

How the chimney-sweeper's cry
   Every blackening church appals,
And the hapless soldier's sigh
   Runs in blood down palace-walls.

But most, through midnight streets I hear
   How the youthful harlot's curse
Blasts the new-born infant's tear,
   And blights with plagues the marriage-hearse.
                William Blake
                 (1757-1827)

MONOPOLISTIC MONOLOGUE

LET us corner up the sunbeams
   Lying all around our path;
Get a trust on wheat and roses,
   Give the poor the thorns and chaff.
Let us find our chiefest pleasure
   Hoarding bounties of the day,
So the poor will have scant measure,
   And high prices have to pay.

Yes, we'll reservoir the rivers,
   And we'll levy on the lakes,
And we'll lay a trifling poll-tax
   On each poor man that partakes;

We'll brand his number on him,
   That he'll carry through his life,
We'll apprentice all his children,
   Get a mortgage on his wife.

We will capture e'en the wind-god,
   And confine him in a cave,
Then through our patent process
   We the atmosphere will save;
Thus we'll squeeze our little brother
   When he tries his lungs to fill,
Put a meter on his wind-pipe,
   And present our little bill.

We will syndicate the starlight
   And monopolize the moon,
Claim royalty on rest days,
   A proprietary noon,
For right of way through ocean's spray
   We'll charge just what it's worth,
We'll drive our stakes around the lakes;
   In fact, we'll own the earth.

                                   E. Bradshaw

TOMORROW'S POOR

HOUSELESS and homeless and Godless as well,
Habitant here of this earth made a hell;
Fearing no other, for what could be worse?—
Living forever 'neath poverty's curse.
God? He's a luxury those can afford
Who have had plenty and feasts at their board.
Hell and hereafter and devils to come?—
Threats that mean nothing to brain that is numb.

Look! He is dressed in the rags that degrade.
Hark! how he pleads—he dares never upbraid.
List! how he curses you under his breath,
Damning your soul to the ultimate death.
Watch! for the gleam of the hate he's suppressed—
Hate that was born of his wrongs unredressed.
Clasp, while you may, his hard hand and be just—
Else, on the morrow, to torment he'll thrust.

Here he was brought, and his burden is great—
Made more unbearable, seeing your state.

Put for a moment yourself in his place;
Think of the future he surely must face;
Plead, as he pleads, for a chance in this world—
Take for your answer the "No" that is hurled.
Crushed and insulted—Why should it surprise
Rich that, rebellious, he some day shall rise?

"Living on garbage and gaunt as a hound,
You would be virtuous, witty, profound?
Doubtless! And you would have reasoned it out
'Living in hovels and doing without
Sanctifies souls'; but you know," he objects,
"Brutes have but bodies, and reason neglects
Brain starved and stunted—Ah! souls, did you say?
Bodies are sure and still potent to slay."

Ah! What a pity tomorrow's poor won't
Stand to be starved and pitied! Pray don't
Look for humanity—we've bred for brutes;
Ask not for love to abide in such suits;
Think not to find when their frenzy is fierce
Kindness controlling their sword-points that pierce.
Mercy? Ah, well! They shall grant what we have shown.
God? Call upon Him! Perchance he will own.

Edwin Arnhold Brenholtz

From THE CRY OF THE CHILDREN

Do YE hear the children weeping, O my brothers,
  Ere the sorrow comes with years?
They are leaning their young heads against their mothers—
  And *that* cannot stop their tears.
The young lambs are bleating in the meadows,
  The young birds are chirping in the nest,
The young fawns are playing with the shadows,
  The young flowers are blowing toward the west—
But the young, young children, O my brothers,
  They are weeping bitterly!
They are weeping in the playtime of the others,
  In the country of the free.

"For oh," say the children, "we are weary,
  And we cannot run or leap;
If we cared for any meadows, it were merely
  To drop down in them and sleep.
Our knees tremble sorely in the stooping,

We fall upon our faces, trying to go;
And, underneath our heavy eyelids drooping,
　　The reddest flower would look as pale as snow.
For, all day, we drag our burden tiring
　　Through the coal dark underground
Or, all day, we drive the wheels of iron
　　In the factories, round and round.

"For, all day, the wheels are droning, turning,—
　　Their wind comes in our faces,—
Till our hearts turn,—our head, with pulses burning,
　　And the walls turn in their places:
Turns the sky in the high window blank and reeling,
　　Turns the long light that drops adown the wall,
Turn the black flies that crawl along the ceiling,
　　All are turning, all the day, and we with all.
And all day, the iron wheels are droning,
　　And sometimes we could pray,
"O ye wheels," (breaking out in a mad moaning),
　　"Stop! be silent for to-day!"
They look up, with their pale and sunken faces,
　　And their look is dread to see,
For they mind you of the angels in high places,
　　With eyes turned on Deity!—
"How long," they say, "how long, O cruel nation,
　　Will you stand, to move the world, on a child's heart,—
Stifle down with a mailed heel its palpitation,
　　And tread onward to your throne amid the mart?
Our blood splashes upward, O gold-heaper,
　　And your purple shows your path!
But the child's sob in the silence curses deeper
　　Than the strong man in his wrath."

Elizabeth Barrett Browning
(1806-1861)

From THE ANTIQUITY OF FREEDOM

O FREEDOM! thou art not, as poets dream,
A fair young girl, with light and delicate limbs,
And wavy tresses gushing from the cap
With which the Roman master crowned his slave
When he took off the gyves. A bearded man,
Armed to the teeth, art thou; one mailed hand
Grasps the broad shield, and one the sword; thy brow,
Glorious in beauty though it be, is scarred
With tokens of old wars; the massive limbs

Are strong with struggling. Power at thee has launched
His bolts, and with his lightnings smitten thee;
They could not quench the life thou hast from heaven.
Merciless Power has dug thy dungeon deep,
And his swart armorers, by a thousand fires,
Have forged thy chain; yet, while he deems thee bound,
The links are shivered, and the prison walls
Fall outward; terribly thou springest forth,
As springs the flame above a burning pile,
And shoutest to the nations, who return
Thy shoutings, while the pale oppressor flies.

William Cullen Bryant
(1794-1878)

THE NEW ROME

A THOUSAND starve, a few are fed,
Legions of robbers rack the poor,
The rich man steals the widow's bread,
And Lazarus dies at Dives' door;
The Lawyer and the Priest adjust
The claims of Luxury and Lust
To seize the earth and hold the soil,
To store the grain they never reap;
Under their heels the white slaves toil,
While children wail and women weep!—
The gods are dead, but in their name
Humanity is sold to shame,
While (then as now) the tinsel'd Priest
Sitteth with robbers at the feast,
Blesses the laden blood-stain'd board,
Weaves garlands round the butcher's sword,
And poureth freely (now as then)
The sacramental blood of Men!

Robert Buchanan
(1841-1901)

LABOR'S RESOLVE

Too LONG have we workers known
The burden of unceasing toil;
Too long have we renounced our own—
From mine and mart, from desk and soil—

The product of our land and brain
  To keep the rich at idle rest.
Henceforth we work to this refrain:
  We mean to have our wrongs redressed!

Too long have we the workers been
  Deprived of leisure, our just due;
But, wiser now, ahead is seen
  A nobler and a worthier view
Of what Life offers in its train
  When we are free men—unoppressed!
Henceforth we rise to this refrain:
  We mean to have our wrongs redressed!

No more we'll suffer stunted lives,
  Devoid of sweetness and of light;
A full return to him who strives
  Should be the guerdon as of right.
For this we'll fight! And not in vain!
  What is not granted us, we'll wrest!
Henceforth we strike to this refrain:
  We mean to have our wrongs redressed!
A. Burfield

A MAN'S A MAN FOR A' THAT

Is THERE, for honest Poverty,
  That hangs his head, an' a' that;
The coward-slave, we pass him by,
  We dare be poor for a' that!
For a' that, an' a' that,
  Our toils obscure an' a' that,
The rank is but the guinea's stamp,
  The Man's the gowd for a' that.

What though on hamely fare we dine,
  Wear hodding-gray, an' a' that;
Gie fools their silks, and knaves their wine,
  A man's a Man for a' that;
For a' that, an' a' that,
  Their tinsel show, an' a' that;
The honest man, the e'er sae poor
  Is king o' men for a' that.

Ye see yon birkie ca'd 'a lord;
  Wha struts, an' stares, an' a' that;

The hundreds worship at his word,
   He's but a coof for a' that:
For a' that an' a' that,
   His ribband, star, an' a' that;
The man o' independent mind
   He looks an' laughs at a' that.

A prince can make a belted knight,
   A marquis, duke and a' that;
But a honest man's aboon his might,
   Gude, faith, he maunna fa' that!
For a' that, an' a' that,
   Their dignities, an' a' that
The pith o' sense, pride o' worth,
   Are higher ranks than o' that.

Then let us pray that come it may,
   As come it will for a' that
That sense and worth, o'er a' the earth,
   May bear the gree, an' a' that
For a' that, and a' that.
   It's comin' yet for a' that;
That Man to Man, the world o'er,
   Shall brothers be for a' that.

Robert Burns
(1759-1796)

From STANZAS

YET FREEDOM! yet thy banner, torn but flying,
Streams like the thunderstorm *against* the wind;
Thy trumpet-voice, though broken now and dying,
The loudest still the tempest leaves behind;
Thy tree had lost its blossoms, and the rind,
Chopp'd by the axe, looks rough and little worth,
But the sap lasts—and still the seed we find
Sown deep, even in the bosom of the North;
So shall a better spring less bitter fruit bring forth.

George Gordon Nöel Byron
(1788-1824)

THE STRENGTH OF TYRANNY

THE tyrant's chains are only strong
   While slaves submit to wear them;
And who could bind them on the throng
   Determined not to bear them?

Then clank your chain, e'en though the links
    Were light as fashion's feather,
The heart which rightly thinks and feels
    Would cast them altogether.

The lords of earth are only great
    While others clothe and feed them!
But what were all their pride and state,
    Should labor cease to heed them?

We toil, we spin, we delve the mine,
    Sustaining each his neighbor;
And who can show a right divine
    To rob us of our labor?
We rush to battle, wear our lot
    In every ill and danger;
And who shall make the peaceful cot
    To homely joy a stranger?

Perish all tyrants far and near,
    Beneath the claims that bind us;
And perish, too, that *servile fear*
    Which makes the slaves they find us.
One grand, one universal claim,
    One peal of moral thunder,
One glorious burst in Freedom's name,
    And rend our bonds asunder!
                Charles Cole

ALL DAY

ALL day, all day the shuttles fly
    Across the noisy room;
All day, all day the maidens sigh
    Adown the busy room.
All day, all day the big machines
    And belted pulleys play;
All day, all day the same old scenes,
    All day, all day.

All day, all day the foreman's eyes
    Sweep o'er the humdrum place,
All day, all day a grim expression lies
    Upon his changeless face.

All day, all day a thousand feet
Tread through the weary way;
All day, all day to labor's beat,
All day, all day.

All day, all day the bent souls yearn
For freedom from the toil;
All day, all day the pulleys turn,
Begrimed with dust and oil.
All day, all day the toiler's fate
'Tis drudge or never pay;
All day, all day the endless gait,
All day, all day.

Joe Cone

THE RED FLAG*

THE people's flag is deepest red,
It sheltered oft our martyred dead;
And ere their limbs grew stiff and cold,
Their hearts' blood dyed in its every fold.

Chorus:
Then raise the scarlet standard high,
Beneath its shade we'll live and die.
Tho' cowards flinch and traitors sneer
We'll keep the red flag flying here!

Look 'round! The Frenchman loves its blaze;
The sturdy German chants its praise;
In Moscow's vaults its hymns are sung;
Chicago swells its surging throng.

It waved above our infant might,
When all ahead seemed dark as night;
It witnessed many a deed and vow;
We must not change its color now.

It well recalls the triumphant past;
It gives the hope of peace at last;
The banner bright, the symbol plain
Of human right, of human gain.

It suits today the weak and base,
Whose minds are fixed on pelf and place,
To cringe before the rich man's frown
And haul the sacred emblem down.

Tune: Maryland, My Maryland.

With heads uncovered swear we all
To bear it onward till we fall;
Come dungeon dark and gallows grim,
This song shall be our parting hymn.

James Connell

THE WATCHWORD OF LABOR

OH, HEAR YE the watchword of labor, the slogan of those who'd be
  free,
That no more to any enslaver must labor bend suppliant knee,
That we on whose shoulders are borne the pomp and the pride of the
  great,
Whose toil they repay with their scorn, must challenge the masters of
  fate.

Chorus:
  Then send aloof on the breeze, boys,
    That watchword, the grandest we've known,
  That labor must rise from its knees, boys,
    And claim the broad earth as its own.

Ay, we who have won by our valor empire for our rulers and lords,
Yet knelt in abasement and squalor to the thing we had made by our
  swords,
Now valor and worth will be blending when, answering labor's
  command,
We arise from our knees and ascending to manhood for freedom take
  the stand.

Chorus:

Then out from the field, from the city, from workshop, from mill and
  from mine,
Despising their wrath and their pity, we workers are moving in line,
To answer the watchword and token that labor gives forth as its own;
Nor pause till our fetters we've broken, and conquered the spoiler and
  the drone.

James Connolly
(1870-1916)

From THE PARISH POOR-HOUSE

THEIR'S yon House that holds the Parish Poor,
Whose walls of mud scarce bear the broken door;
There, where the putrid vapors flagging play,
And the dull wheel hums doleful through the day;

There children dwell who know no parent's care;
Parents who know no children's love dwell there;
Heart-broken matrons on their joyless bed,
Forsaken wives and mothers never wed;
Dejected widows with unheeded tears,
And crippled age with more than childhood-fears;
The lame, the blind, and—far the happiest they!—
The moping idiot and the madman gay.
Here too the sick their final doom receive,
Here brought amid the scenes of grief, to grieve;
Where the loud groans from some sad chamber flow,
Mixed with the clamors of the crowd below;
Here, sorrowing, they each kindred sorrow scan,
And the cold charities of man to man!
Whose laws indeed for ruined age provide,
And strong compulsion plucks the scrap from pride;
But still that scrap is bought with many a sigh,
And pride imbitters what it can't deny.
Say ye, oppressed by some fantastic woes,
Some jarring nerve that baffles your repose;
Who press the downy couch while slaves advance,
With timid eye, to read the distant glance;
Who with sad prayers the weary doctor tease
To name the nameless ever-new disease;
Who with mock patience dire complaints endure,
Which real pain and that alone can cure:
How would ye bear in real pain to lie,
Despised, neglected, left alone to die?
How would ye bear to draw your latest breath
Where all that's wretched paves the way for death?

George Crabbe
(1754-1832)

SONG FOR LABOR DAY

I

Like the voice of many waters,
  Hear the tongues of every land!
Gather Labor's sons and daughters
  With one heart to understand.

  Sound upon the pipe and tabor!
    Blow the trumpet, beat the drum!
  Leave your toil, ye sons of Labor!
    Come a-maying, toilers, come!

II

From the field and from the city,
   See the highway thronged with folk,
Fain to win one day, for pity,
   From beneath the factory smoke.
     Sound, &c.

III

March they not in shining warfare,
   No sword they bear, or flashing blade;
But the pruning hook and ploughshare,
   But the worn wealth-winner's spade.
     Sound, &c.

IV

Winged to bear the torch afar,
   With dancing flame doth Freedom **lead,**
Shining in each heart a star,
   Scatt'ring o'er the earth her seed.
     Sound, &c.

V

As the horse with loosened traces
   Feels no more the wheels that grind,
So this day of days your faces
   Turn to hope—leave care behind!
     Sound, &c.

VI

See the floating standard, borne
   By stalwart arms and courage good,
Red with all the hopes of morn—
   The Banner of Man's Brotherhood.
     Sound, &c.

VII

Not like patient oxen, bearing
   Fruits of earth for idlers' hands,
But like men and women, sharing
   Commonwealth and common lands.
     Sound, &c.

VIII

Fruits of earth and fruits of ocean,
   Spade and trident side by side;
Like the sea's resistless motion,
   Around the world sweeps Labor's tide.
     Sound, &c.

IX

Hand to hand, let every toiler
　Make a circlet 'round the world:
Break the bonds of slave and spoiler
　Beneath the heart-hued flag unfurled!
　　Sound, &c.

X

Rejoice, then, weary-hearted mothers,
　That your little ones shall see
Brighter days—O men and brothers—
　When Life and Labor ye set free!

　Sound upon the pipe and tabor!
　　Blow the trumpet, beat the drum!
　Leave your toil, ye sons of Labor!
　　Come a-maying, toilers, come!

　　　　　　　Walter Crane
　　　　　　　(1845-1915)

NINETY-NINE IN THE SHADE

As I look up to the stars, lo, behold!
Comes to my ear, as to shepherds of old,
Strains, as it were, from a heavenly choir,
Singing, "O brothers who toil, never tire!
Justice will come if you look for it higher!"

WALK with me down through the furnace-like street,
Feel the hot paving-stones under my feet;
Breathe the dead air; smell the vile human smells;
Don't lag behind though your stomach rebels.
Now it is night, and the sun has long set;
Still how its rays seem to blister us yet.
Elbow your way through the sweltering mass,
Moist, pallid faces are turned as we pass.
Some are of men who have toiled all day.
Children are screaming in dearth as they play;
Woe-begone women, with babes at the breast,
Sit in the doorways unkempt and half dressed.
All talk at once; the night passes in din.
Soon will the work of a new day begin.
Ah, 'tis enough to make angels despair;
This the thing they call taking the air!
Enter this hallway; climb five flights of stairs;
Visit the dens where the poor have their lairs,—
Kitchen and bedroom and parlor in one,

Cooking the life that was left by the sun,—
Windowless cupboards where men try to sleep,
Heedless of roaches and bugs as they creep.
Some born with fever, and here they must die,
Crowded like litters of pigs in a sty.
One narrow house, rising floor above floor,
Holds a few hundred of mortals or more.
Up on a roof see a score or two lie,
Seeking for slumber beneath the dull sky.
Let us be proud of the city we've made,
After a day of ninety-nine in the shade.

Follow me now to the streets near the Park.
Palace and mansion loom up in the dark.
Windows are closed; all the people have fled.
Surely this seems like a town of the dead.
Gone to the mountains or gone to the sea,
Traveling to Europe for two months or three;
Here they have left in the heat and the gloom
Houses as empty of life as the tomb.
Come, I've a latch-key, let's go in the room
Ghost-like through halls of what once was a home.
Look at the tables and pictures and all
Covered each one like a corpse with its pall.
Beds of the softest invitingly stand,
Luxury wickedly cumbering the land.
Here, were the waifs of the slums to repose,
Soon they'd forget all their trials and woes.
Think what a blessing,—I say it with wrath,—
Could they but dip in this porcelain bath.
Miles upon miles of such houses stretch forth,
Bolted and barred from the south to the north.
Children may perish like flies in the heat,
How could we let them pollute a fine street?
Let us be proud of the city we've made,
After a day of ninety-nine in the shade.

Down on the curb again, what do I hear?
Up from the sewer comes a song harsh and clear.
List to the words of the devil's own choir,
"Sodom, Gemorrah, with Sidon and Tyre,
Wait for New York in the depths of hell-fire."

Ernest Crosby
(1856-1907)

TO THE GENERATION THAT IS KNOCKING
AT THE DOOR

BREAK—break it open; let the knocker rust:
Consider no "shalt not," no man's "must."
And, being entered, promptly take the lead,
Setting aside tradition, custom, creed;
Nor watch the balance of the huckster's beam;
Declare your hardiest thoughts, your proudest dream;
Await no summons; laugh at all rebuff;
High hearts and you are destiny enough.
The mystery and power enshrined in you
Are old as time and as the moment new;
And none but you can tell what part you play,
Nor can you tell until you make assay,
For this alone, this always, will succeed:
The miracle and magic of the deed.

John Davidson

From THE TESTAMENT OF A MAN FORBID

THIS Beauty, this Divinity, this Thought,
This hallowed bower and harvest of delight
Whose roots ethereal seemed to clutch the stars,
Whose amaranths perfumed eternity,
Is fixed in earthly soil enriched with bones
Of used-up workers; fattened with the blood
Of prostitutes, the prime manure; and dressed
With brains of madmen and the broken hearts
Of children. Understand it, you at least
Who toil all day and writhe and groan all night
With roots of luxury; a cancer struck
In every muscle: out of you it is
Cathedrals rise and Heaven blossoms fair;
You are the hidden putrefying source
Of beauty and delight, of leisured hours,
Of passionate loves and high imaginings;
You are the dung that keeps the roses sweet.
I say, uproot it; plough the land; and let
A summer-fallow sweeten all the World.

John Davidson
(1857-1909)

From A BALLAD OF FREEDOM

THE Frenchman sailed in freedom's name to smite the Algerine,
The strife was short, the crescent sunk, and then his guile was seen;
For, nestling in the pirate's hold—a fiercer pirate far—

He bade the tribes yield up their flocks, the towns their gates unbar.
Right on he pressed with freemen's hands to subjugate the free,
The Berber in old Atlas glens, the Moor in Titteri;

* * *

The Englishman for long, long years, had ravaged Ganges' side;
A dealer first, intriguer next, he conquered far and wide,
Till, hurried on by avarice, and thirst of endless rule,
His sepoys pierced to Candahar, his flag waved in Cabul;
But still within the conquered land was one unconquered man,
The fierce Pushtani* lion, the fiery Akhbar Khan—
He slew the sepoys on the snow, till Scindh's full flood they swam it
Right rapidly, content to flee the son of Dost Mohammed,
The son of Dost Mohammed! and brave old Dost Mohammed.

* * *

But Russia preys on Poland's fields, where Sobieski reigned,
And Austria on Italy—the Roman eagle chained—
Bohemia, Servia, Hungary within her clutches gasp.
And Ireland struggles gallantly in England's loosening grasp.
Oh! would all these their strength unite, or battle on alone,
Like Moor, Pushtani, and Cherkess, they soon would have their own!
Hurrah! hurrah! it can't be far, when from the Scindh to Shannon
Shall gleam a line of freemen's flags begirt by freemen's cannon!
The coming day of freedom—the flashing flags of freedom.

Thomas Davis
(1814-1845)

*Afghan.

OUT OF THE DARKNESS

WHO am I? Only one of the common people,
Only a worked-out body, a shriveled and withered soul.
What right have I to sing, then? None; and I do not, I cannot.
Why ruin the rhythm and rhyme of the great world's songs with
    moaning?
I know not—nor know why whistles must shriek, wheels ceaselessly
    mutter;
Nor why all I touch turns to clanging and clashing discord;
I know not; I know only this—I was born to this, live in it hourly,
Go round with it, hum with it, curse with it, would laugh with it
    had it laughter;
It is my breath—and breath goes outward from me in moaning.

Oh, you, up there, I have heard you; I am "God's image defaced,"
"In heaven reward awaits me"—"hereafter I shall be perfect";
Ages you have sung that song—but what is it to me, think you?
If you heard down here in the smoke and the smut, the sneer **and**
    the offal,

In the dust, in the mire, in the grime and the slime, the hideous
    darkness,
How the wheels turn your songs into sounds of horror and loathing
    and cursing.
The offer of lust, the sneer of contempt and acceptance, thieves'
    whispers,
The laugh of the gambler, the suicide's gasp, the yell of the drunkard,
If you heard them down here you would say the reward of such is
    damnation,
If you heard them, I say, your song of "reward hereafter" would fail.

You too, with your science, your titles, your books and your long
    explanations
That tell me how I am come up out of the dust of the cycles,
Out of the sands of the sea—out of the unknown primeval forests;
Out of the growth of the world have become the bud and the promise,
Out of the race of beasts have arisen, proud and triumphant;
You, if you knew how your words rumble around the wheels of labor,
If you knew how many hammering hearts beat: "Liar! Liar! You lie!
Out of all the earth we are the most blasted and blighted;
What beast of all the beasts is not prouder and freer than we?"

You too, who sing in high woods of the glory of Man Universal,
Sacrifice beauty, the debt of the future, the Present mortal,
The glory of use, absorption by Death of the being in Being.
You, if you knew what jargon it makes down here, would be quiet.
Oh, is there not one to find or to speak a meaning to me,
To me, as I am—the hard, the ignorant, withered-souled worker,
To me upon whom God and Science alike have stamped "failure,"
To me who know nothing but labor, nothing but sweat, dirt and
    sorrow,
To me who can scorn and despise you up there who sing while I moan,
To me as I am, for me as I am—not dying but living;
Not my future, my present? My body, my needs, my desires.

        Is there no one

In the midst of this rushing of phantoms of Gods, of Science, of Logic,
Of Philosophy, Morals, Religion, Economy—all this that helps not,
All these ghosts at whose altars you worship, these ponderous marrow-
    less fictions,
Is there no one who thinks, is there nothing to help this dull moaning
    of men?

Voltairine de Cleyre
(1866-1912)

THE STREET DIGGERS

STRAINING and striving and digging where the earth is clammy and
    brown,
Laughing and sighing and singing, the toilers are struggling down
Through the crust where a million foot-falls have tramped through the
    braved years
And the grief of a million mourners has sprinkled the way with tears.

The city is grim and heartless to the ways where toilers delve—
A thought for the task in motion and a thousand more for self.
Who recks if a heart is racking; who cares if a mind is scarred?
The click of the pick is the minute tick, where the lip of the pit is
    bared.
The click of the pit keeps growing apace where the muscles and sinew
    and thew
Are throbbing in aching protest where the click of the pick is true.
And the sun in bundles of burning brands and in broiling shafts
    shoots down
On hands that are bronzed and ready and rough, in the eyes of the
    seething town.

So the pit and the night are the price by right and the song and the
    sigh go on
While the clouds they hover above and around and frown as the task
    is done.
And the pit is the grave of a thousand hopes that have harried with
    noiseless feet;
Far away to the heart of the lightless land from the lip of the pit
    in the street.

                       S. J. Donleavy

A DREAM

I DREAMED one night a wondrous dream, another world I saw
And it most marvelous did seem, no government or law,
No kings or presidents were there, no emperors or czars,
No despots waving sword in air, no followers of Mars.

The people scarce did work at all, abundantly seemed blest;
No enemies there to cringe and crawl, at tyranny's behest;
The men and women eye to eye did upright stand and look,
And no one could deceive or lie, each mind an open book.

I strolled among the merry bands of children on the green;
They danced and sang while holding hands, a truly fairy scene.
An edifice imposing grand, which crowned a low green hill,
Gave sweet music from a band which made the heart-strings thrill.

Such splendor charmed me and amazed, delighted eye and mind.
And thus entranced I stood and gazed, fresh wonders still did find:
What magic scenery was this, what kindly fairy wand
That scattered broadcast perfect bliss? I could not understand.

So simple was it when explained, one scarce could realize
That other systems once obtained, slave systems based on lies,
Slave systems that were overthrown by causes, in them bred;
The wage-slave system, be it known, was numbered with the dead.

Experience did educate for that which came to pass;
Themselves did they emancipate—the mighty working class—
In mills and mines, on ships and farms, all wealth did they create;
At last, in spite of false alarms, they struck and felled the State.

L. E. Drake

I HAVE COME

Out of the Void, the mist and slime,
  Out of the Mighty Past,
Out of the hidden holes of Time
  I am as I am cast.

Millions of years are behind me,
  And millions, perhaps, before;
But the forces that once confined me
  Now let me move on—and more.

Millions I have met in my struggle—
  Millions of species—aye;
Some of them lived for a future time,
  But most of them lived to die.

Battle and bloodshed and sorrow
  Mark the sad tale of my life;
But I am Building the Future, To-Morrow—
  The Product of Time and its strife.

Louis Duchez

THE SONG OF TOIL

Let him who will rehearse the song
  Of gentle love and bright romance—
Let him who will, with tripping tongue,
  Lead gleaming thoughts to fancy's dance;

But let me strike mine iron harp
    As northern harps were struck of old—
And let its music, stern and sharp,
    Arouse the free and bold!

My hands that iron harp shall sweep,
    Till from each stroke new strains recoil,
And forth the sounding echoes leap,
    To join the rousing Song of Toil.
Till men of thought their thoughts outspeak
    And thoughts awake in kindred mind;
And stirring words shall arm the weak,
    And fetters cease to bind.

And crashing soon, o'er soul and sense,
    That glorious harp, whose iron strings
Are Labor's mighty instruments,
    Shall shake the thrones of mortal kings!
And ring of axe, and anvil note,
    And rush of plough, through yielding soil,
And laboring engine's vocal throat
    Shall swell the Song of Toil!

A. Dugganne
(1823-1884)

A WINTER'S DAY

Across the hills and down the narrow ways,
    And up the valley where the free winds sweep,
    The earth is folded in an ermined sleep
That mocks the melting mirth of myriad Mays.
Departed her disheartening duns and grays,
    And all her crusty black is covered deep.
    Dark streams are locked in winter's donjon-keep,
And made to shine with keen, unwanted rays.
O icy mantle and deceitful snow!
    What world-old liars in your hearts you are!
    Are there not still the darkened seam and scar
Beneath the brightness that you fain would show?
Come from the cover with thy blotch and blur,
O reeking Earth, thou whited sepulchre!

Paul Laurence Dunbar
(1872-1906)

A NEW NATIONAL HYMN

WE ARE marching on to glory with the bible in our hands,
We are carrying the gospel to the lost in foreign lands;
We are marching on to glory, we are going forth to save
With the zeal of ancient priest, with the prayer of modern knave;
We are robbing Christian churches in our missionary zeal,
And we carry Christ's own message in our shells and bloody steel.
By the light of burning roof-trees they may read the Word of Life,
In the mangled forms of children they may see the Christian Strife.
We are healing with the gatling, we are blessing with the sword;
For the Honor of the Nation and the Glory of the Lord.

Then march on, Christian soldiers! with sword and torch in hand,
And carry free salvation to each benighted land!
Go, preach God's Love and Justice with steel and shot and shell!
Go, preach a future Heaven and prove the present Hell!
Baptize with blood and fire, with every gun's last breath,
Teach them to love the Father, and make them free in Death;
Proclaim the newer gospel; the cannon giveth peace,
Christ rides upon the warship his army to increase.
So bless them with the rifle and heal them with the sword—
For the Honor of the Nation and the Glory of the Lord!

William G. Eggleston

THE UNIVERSAL SONG

LET me go where'er I will,
I hear a sky-born music still:
It sounds from all things old,
It sounds from all things young,
From all that's fair, from all that's foul,
Peals out a cheerful song.
It is not only in the rose,
It is not only in the bird,
Not only where the rainbow glows,
Nor in the song of woman heard,
But in the darkest, meanest things,
There alway, alway something sings.
'Tis not in the high stars alone,
Nor in the cups of budding flowers;
Nor in the redbreast's mellow tone,
Nor in the bow that smiles in showers,
But in the mud and scum of things
There alway, alway something sings.

Ralph Waldo Emerson
(1803-1882)

WHO CAN BLAME?

WHEN the mills of men have ground us
  To the fighting edge of fate,
Who can blame if lying around us
  Is the wreckage of blind hate?

When for dollars we are broken
  Like a faggot for a fire,
Who can blame if by that token
  We inflame in razing ire?

When with being slave and chattel
  For a pittance we have done,
Who can blame if we give battle?
  We are many, they are one!

Herbert Everett

TO THE WORKERS

YOUR kings and your countries need you—
  You, the sons of honest toil;
But your countries have been stolen,
  You're needed to guard the spoil.

Flower of the nation's manhood,
  They need you but a day;
Mayhap, the morning's sun will rise
  On heaps of bleeding clay.

I see the bloody plains of war
  Swept clear with shot and shell;
Death's scythe is sweeping quickly past;
  Gape wide the jaws of hell.

I hear the cannon's roar,
  The cry of souls in anguish;
And maimed and mangled, friend and foe,
  Are left to die in anguish.

O men, where does the honor lie,
  In deeds of foulest murder;
To rob a mother of her son,
  Or children of their father?

You build the ships, the ships of war,
  To dominate the foam;
To guard the land you don't possess,
  And your hovel, called a home.

You build the lofty palace hall,
    You build the prison cell;
You forge the tatters of the chain
    To bind yourselves in hell.

You toil and sweat, you spin and weave,
    You plow the fertile lands,
Yet in the fruitful summer-time
    You stand with empty hands.

Remember this: the great are great
    Whilst you on knee are bended;
But stand and act and think like men,
    The tyrant's day is ended.

Frank A. Fearnley

From A NEW YEAR'S CAROL

Awake, awake! The world is young,
For all its weary years of thought:
The starkest fights must still be fought,
The most surprising songs be sung.

Then hear the shouting voice of men
Magniloquently rise and ring:
Their flashing eyes and measured swing
Prove that the world is young again.

O stubborn arms of rosy youth,
Break down your other Gods, and turn
To where her dauntless eyeballs burn—
The silent pools of Light and Truth.

James Elroy Flecker
(1884-1915)

FREEDOM FOR THE MIND*

High walls and huge the body may confine,
And iron grates obstruct the prisoner's gaze,
And massive bolts may baffle his design,
And vigilant keepers watch his devious ways:
Yet scorns the immortal mind this base control!
No chains can bind it, and no cell enclose:
Swifter than light, it flies from pole to pole,
And, in a flash, from earth to heaven it goes!
It leaps from mount to mount—from vale to vale

*Written while in prison for opposing Negro slavery in the United States.—M. G.

It wanders plucking honeyed fruits and flowers;
It visits home, to hear the fireside tale,
Or in sweet converse pass the joyous hours.
'Tis up before the sun, roaming afar,
And, in its watches, rises every star.

William Lloyd Garrison
(1805-1879)

THE CRAZY WORLD

THE world did say to me,
  "My bread thou shalt not eat,
I have no place for thee
  In house nor field nor street.

"I have no land nor sea
  For thee nor home nor bread,
I scarce can give to thee
  A grave when thou art dead."

"O crazy World," said I,
  "What is it thou canst give,
Which wanting, I must die,
  Or having, I shall live?

"When thou thy all hast spent,
  And all thy harvests cease,
I still have nutriment
  That groweth by decrease.

"Thy streets will pass away,
  The towers of steel be rust,
Thy heights to plains decay,
  Thyself be wandering dust;

"But I go ever on
  From prime to endless prime,
I sit on Being's throne,
  A lord o'er space and time."

"Then, crazy World," said I,
  "What is it thou canst give,
Which wanting I must die,
  Or having I shall live?"

William Gay
(1865-1897)

REVOLUTION

Lo, THEY come with hope abounding;
   Their march is in the street;
Oppression's doom is sounding
   In the tramping of their feet.

They, the toilers of the city;
   They, the toilers of the field;
For whom Mercy had no pity
   And Justice had no shield.

They march, their hearts are glowing
   With the fire of freedom's breath;
Their hands have the bestowing
   Of the gift of life or death.

Their hopes are as the morning,
   As the quieting of the night—
As a clarion blast of warning,
   As a sweet song of delight.

For a vision shines before them
   Making all daylight dim:
And its glory trembles o'er them
   Like the flight of cherubim.

And within its bright unfolding,
   The "Glorious times to be,"
Which long in dark beholding
   Now in the noontide light they see.

The heroic dead arisen
   March exultant by their side;
And from exile and from prison
   Come their comrades glorified.

               J. Bruce Glasier
               (1859-1920)

From THE DESERTED VILLAGE

WHERE THEN, ah! where, shall poverty reside,
To 'scape the pressure of contiguous pride?
If to some common's fenceless limits stray'd,
He drives his flock to pick the scanty blade,
Those fenceless fields the sons of wealth divide,
And even the bare-worn common is denied.

If to the city sped—What waits him there?
To see profusion that he must not share;
To see ten thousand baneful arts combined
To pamper luxury, and thin mankind;
To see those joys the sons of pleasure know
Extorted from his fellow-creature's woe.
Here, while the courtier glitters in brocade ,
There the pale artist plies the sickly trade;
Here, while the proud their long-drawn pomps display,
There the black gibbet glooms beside the way.
The dome where Pleasure holds her midnight reign
Here, richly deck'd, admits the gorgeous train;
Tumultuous grandeur crowds the blazing square—
The rattling chariots clash, the torches glare.
Sure scenes like these no troubles e'er annoy!
Sure these denote one universal joy!

  * * * * *

O luxury! thou curs'd by Heaven's decree,
How ill exchang'd are things like these for thee!
How do thy potions, with insidious joy
Diffuse their pleasures only to destroy!
Kingdoms, by thee, to sickly greatness grown,
Boast of a florid vigor not their own.
At every drought more large and large they grow,
A bloated mass of rank unwieldy woe;
Till sapped their strength, and every part unsound,
Down, down they sink, and spread a ruin round.

Oliver Goldsmith
(1728-1774)

ANARCHIST

As ONE upon no mission bent
I came—no sacerdotal cause
Save just to live by nature's laws,
And her direct arbitrament.
To hold in awe; to please myself,
And thus the world a service do;
To drive devoid the greed of pelf,
The product of my labor mine.
To crouch to none, to crave no sway,
But inward from the leagues of blue
To drink the gladness of the lovely day,
To dwell in peace, and bear no fruitless pain.

But I—who love the wood and stream,
The winning voice of Day and Night,

And Man and Beast, and Art and Song;
And fain would wander in a dream
Of life and love, and seek delight
In gentle woods, forgetting wrong,
Musing o'er mellow sunsets lost
In contemplation's misty deep—
I, who would ever seek to find
The mystery that lurks behind
Fair nature's apparition, must
Into this bitter warfare leap,
The unaccustomed steel upon me bind
And, facing Hell, give biting thrust for thrust.

William Walston Gordak

FREETHOUGHT

GREAT word, that fill'st my mind with calm delight,
I love to feel, but cannot hope to tell,
How, like the noonday sun, thou dost dispel
The mists of error that impede our sight!
What noble dreams, what yearning hopes excite!
What memories too awake at sound of thee,
Like myriad ripples on a wind-swept sea!
How full and irresistible thy might!
Thou causest to grow pale the tyrant's cheek;
Thou art the knell that loud proclaims the fall
Of despots and of priests, and those who seek
To crush the human mind beneath their thrall:
Thou dost avenge all wrong, make strong the weak—
Nobility and heritage of all!

Edward H. Guillaume

WE AND YE

WE of the hut and the hovel,
  We of the grime and sweat,
To you of the purple and linen fine,
Of the palace home and the sparkling wine,
  Are exceedingly in debt!

For our bread we are indebted
  To you of the banquet spread,—
For the crumbs that fall when ye need no more,
For the hunger howls of the wolf at the door,
  Ye, for our famished dead!

For our lives we are indebted
    To ye that lord the earth!
Our lives! Ha, ha! Look on and see
For the gift how thankful we should be!
    Ye gods! Is it not worth?

For its round of ceaseless travail,
    Of knavish fears and cares,
For darkened mind and stunted frame,
For childhood lost and blotted name,
    We owe you, O Millionaires!

For many a long-drawn contest,
    Our hunger against your gold,—
Your gold and the right arm of the law,
And the breath of Famine's gasping maw,
    'Gainst us, O ye Warriors bold!

Red Cœur d'Alene and Homestead
    Were yours, Victorious Foe,
And the cities twain beside the Lakes,
Where brothers fell e'en for our sakes!
    But ours was the debt and woe!

For ever and ever it crieth,
    And we may not forget,
The blood of the murdered Twenty-four!*
Say, shall we pay you with golden ore,
    O Plutocrats, this deep debt?

Yea, but our debts be many,
    We of the grime and sweat.
Awake, O Sleepers, O Blind, and think!
'Tis not well to dream on the crater's brink!
    We love not to be in debt!

Margaret Haile

*In the steel strike of 1892-1893.—M. G.

THE STRAIGHT ROAD

THEY GOT Y', kid: they got y'—just like I said they would.
    You tried to walk the narrow path,
    You tried, and got an awful laugh;
And laughs are all y' did get, kid—they got y' good!

They never knew the little kid—the kid I used to know;
    The little bare-legged girl back home,
    The little kid that played alone—
They don't know half the things I know, kid, ain't it so?

They got y', kid, they got y'—you know they got y' right;
    They waited till they saw y' limp,
    Then introduced y' to the pimp—
Ah, you were down then, kid, and couldn't fight!

I guess y' know what some don't know, and others know damn well—
    That sweatshops don't grow angels' wings,
    That workin' girls is easy things,
And poverty's the straightest road t' Hell!

Paul Hanna
(1882-1925)

THE MAN HE KILLED

"HAD HE and I but met
    By some old ancient inn,
We should have sat us down to wet
    Right many a nipperkin!

"But ranged as infantry,
    And staring face to face,
I shot at him as he at me,
    And killed him in his place.

"I shot him dead because—
    Because he was my foe,
Just so: my foe of course he was;
    That's clear enough; although

"He thought he'd 'list perhaps,
    Off-hand like—just as I—
Was out of work—and sold his traps—
    No other reason why.

"Yes; quaint and curious war is!
    You shoot a fellow down;
You'd treat if met where any bar is,
    Or help to half-a-crown."

Thomas Hardy

GOING AND STAYING

THE MOVING sun-shapes on the spray,
The sparkles where the brook was flowing,
Pink faces, plightings, moonlit May,
These were the things we wished would stay;
    But they were going.

Seasons of dankness as of snow,
The silent bleed of a world decaying,
The moan of multitudes in woe,
These were the things we wished would go;
    But they were staying.

Thomas Hardy
(1840-1928)

THE WORKERS' SONG OF THE SPRINGTIDE

WE HAVE heard that the spring is lovely,
    That the whole earth leaps with glee
When the young May brings to the woodlands
    The rapture of being free;
But we know when the springtime cometh
    Though we cannot see its grace,
For our prisoning walls grow closer
    With the sun's glare in our face.

For us, in the spring, not the singing
    Of birds, but the whirling of wheels,
And the shrieking of noisy engines
    Till our brain with discord reels;
And the stifling air of our work cells
    Grows hotter and fiercer far:
Oh, curse we the sultry springtide
    Where pests and hot fever are.

We have heard of the happy forests
    Where the gurgling streamlets play,
And the merry flowers listen
    To the song of the birds all day;
But for us, in our homes in slumland,
    What beauty is there at all,
Where the very skies above us
    Are black with the smoke's cursed pall?

We know there are some with leisure,
    Who roam where the world is sweet,

But we to our factory prisons
  Are chained by the hands and feet;
For the cry of our babes is sounding
  Forever within our ears,
And we toil for the bread to feed them,
  With a toil that is full of fears.

We built the homes of our masters,
  Where always at ease they dwell;
And the sound of music greets them,
  'Midst the comfort they love so well;
But we know that their ease is builded
  On the hunger and pain we bear,
Their pleasure upon our toiling,
  Their hope upon our despair.

The song of the merry springtide
  Is sweet to them indeed,
These wealthy whom we are clothing,
  Whose little ones we feed;
But to us is the sun a furnace,
  The spring but a scorching hell,
The sky but a burning cauldron,
  And life but a prison cell.

But the time will come when the beauties
  Of earth shall be for all,
When none on his brother's slavehood
  Shall base his freedom from thrall,
When the spring shall bring us gladness,
  And pleasure in place of pain,
To us who have toiled and sorrowed,
  Nor tasted our toiling's gain!

Fred Henderson

INVICTUS

OUT OF the night that covers me,
  Black as the pit from pole to pole,
I thank whatever gods may be
  For my unconquerable soul.

In the fell clutch of circumstance
  I have not winced nor cried aloud.
Under the bludgeonings of chance
  My head is bloody, but unbowed.

Beyond this place of wrath and tears
  Looms but the horror of the shade,
And yet the menace of the years
  Finds, and shall find me, unafraid.

It matters not how strait the gate,
  How charged with punishments the scroll,
I am the master of my fate:
  I am the captain of my soul.

William Ernest Henley
(1849-1903)

From SONGS OF NEW LONDON

LET US pull London down and stand
Once more 'neath skies, and walk on land!
Let us pull London down and make
A place to keep the soul awake.
Destroy the city and forget
A new one in its room to set!

Th' invading sun, besieging trees,
Would purge the town of all disease.
Fireless and bedless, Bloomsbury cats
Would kill each other on Thames' flats,
And all the mice of Mount Street flock
To drown in cages of baroque.

Robert Herrick

MAKE THE WORLD

OH, COME, ye toilers of the earth,
  Ye who for masters sow and reap,
Who make and dye, but have no cloth,
  Whose fruits are but the tears ye weep.

Come, ye who build but homeless are,
  Who are as cattle bought and sold,
Whose souls and bodies are but grist,
  Your children, too, but ground to gold.

Come, ye creators of the world,
  To whom the world as aye belonged,
Yet are yoked by what ye work,
  By your creation robbed and wronged.

Come, victims of the lawless laws
  Your masters make to keep you bound,

And ye who went out after priests,
Yet neither faith nor virtue found.

Oh, come, ye outcasts of the earth,
And let us end the human night,
The priests and masters, yokes and lies,
And build for love the world of light.

Oh, piteous processions, come,
Yoke-bearers of the human night,
And let's make the world a home,
A fellowship of love and light.

George D. Herron
(1862-1925)

THOUGHTS

I WISH 'twas six; the factory bell, oh! will it ever ring?
I wish the time would pass away, the spindles cease to spin.
Oh, if the big machine would break, the pulley shaft or cone.
I want to quit at six o'clock and then to hurry home.

I wish 'twas six; the factory grime would fall from my haggard
face.
My head is aching, tho I hear there are plenty to fill my place;
My lungs are inhaling the factory dust, I hear the foreman say,
"Faster, faster you must, you must, no need for this delay!"

I gazed through the open window, and grazing in the grass,
To my surprise I recognized the mirage of an ass,
And he seemed to be free and happy, so far as I could see,
I could easily call him a jackass, but what could he call me?

Edw. Higgins

THE PREACHER AND THE SLAVE*

LONG-HAIRED preachers come out every night,
Try to tell you what's wrong and what's right;
But when asked how 'bout something to eat
They will answer with voices so sweet:

Chorus:

You will eat, bye and bye,
In that glorious land above the sky;
Work and pray, live on hay,
You'll get pie in the sky when you die.

*The above song (tune "Sweet Bye and Bye") is one of the most characteristic
parodies written by Joe Hill, who was killed by the State of Utah in the year 1915.
It is still popular with the I. W. W., (Industrial Workers of the World) of which
organization Hill was a member.—M.G.

And the Starvation Army they play,
And they sing and they clap and they pray,
Till they get all their coin on the drum,
Then they'll tell you when you're on the bum: (*Chorus*)

If you fight hard for children and wife—
Try to get something good in this life—
You're a sinner and bad man, they tell,
When you die you will sure go to hell.   (*Chorus*)

Working men of all countries, unite,
Side by side we for freedom will fight;
When the world and its wealth we shall gain
To the grafters we'll sing this refrain:

Chorus:
You will eat bye and bye,
    When you've learned how to cook and fry;
Chop some wood, 'twill do you good,
    And you'll eat in the sweet bye and bye.

Joe Hill (Joseph Hillstrom)
(1882-1915)

MISS KILMANSEGG: HER MORAL*

Gold! Gold! Gold! Gold!
Bright and yellow, hard and cold,
Molten, graven, hammer'd, and roll'd;
Heavy to get, and light to hold;
Hoarded, barter'd, bought, and sold,
Stolen, borrow'd, squander'd, doled:
Spurn'd by the young, but hugg'd by the old
To the very verge of the churchyard mould;
Price of many a crime untold:
Gold! Gold! Gold! Gold!
Good or bad a thousand-fold!

How widely its agencies vary—
To save—to ruin—to curse—to bless—
As even its minted coins express,
Now stamp'd with the image of Good Queen Bess,
    And now of a bloody Mary.

Thomas Hood

*From *Miss Kilmansegg and Her Precious Leg*

THE SONG OF THE SHIRT

WITH fingers weary and worn,
  With eyelids heavy and red
A woman sat, in unwomanly rags,
  Plying her needle and thread—
    Stitch! stitch! stitch!
In poverty, hunger and dirt,
  And still with a voice of dolorous pitch
She sang the "Song of the Shirt!"

"Work! work! work!
While the cock is crying aloof!
  And work—work—work—
Till the stars shine through the roof!
It's O! to be a slave
  Along with the barbarous Turk,
Where woman has never a soul to save,
  If this is Christian work!

"Work—work—work—!
Till the brain begins to swim!
Work—work—work—
  Till the eyes are heavy and dim!
Seam, and gusset, and band,
  Band, and gusset, and seam,
Till over the buttons I fall asleep,
  And sew them on in a dream.

"O men with sisters dear!
  O men with mothers and wives!
It is not linen you're wearing out,
  But human creatures' lives!
    Stitch—stitch—stitch—
In poverty, hunger, and dirt,
Sewing at once with a double thread,
  A Shroud as well as a Shirt!

"But why do I talk of Death?
  That phantom of grisly bone.
I hardly fear his terrible shape,
  It seems so like my own—
    It seems so like my own,
  Because of the fasts I keep;
O God! that bread should be so dear,
  And flesh and blood so cheap!

"Work—work—work
My labor never flags;
And what are its wages? A bed of straw,
   A crust of bread—and rags.
That shatter'd roof—and this naked floor—
   A table—a broken chair—
And a wall so blank, my shadow I thank
   For sometimes falling there!

Work—work—work—!
   From weary chime to chime,
Work—work—work—
   As prisoners work for crime!
Band, and gusset, and seam,
   Seam, and gusset, and band,
Till the heart is sick, and the brain benumb'd,
   As well as the weary hand.

"Work—work—work—
In the dull December light,
   And work—work—work—
When the weather is warm and bright—
While underneath the eaves
   The brooding swallows cling,
As if to show me their sunny backs
   And twit me with the spring.

"O but to breathe the breath
Of the cowslip and primrose sweet—
   With the sky above my head,
And the grass beneath my feet;
For only one short hour
   To feel as I used to feel,
Before I knew the woes of want
   And the walk that costs a meal.

"O but for one short hour!
   A respite however brief!
No blessed leisure for Love or Hope,
   But only time for Grief—
A little weeping would ease my heart,
   But in their briny bed
My tears must stop, for every drop
   Hinders needle and thread!"

"Seam, and gusset, and band,
Band, and gusset, and seam,

Work, work, work
Like the Engine that works by Steam!
A mere machine of iron and wood
   That toils for Mammon's sake—
Without a brain to ponder and craze,
   Or a heart to feel and break!

With fingers weary and worn,
   With eyelids heavy and red,
A woman sat, in unwomanly rags,
   Plying her needle and thread—
      Stitch! stitch! stitch!
   In poverty, hunger, and dirt,
And still with a voice of dolorous pitch,—
Would that its tone could reach the Rich!—
   She sang this "Song of the Shirt!"

Thomas Hood
(1799-1845)

From AT THE END OF THE DAY

THERE is no escape by the river,
There is no flight left by the fen;
We are compassed about by the shiver
Of the night of their marching men.
Give a cheer!
For our hearts shall not give way.
Here's to a dark to-morrow,
And here's to a brave to-day!

The tale of their hosts is countless,
And the tale of ours a score;
But the palm is naught to the dauntless,
And the cause is more and more.
Give a cheer!
We may die, but not give way.
Here's to a silent morrow
And here's to a stout to-day!

Richard Hovey
(1864-1900)

THE SONG OF THE WAGE-SLAVE

THE LAND it is the landlord's,
   The trader's is the sea,
The ore the usurer's coffer fills—
   But what remains for me?

The engine whirls for master's craft;
  The steel shines to defend,
With labor's arms, what labor raised,
  For labor's foe to spend.
The camp, the pulpit, and the law
  For rich men's sons are free;
Theirs, theirs the learning, art, and arms—
  But what remains for me?
    The coming hope, the future day,
      When wrong to right shall bow,
    And hearts that have the courage, man,
      To make that future _now_.

I pay for all their learning,
  I toil for all their ease;
They render back, in coin for coin,
  Want, ignorance, disease:
Toil, toil—and then a cheerless home,
  Where hungry passions cross;
Eternal gain to them that give
  To me eternal loss!
The hour of leisured happiness
  The rich alone may see;
The playful child, the smiling wife—
  But what remains for me?
They render back, those rich men,
  A pauper's niggard fee,
Mayhap a prison—then a grave,
  And think they are quits with me;
But not a fond wife's heart that breaks,
  A poor man's child that dies,
We score not on our hollow cheeks
  And in our sunken eyes;
We read it there, where'er we meet,
  And as the sun we see,
Each asks, "The rich have got the earth,
  And what remains for me?"

We bear the wrong in silence,
  We store it in our brain;
They think us dull, they think us dead,
  But we shall rise again:
A trumpet through the lands will ring;
  A heaving through the mass;
A trampling through their palaces
  Until they break like glass:

We'll cease to weep by cherished graves,
From lonely homes we'll flee;
And still, as rolls our million march,
Its watchword brave shall be—
The coming hope, the future day,
When wrong to right shall bow,
And hearts that have the courage, man,
To make that future *now*.

Ernest Jones
(1819-1868)

WHEN FREEDOM MOURNS

WHEN hordes with lance and sabre
Spread desolation wide,
And bloody murder revels
Along the crimson tide.

When hungry famine follows
The devastating flame,
And tender children vainly call
A slaughtered father's name.

When homes are burned and plundered,
And widowed women weep,
Distorted lie the mangled dead
In their eternal sleep.

Then desolated Freedom mourns
Her immolated sons;
And lamentations mingle with
The echoes of the guns.

Daniel Kerr

From ROOFS

I NEVER have seen a vagabond who really liked to roam
All up and down the streets of the world and not to have a home:
The tramp who slept in your barn last night and left at break of day
Will wander only until he finds another place to stay.

From THE APARTMENT HOUSES

SEVERE against the pleasant arc of sky
The great stone box is cruelly displayed.
The street becomes more dreary from its shade,

And vagrant breezes touch its walls and die.
Here sullen convicts in their chains might lie;
   Or slaves toil dumbly at some dreary trade.
   How worse than folly is their labor made
Who cleft the rocks that this might rise on high!

Joyce Kilmer
(1886—1918)

STRUGGLE

MY SOUL is like the oar that momently
   Dies in a desperate stress beneath the wave,
Then glitters out again and sweeps the sea:
   Each second I'm new-born from some new grave.

Sidney Lanier

A SONG OF THE FUTURE

   SAIL fast, sail fast,
Ark of my hopes, Ark of my dreams;
Sweep lordly o'er the Past,
Fly glittering through the sun's strange beams;
   Sail fast, sail fast.
Breaths of new buds from off some dying lea
With news about the Future scent the sea:
My brain is beating like the heart of Haste:
I'll loose me a bird upon this Present waste;
   Go, trembling song,
   And stay not long:
Thou 'rt a gray and sober dove,
But thine eye is faith and thy wing is love.

Sidney Lanier
(1842-1881)

"SEVENTY-ONE"

How memory through the lapse of years recalls the commune's rattle,
   Brings back the time so grandly dread;
When Paris rose in Labor's name and gave the foeman battle,
   And sealed her fate with hecatombs of dead.

Yes, memory loves to dwell upon the great defeat victorious
   Made holy by the life-blood of the brave,
The sacrifice triumphant, for the peerless cause, the glorious,
   And the radiant resurrection from the grave.

The blood goes surging through the heart, we hear the loud defiance,
  The cry "To arms!" ringing over France,
And Paris calls the workingmen of Europe to alliance
  And breaks the spell of twenty years of trance.

The chivalry are charging from the lowly homes of Labor,
  Hear the shock, the shout of conquest from the hill,
When the trained assassins meet their match and fly with shivered sabre
  From the heroes of the workroom and the mill.

See spreading far to left and right the battle line extended;
  The fury of the onset—how the green
And blossom of the fair fresh fields becomes so darkly blended
  With the crimson dye along the banks of the Seine.

The battles on the Versailles plain we see their grim emblazon;
  The din, the crash of combat, smoke and flame;
And night and day the fortress guns strike loud the diapason
  In the madness-moving music of War's game.

The two months! How many times the enemy's lines were routed
  'Midst thunder from the cannon came the May,
Yet Paris held the Red Flag high, and still defiance shouted,
  With the life-blood ebbing from her in the fray.

Fate's fearful shade grows blacker still, contracts the ring of fire,
  Though fearlessly is given blow for blow;
And Paris, Labor's Mecca shrine, becomes a blazing pyre,
  And nearer, ever nearer, comes the foe.

The line of battle broke at last; in every street and alley
  Unflinchingly are crossed the bayonet blades,
And every inch of ground is fought where Freedom still can rally
  A single man behind the barricades.

Not yet the time! The curtain falls, and, 'midst the lurid darkness,
  Death looks on freedom's soldiers face to face;
And now, the time to try men's souls, in all his ghastly starkness
  They meet him with the daring of their race.

But who can tell the story of the strife so great, Titanic?
  Or who depict the glory of the fall
That shook the globe and scattered wide the dragon's teeth volcanic
  To grow the armed crop to break the thrall?

We treasure in remembrance, too, the week of slaughter
  When the butchers in their fury killed amain;
The murder of the thousands of the people's sons and daughters,
  And the mitraillades and Satory's plain.

The glorious dead! They left their flag and willed us to preserve it
  As red as when from their dead hands it fell,
To keep it free from spot and stain, and loyally to serve it,
  As they did 'gainst the powers of earth and hell.

The Blood-Red Flag of Liberty! We'll guard it from pretenders,
  From those who its red meaning would impugn,
And when it floats in battle breeze prove we as true defenders
  As those who fought and died in the Commune.

John Leslie

From THE ARSENAL AT SPRINGFIELD

This is the Arsenal. From floor to ceiling,
  Like a huge organ, rise the burnished arms;
But from their silent pipes no anthem pealing
  Startles the villages with strange alarms.

Ah! what a sound will rise, how wild and dreary,
  When the death-angel touches those swift keys!
What loud lament and dismal Miserere
  Will mingle with their awful symphonies!

I hear even now the infinite fierce chorus,
  The cries of agony, the endless groan,
Which, through the ages that have gone before us,
  In long reverberations reach our own.

Is it, O man, with such discordant noises,
  With such accursed instruments as these,
Thou drownest Nature's sweet and kindly voices,
  And jarrest the celestial harmonies?

Were half the power that fills the world with terror,
  Were half the wealth bestowed on camps and courts,
Given to redeem the human mind from error,
  There were no need of arsenals or forts.

The warrior's name would be a name abhorred!
  And every nation that should lift again
Its hand against a brother, on its forehead
  Would wear for evermore the curse of Cain!

Henry Wadsworth Longfellow
(1807-1882)

STANZAS ON FREEDOM

MEN! whose boast it is that ye
Come of fathers brave and free,
If there breathe on earth a slave,
Are ye truly free and brave?
If ye do not feel the chain,
When it works a brother's pain,
Are ye not base slaves, indeed,
Slaves unworthy to be freed?

Women! who shall one day bear
Sons to breathe New England air,
If ye hear without a blush
Deeds to make the roused blood rush
Like red lava through your veins,
For your sisters now in chains,—
Answer! are ye fit to be
Mothers of the brave and free?

Is true Freedom but to break
Fetters for our own dear sake,
And with leathern hearts forget
That we owe mankind a debt?
No! true Freedom is to share
All the chains our brothers wear,
And with heart and hands to be
Earnest to make others free!

They are slaves who fear to speak
For the fallen and the weak;
They are slaves who will not choose
Hatred, scoffing and abuse,
Rather than in silence shrink
From the truth they needs must think;
They are slaves who dare not be
In the right with two or three.

James Russell Lowell
(1819-1891)

ALBERT RICHARD PARSONS*

"Caesar kept me awake till late at night with the noise (music) of hammers and saws erecting his throne, my scaffold."—A. R. Parsons, Nov. 11, 1887.

THE DOOMED man waits the morning light while busy hammers ply,
Erecting for the Caesar State its sacrificial throne:
For he had dared to let his thoughts far in the future fly,
And in the name of the oppressed has made their cause his own.
Without the mob of Church and State await the coming day
For him who dared to bid defiance to the commonplace;
Within, their victim, calm, self-poised, whom naught can now dismay,
With pity smiles at Caesar's strokes, as strokes of time creep on apace.

His thoughts fly backward o'er the past, the scenes of busy life
(The cause so proudly made his own, the weak against the strong),
Of childhood's days and manhood's friends, of home, his children, wife
—And then the corridors resound with "Annie Laurie" song.

His heart swells high, exultingly, his eyes with conscious pride
Behold his last day's morning light; for him the martyr's rest,
For him the path so often trod where man for man has died;
For him upon the scaffold-throne his honor manifest.

What though the mob of Church and State raise loud a frenzied shout,
And able editors compete to prostitute their brains,
Yet on the scaffold, Caesar's throne, his face betrays no doubt,
Prouder than king to give his life to break a people's chains.

In after years the people's voice, no longer choked, unheard,
Will sound through plutocratic halls the warning of the dead;
And in the day of Freedom's birth there'll be no clearer word
Than Parsons' name, a willing sacrifice where Freedom led.

Dyer D. Lum

*Albert Richard Parsons was one of the five Anarchists hanged in Chicago, November 11, 1887. Parsons, whose whereabouts was unknown, voluntarily walked into the court room as the trial, which terminated in his death, was going on.—M. G.

THE CHILDREN'S AUCTION

WHO bids for the little children—
    Body and soul and brain?
Who bids for the little children—
    Young and without a stain?

"Will no one bid," said England
   "For their souls so pure and white,
And fit for all good or evil
   The world on their page may write?"

"We bid," said Pest and Famine;
   "We bid for life and limb;
Fever and pain and squalor
   Their bright young eyes shall dim.
When the children grow too many,
   We'll nurse them as our own,
And hide them in secret places
   Where none may hear their moan."

"I bid," said Beggary, howling;
   "I bid for them one and all!
I'll teach them a thousand lessons—
   To lie, to skulk, to crawl!
They shall sleep in my lair like maggots,
   They shall rot in the fair sunshine;
And if they serve my purpose
   I hope they'll answer thine."

"I'll bid you higher and higher,"
   Said Crime, with a wolfish grin;
"For I love to lead the children
   Through the pleasant paths of sin.
They shall swarm in the streets to pilfer,
   They shall plague the broad highway,
They shall grow too old for pity
   And ripe for the law to slay.

"Give me the little children,
   Ye good, ye rich, ye wise,
And let the busy world spin round
   While ye shut your idle eyes:
And your judges shall have work,
   And your lawyers wag the tongue,
And the jailers and policemen
   Shall be fathers to the young!"

                    Charles Mackay
                    (1814-1889)

A VICTIM

O! I AM tired of factory toil,
    Of starveling virtue, tired am I;
It's so hard to be poor and good,
    It is so hard by degrees to die;
Easier it were to take heart and drown
    In the river that winds the factory town.

The factory air is choking close:
    Without in the streets it's cool and sweet—
And the factory bully, that comes and goes,
    Has never a word—save a curse—to greet.
It is not so in the streets without,
    Where all are free to go gaily about.

My cheeks are pallid, they once were red;
    My eyes are saddened, they once were bright;
And weary and faint the steps I tread,
    Though once I carried me firm and light;
The breath of the grave has damped my brow,
    But the world never seemed so fair as now.

O what in return does virtue give?
    She has stolen my hopes away;
She has stolen (and sore I grieve)
    The laugh from my lips and the light from my day!
And naught in return does virtue give
    But a tomb—and a toil while her votaries live.

If toil and the tomb be virtue's lot,
    If vice be ever the world's elect,
They may be chaste who are tempted not,
    Or have the means to be circumspect;
But let them not of temptation tell,
    Till they look at the streets from a factory hell!

'Tis but a step from the factory door
    To the streets—to laughter and song and wine,
To the sullen river but one step more,
    And there is an end to this life of mine.
Through one or the other must I one day
    Pass from this with my shadow away!

T. Maguire.

MAMMON

HAIL, puissant god, lord of all the gods,
The pillars of the world uprear thine hall;
Nations supply thy loaded table's feast
And thou, O pitiless, devourest all.
What meat thro' ages has not filled thy maw—
Brave glutton—sweeter for men's agonies?
O Mammon, thou hast many sacrifices.
The smoke of thy altars overwhelms the skies.

The groan of starvelings and the sweat of toil,
Success and failure; centuries of strife;
Drink, death, disease, and every rottenness;
Joy, beauty, strength, the flower, the weed of life;
Round up thy nostrils, water thy foul lips;
Go to thy pot and steam thy swollen eyes.
O Mammon, thou hast many sacrifices,
The smoke of thy altars overwhelms the skies.

Thy feet are planted firm in hell; thy head
Pillows the stars; thy tongue licks up its prey.
Thy swart legs straddle over all the earth.
We are thy slaves; we tremble and obey.
Who shall withstand thee, O implacable,
Or crowd thy belly till it putrifies?
O Mammon, thou hast many sacrifices,
The smoke of thy altars overwhelms the skies.

Harold Massingham

SOULS*

SOULS for sale! Souls for sale!
Souls for sale! Who'll buy?
In the pent-up city, through the wild rush of human hearts, I hear
    this unceasing, haunting cry:
Souls for sale! Souls for sale!
Through mist and gloom,
Through hate and love,
Through peace and strife,
Through wrong and right,
Through life and death,
The hoarse voice of the world echoes up the cold gray sullen river of
    life.

Adah Isaacs Menken
(1835-1868)

*Fragment from *Battle of the Stars*

RIEL, THE REBEL*

HE DIED at dawn in the land of snows;
  A priest at the left, a priest at the right;
The doomed man praying for his pitiless foes,
  And each priest holding a low dim light,
    To pray for the soul of the dying.
      But Windsor Castle was far away;
      And Windsor Castle was never so gay
    With her gorgeous banners flying!

The hero was hung in the windy dawn—
  'Twas splendidly done, the telegraph said;
A creak in the neck, then the shoulders drawn;
  A heave of the breast—and the man hung dead.
  And, oh! never such valiant dying!
      While Windsor Castle was far away
      With its fops and fools on that windy day,
    And its thousand banners flying!

Some starving babes where a stark stream flows
  'Twixt windy banks by an Indian town,
A frenzied mother in the freezing snows,
  While softly the pitying snow came down
    To cover the dead and the dying.
      But Windsor Castle was gorgeous and gay
      With lion banners that windy day—
    With lying banners flying.

Joaquin Miller
(1841-1913)

*Louis Riel was executed in 1885 for leading an insurrection of Franco-Indians in the northwest of Canada.

PANDORA'S SONG*

OF WOUNDS and sore defeat
I made my battle stay;
Winged sandals for my feet
I wove of my delay;
Of weariness and fear
I made my shouting spear;
Of loss, and doubt, and dread,
And swift oncoming doom
I made a helmet for my head
And a floating plume.
From the shutting mist of death,
From the failure of the breath,

*From *The Fire-Bringer*

I made a battle-horn to blow
Across the vales of overthrow.
O hearken, love, the battle-horn!
The triumph clear, the silver scorn!
O hearken where the echoes bring,
Down the grey disastrous morn,
Laughter and rallying.

William Vaughn Moody
(1869-1910)

NO MASTER

SAITH man to man, We've heard and known
   That we no master need
To live upon this earth, our own,
   In fair and manly deed;
The grief of slaves long passed away
   For us hath forged the chain,
Till now each worker's patient day
   Builds up the House of Pain.

And we, shall we too crouch and quail,
   Ashamed, afraid of strife;
And lest our lives untimely fail
   Embrace the death in life?
Nay, cry aloud and have no fear;
   We few against the world.
Awake! arise! the hope we bear
   Against the curse is hurl'd.

It grows, it grows: are we the same,
   The feeble band, the few?
Or what are those with eyes aflame,
   And hands to deal and do?
This is the last that bears the word,
   No Master, High or Low,
A lightning flame, a shearing sword,
   A storm to overthrow.

William Morris

A DEATH SONG

WHAT cometh here from west to east awending?
And who are these, the marchers stern and slow?
We bear the message that the rich are sending
Aback to those who bade them wake and know.
*Not one, not one, nor thousands must they slay
But one and all if they would dusk the day.*

We asked them for a life of toilsome earning,
They bade us bide their leisure for our bread;
We craved to speak, to tell of our woeful learning:
We come back speechless, bearing back our dead.
Not one, not one, nor thousands must they slay
But one and all if they would dusk the day.

They will not learn; they have no ears to hearken.
They turn their faces from the eyes of fate;
Their gay-lit halls shut out the skies that darken.
But, lo! this dead man knocking at the gate.
Not one, not one, nor thousands must they slay
But one and all if they would dusk the day.

Here lies the sign that we shall break our prison;
Amidst the storm he won a prisoner's rest;
But in the cloudy dawn the sun arisen
Brings our day of work to win the best,
Not one, not one, nor thousands must they slay
But one and all if they would dusk the day.

William Morris

From THE DAY IS COMING

COME hither, lads, and hearken,
for a tale there is to tell,
Of the wonderful days a-coming, when all
shall be better than well.

And the tale shall be told of a country,
a land in the midst of the sea,
And folk shall call it England
in the days that are going to be.

There more than one in a thousand
in the days that are yet to come,
Shall have some hope of the morrow,
some joy of the ancient home.

*   *   *   *

For then, laugh not, but listen,
to this strange tale of mine,
All folk that are in England
shall be better lodged than swine.

Then a man shall work and bethink him,
and rejoice in the deeds of his hand,
Nor yet come home in the even
too faint and weary to stand.

Men in that time a-coming
shall work and have no fear
For tomorrow's lack of earning
and the hunger-wolf anear.

I tell you this for a wonder,
that no man then shall be glad
Of his fellow's fall and mishap
to snatch at the work he had.

For that which the worker winneth
shall then be his indeed,
Nor shall half be reaped for nothing
by him that sowed no seed.

O strange new wonderful justice!
But for whom shall we gather the gain?
For ourselves and for each of our fellows,
And no hand shall labor in vain.

Then all Mine and all Thine shall be Ours,
and no more shall any man crave
For riches that serve for nothing
but to fetter a friend for a slave.

*   *   *   *

And what wealth then shall be left us
when none shall gather gold
To buy his friend in the market,
and pinch and pine the soul?

Nay, what save the lovely city,
and the little house on the hill,
And the wastes and the woodland beauty,
and the happy fields we till;

And the homes of ancient stories,
the tombs of the mighty dead;
And the wise man seeking out marvels
and the poet's teeming head;

And the painter's hand of wonder;
and the marvelous fiddle-bow,
And the banded choirs of music:
all those that do and know.

For all these shall be ours and all men's,
nor shall any lack of a share
Of the toil and the gain of living
in the days when the world grows fair.

William Morris
(1834-1896)

A MILLION JOBLESS MEN

A MILLION jobless men—
    On twenty-three hundred million acres of idle earth
    Rich with unworked mines,
    Webbed with highways and railroads,
    Watered with rivers and brooks
    Under snow-capped peaks and mountain lakes.

A million jobless men—
    In an idle, unused, vacant fertile land
    Dotted here and there with villages and cities
    In which a hundred million mouths want food
    And a hundred million needs
    Are not half supplied.

A million jobless men—
    Idle, hungry, roofless, shabby men
    With ten million women and children dependent upon them,
    Wandering aimlessly over twenty-three hundred million acres
    Of land that is mostly fertile and mostly idle—
    Idle, vacant, unused land—and a starving people!

A million jobless men—
    In an idle, vacant, unused land broad enough
    To house without crowding every human being in the world—
    Rich enough to support without exhausting
    All the population of the world—
    Its own few people but partly housed, fed and clothed!

A million jobless men—
    Clerks, bookkeepers, artisans, laborers, all the professions—
    Men with nothing to do, who can find no work,
    While two million stunted children labor in mine and mill
    And needy women must sell their sex for food—
    A million or maybe six million jobless men!

A million jobless men—
  And ten million poorly paid men who get barely enough to sustain
      their families,
  And a million women on the streets, and a million hungry children,
  Plus a million mortgaged homes, and a million business bankrupts,
  In twenty-three hundred million acres of inexhaustible richness not
      a thousandth part of which has been touched!

A million jobless men—
  And twenty million human dolts content to live in hell—
  To lecture, write, legislate, investigate, resolve and vote
  To "cure unemployment!" with a learned President
  And a cabinet and a congress of economic students
  Who institute Employment Bureaus! to feed the hungry, jobless,
      idle men tramping over idle, vacant, undeveloped land!

A million jobless men—
  And ten million legislators, judges, detectives, soldiers, sheriffs, con-
      stables and policemen
  With clubs, guns, bayonets, legal process, penal code, prisons, hand-
      cuffs, dungeons, and gallows
  To keep these million jobless men from going on the idle, naked,
      fertile acres
  And feeding themselves, their women and children!

Luke North

A CREED

WHEN ships of war no longer curse the sea;
When force of arms disgraces not the earth;
When caste and class distinctions cease to be;
When money is not master over worth;

When man is not required to fawn and cringe
To gain a portion of his daily bread;
When hope for merited success shall hinge
On worth alone; when lying art is dead;

When needed aid is not given for gain;
When golden altared churches help the poor;
When sympathy extends to all in pain;
And skilled physicians, though unpaid, will cure;

When courts of law no longer cast their blight
O'er dealings of fair minded men who deem,
The only court of justice is the right
Presided o'er by conscience, judge supreme;

When all the follies and the shams of state—
Their puppet kings and princes, useless toys—
Shall for the wise be forced to abdicate—
Then, not till then, shall man know freedom's joys.

W. B. Northrop

THE STATE

OH, CHILD of superstition that calls itself the State,
Whence came thy right assumed to pose as potentate;
Art thou the creator of land and air, and sea,
Or a blown-up bubble that just affects to be?
Does nature bend to thee—like men thy laws obey,
Or art thou bravado, that seeks with fools to play?

Come, tell us, great mogul, to whom weak subjects bow,
Where in thy book of law. thy crimes are marked—and how;
Art parent of the law that festers in thy womb;
And could this brat of thine be bribed to speak thy doom,
Thou trickster of the day that fattens on man's fears,
Parody on justice that laughs at human tears?

Tell us of thy greatness, just how it came about,
What promises were made to lay all fear and doubt,
How first thy agents took to ruling earth and man,
What argument was used to force such robber plan.
Were all mankind weak fools, or blind, when thou wast born,
That they didn't foresee, within the trick—the harm?

O twin of monarchy that lives to rob and kill,
What deviltry here that prostitutes at will,
That keeps a robber gang in kingly rights enthroned
Then turns their robberies to legal acts condoned?
Is not the blood as pure of him who lives by toil
As he who waxes fat—on idleness and spoil?

Are they of whiter clay who murder through the law
Than he who hurled a bomb—when he rank injustice saw?
Freak of idle fancy, where hatched these laws for man;
Dost serve thy time below and steal the devil's plan?
Oh, tell us, modern Sphinx, dost serve thy time so well
That back to earth wast sent to teach the tricks of hell?

Be gone, thou worthless churl that breed'st class of drones,
Emblem of hate and fear, grinder of human bones,
From whence thou cam'st, go back, and his honor tell
That we can get along without thy aid from hell.

L. S. Olliver

RESURGITE!

Now, for the faith that is in ye,
  Polander, Sclav, and Kelt!
Prove to the world what the lips have hurled,
  The hearts have grandly felt.

Rouse, ye races in shackles!
  See, in the East, the glare
Is red in the sky, and the warning cry
  Is sounding—"Awake! Prepare!"

A voice from the spheres—a hand downreached
  To hands that would be free,
To rend the gyves from the fettered lives
  That strain toward Liberty!

Greece! to the grasp of heroes,
  Flashed with thine ancient pride,
Thy swords advance; in the passing chance
  The great of heart are tried.

Poland! thy lance-heads brighten:
  The Tartar has swept thy name
From the schoolman's chart, but the patriot's heart
  Preserves its lines in flame.

Ireland! mother of dolors,
  The trial of thee descends:
Who quaileth in fear when the test is near,
  His bondage never ends.

Oppression, that kills the craven,
  Defied, is the freeman's good:
No cause can be lost forever whose cost
  Is coined from Freedom's blood.

Liberty's wine and altar
  Are blood and human right;
Her weak shall be strong, while the struggle with wrong
  Is a sacrificial fight.

Earth for the people—their laws their own—
  An equal race for all:
Though shattered and few, who to this are true
  Shall flourish the more they fall.

                    John Boyle O'Reilly
                    (1844-1890)

MINERS

THERE was a whispering in my hearth,
  A sigh of the coal,
Grown wistful of a former earth
  It might recall.

I listened for a tale of leaves
  And smothered ferns,
Proud-forests, and the low sly lives
  Before the fawns.

My fire might show steam-phantoms simmer
  From Time's old cauldron,
Before the birds made nests in summer,
  Or men had children.

But the coals were murmuring of their mine,
  And moans down there,
Of boys that slept wry sleep, and men
  Writhing for air.

I saw white bones in the cinder-shard,
  Bones without number.
For many hearts with coal are charred,
  And few remember.

I thought of all that worked dark pits
  Of war, and died
Digging the rock where Death reputes
  Peace lies indeed:

Comforted years will sit soft-chaired,
  In rooms of amber,
The years will stretch their hands, well cheered
  By our life's ember;

The centuries will burn rich loads
  With which we groaned,
Whose warmth shall lull their dreamy lids,
  While songs are crooned;
But they will not dream of us poor lads
  Lost in the ground.

                    Wilfred Owen
                    (1893-1918)

THE WAR SPIRIT

I HATE that drum's discordant sound,
   Parading round and round and round;
To thoughtless youth it pleasure yields,
   And lures from cities, farms and fields,
To sell their liberties for charms
   Of tawdry lace and glittering arms,
And, when the ambitious voice commands,
   To march, and fight and fall in foreign lands.

I hate that drum's discordant sound,
   Parading round and round and round;
To me it speaks of ravaged plains,
   Of burning towns and ruined swains;
Of mangled forms and broken bones;
   Of widows' tears and orphans' moans,
And all that misery's hand bestows
   To swell the catalogue of human woes.

Thomas Paine
(1737-1809)

LAST WORDS*

COME not to my grave with your mournings,
With your lamentations and tears,
With your sad feelings and fears!
When my lips are dumb
Do not thus come.

Bring no long train of carriages,
No horses crowned with waving plumes,
Which the gaunt glory of death illumes;
But with my hands on my breast
Let me rest.

Insult not my dust with your pity,
Ye who're left on this desolate shore
Still to live and lose and deplore.
'Tis I should, as I do,
Pity you.

For me no more are the hardships,
The bitterness, heartaches, and strife,
The sadness and sorrows of life,
But the glory divine—
This is mine.

   *Albert Richard Parsons was one of the five Anarchists "legally" hanged in Chicago, November 11, 1887.—M. G.

Poor creatures! Afraid of the darkness,
Who groan at the anguish to come.
How silent I go to my home!
Cease your sorrowful bell—
I am well.

Albert Richard Parsons
(1848-1877)

ELDORADO

GAILY bedight,
A gallant knight,
In sunshine and in shadow
Had journeyed long,
Singing a song,
In search of Eldorado.

But he grew old,
This knight so bold,
And o'er his heart a shadow
Fell as he found
No spot of ground
That looked like Eldorado.

And, as his strength
Failed him at length,
He met a pilgrim shadow.
"Shadow," said he,
"Where can it be,
This land of Eldorado?"

"Over the Mountain
Of the Moon,
Down the valley of the Shadow,
Ride, boldly ride,"
The shade replied,
"If you seek for Eldorado."

Edgar Allan Poe
(1809-1849)

THE LIE*

Go, SOUL, the Body's guest,
Upon a thankless errand;
Fear not to touch the best;
The truth shall be thy warrant:
Go since I needs must die,
And give the world the lie.

*Written shortly before the author's execution.—M. G.

Say to the Court it glows
   And shines like rotten wood;
Say to the Church it shows
   What's good and doth no good:
If Court and Church reply,
Then give them both the lie.

Tell Potentates, they live
   Acting by others' action,
Not loved unless they give,
   Not strong but by affection:
If Potentates reply,
Give Potentates the lie.

Tell men of high condition
   That manage the Estate,
Their purpose is ambition,
   Their practice, only hate:
And if they once reply,
Then give them all the lie.

Tell them that brave it most,
   They beg for more by spending,
Who, in their greatest cost,
   Seek nothing but commanding:
And if they make reply,
Then give them all the lie.

Tell Zeal it wants devotion,
   Tell Love it is but lust;
Tell Time it is but motion
   Tell Flesh it is but dust:
And wish them not reply,
For thou must give the lie.

Tell Age it daily wasteth;
   Tell Honor how it alters;
Tell Beauty how she blasteth;
   Tell Favor how it falters.
And as they shall reply,
Give everyone the lie.

Tell Wit how much it wrangles
   In tickle points of niceness;
Tell Wisdom she entangles
   Herself in overwiseness:
And when they do reply,
Straight give them both the lie.

Tell Physic of her boldness;
  Tell Skill it is pretension;
Tell Charity of coldness;
  Tell Law it is contention:
And as they do reply,
So give them still the lie.

Tell Fortune of her blindness;
  Tell Nature of decay;
Tell Friendship of unkindness;
  Tell Justice of delay:
And if they will reply,
Then give them both the lie.

Tell Arts they have no soundness,
  But vary by esteeming;
Tell Schools they want profoundness,
  And stand too much on seeming:
If Arts and Schools reply,
Give Arts and Schools the lie.

Tell Faith it's fled the City;
  Tell how the Country erreth,
Tell Manhood shake off pity;
  Tell Virtue least preferred:
And if they do reply,
Spare not to give the lie.

So when thou hast, as I
  Commanded thee, done blabbing,
Although to give the lie
  Deserves no less than stabbing,—
Yet, stab at thee that will,
No stab the soul can kill.

        Sir Walter Raleigh
         (1552-1618)

EN PASSANT*

THEY lie beneath the stone and beating sea—six hundred fathoms deep;
The last "shift" spent, their last "tub" filled; they rest in death's
    long sleep.

Their "tally-checks" are "handed in"; they have made their last "trip
    down,"

*Suggested by a mine cave-in.

No more they'll haste to "catch" their "cage" at buzzer's warning
    sound.

No monuments to mark their graves; no crapings drape their biers;
Their mausoleums are orphans' cries, their craping, widows' tears.

No pageants gather from afar as for a nation's chief;
The flaming gas their funeral scene; their pomp—their comrades' grief.

No minute guns to sound "good-bye," no scurrying to and fro;
Their booming guns the gas flame's roar, in a coal seam down below.

No massed bands render martial sound, or play with sad refrain;
No martial sounds or services they'll ever need again.

No panegyrics to their lives, no catafalque august;
Their lives pertained to lowliness, their tomb—the coal's black dust.

No flags float from black-draped mast to mark their passing by,
For they did naught but work to live; to work and then to die.

No promulgated holiday to give the nation's pause;
They were but pawns in life's rough game to move in humble cause.

Joseph Ralph

PROUD NEW YORK

By proud New York and its man-piled Matterhorns
The hard blue sky overhead and the west wind blowing,
Steam-plumes waving from sun-glittering pinnacles,
And deep street shaking to the million-river:

Manhattan, zoned with ships, the cruel
    Youngest of all the world's great towns,
Thy bodice bright with many a jewel,
    Imperially crowned with crowns—

Who that has known thee but shall burn
    In exile till he come again
To do thy bitter will, O stern
    Moon of the tides of men!

John Reed
(1887-1920)

IS THERE A GOD?

Is THERE a God—who rules o'er the land,
Who moulds the very destiny of man,
Who sets the state of every creature's birth,
And with his loving care guards o'er the earth?

Is there a God—who notes the sparrow's fall,
And will not listen to the orphan's call;
Who paints the glory of the lily's breast
And will not give little children rest?

Is there a God—God of the low and meek,
Who puts the ermine in the rose's cheek,
Who rules the earth from high and holy skies
And takes the sparkle from my baby's eyes?

Is there a God—who rides above the storm,
And gives to us the glories of the morn;
While the radiance of my darling's cheek
Is woven in the garments of the sleek?

Is there a God—who tunes the harps of gold,
Who stoned and slew the Amelikites of old,
Who sees from lofty places in the skies,
The child-laugh of our children turned to sighs?

Is there a God—poised bolts of wrath in hand,
Who fails to strike and slay the heartless man
That heavy burdens binds upon the weak
And thrusts the widow out into the street?

Is there a God—friend, father of the poor,
That will not keep the gaunt wolf from the door,
Who will not even lift his powerful hand
To stay his inhumanity to man?

N. K. Richardson

From FOR THE PEOPLE

WE ARE the hewers and delvers who toil for another's gain,—
The common clods and the rabble, stunted of brow and brain.
What do we want, the gleaners, of the harvest we have reaped?
What do we want, the neuters, of the honey we have heaped?

Ye have tried and failed to rule us; in vain to direct have tried,
Not wholly the fault of the ruler, not utterly blind the guide;
Mayhap there needs not a ruler, mayhap we can find the way.
At least ye have ruled to ruin, at least ye have led astray.

What matter if king or consul or president holds the rein,
If crime and poverty ever be links in the bondman's chain?
What careth the burden-bearer that Liberty packed his load,
If Hunger presseth behind him with a sharp and ready goad?

There's a serf whose chains are of paper; there's a king with a parch-
      ment crown;
There are robber knights and brigands in factory, field, and town.
But the vassal pays his tribute to a lord of wage and rent;
And the baron's toll is Shylock's, with a flesh-and-blood per cent.

The seamstress bends to her labor all night in a narrow room;
The child, defrauded of childhood, tiptoes all day at the loom.
The soul must starve, for the body can barely on husks be fed
And the loaded dice of a gambler settle the price of bread.

Ye have shorn and bound the Samson and robbed him of learning's
      light;
But his sluggish brain is moving, his sinews have all their might.
Look well to your gates of Gaza, your privilege, pride and caste!
The Giant is blind and thinking, and his locks are growing fast.

James Jeffrey Roche
(1847-1908)

THE DAWN OF PEACE

PUT OFF, put off your mail, O Kings,
   And beat your brands to dust!
Your hands must learn a surer grasp,
   Your hearts a better trust.

Oh, bend aback the lance's point,
   And break the helmet bar;
A noise is in the morning wind,
   But not the note of war.

Upon the grassy mountain paths
   The glittering hosts increase—
They come! They come! How fair their feet!
   They come who publish peace.

And victory, fair victory,
   Our enemies are ours!
For all the clouds are clasped in light,
   And all the earth with flowers.

Aye, still depressed and dim with dew!
  But wait a little while,
And with a radiant deathless rose
  The wilderness shall smile.

And every tender living thing
  Shall feed by streams of rest;
Nor lamb shall from the flock be lost,
  Nor nestling from the nest.

John Ruskin
(1819-1900)

THE CHALLENGE

NOT BY my will I came into this world,
  Into a world-wide labyrinth of Law,
Where, hydra-headed, serpent-wise upcurled,
  Lurks Property with never-sated maw.

To slavedom's scroll I have not set my hand;
  I spurn the dead past's deadly legacy—
The might-born right of some to own the land
  Or aught required for life in liberty.

Freedom from all external rule I claim;
Freedom to work, to love, to live my life;
Freedom for selfhood's growth and self-control:

Yea, and for others I demand the same.
For each and all, accord instead of strife;
Bread for the body, Beauty for the soul.

Tom Senhouse

HISTORY

THERE is a history in all men's lives,
Figuring the nature of the time deceased;
The which observed, a man may prophesy,
With a near aim, of the main chance of things
As not yet come to life.

William Shakespeare

TO THE POOR

FAMINE is in thy cheeks.
Need and oppression stareth in thine eyes,
Upon thy back hangs ragged misery;

The world is not thy friend; nor the world's laws.
The world affords no law to make thee rich;
Then be not poor, but break it.

William Shakespeare
(1564-1616)

THE ROYAL MASQUE*

Ay, there they are—

NOBLES, and sons of nobles, patentees,
Monopolists, and stewards of this poor farm,
On whose lean sheep sit the prophetic crows.
Here is the pomp that strips the houseless orphan,
Here is the pride that breaks the desolate heart,
These are the lilies glorious as Solomon,
Who toil not, neither do they spin,—unless
It be the webs they catch poor rogues withal.
Here is the surfeit which to them who earn
The niggard wages of the earth, scarce leaves
The tithe that will support them till they crawl
Back to its cold hard bosom. Here is health
Followed by grim disease, glory by shame,
Waste by lank famine, wealth by squalid want,
And England's sin by England's punishment.
And, as the effect pursues the cause foregone,
Lo, giving substance to my words, behold
At once the sign and the thing signified—
A troop of cripples, beggars and lean outcasts,
Horsed upon stumbling shapes, carted with dung,
Dragged for a day from cellars and low cabins
And rotten hiding-holes, to point the moral
Of this presentment, and bring up the rear
Of painted pomp with misery!

Percy Bysshe Shelley

*From *Charles the First*

TO THE MEN OF ENGLAND

MEN of England, wherefore plough
For the lords who lay ye low?
Wherefore weave with toil and care
The rich robes your tyrants wear?

Wherefore feed, and clothe, and save,
From the cradle to the grave,
Those ungrateful drones who would
Drain your sweat—nay, drink your blood!

Wherefore, Bees of England, forge
Many a weapon, chain and scourge,
That these stingless drones may spoil
The forced produce of your toil?

Have ye leisure, comfort, calm,
Shelter, food, love's gentle balm?
Or what is it ye buy so dear
With your pain and with your fear?

The seed ye sow, another reaps;
The wealth ye find, another keeps;
The robes ye weave, another wears;
The arms ye forge, another bears.

Sow seed,—but let no tyrant reap;
Find wealth,—let no impostor heap;
Weave robes,—let no idler wear;
Forge arms,—in your defense to bear.

Shrink to your cellars, holes, and cells;
In halls ye deck, another dwells.
Why shake the chains ye wrought?   Ye see
The steel ye tempered glance on ye.

With plough, and spade, and hoe and loom,
Trace your grave, and build your tomb,
And weave your winding-sheet, till fair
England be your sepulchre.

Percy Bysshe Shelley

THE TRINITY*

KINGS, *priests* and *statesmen* blast the human flower,
Even in its tender bud; their influence darts
Like subtle poison through the bloodless veins
Of desolate society. . . .
Let priest-led slaves cease to proclaim that man
Inherits vice and misery, when force
And falsehood hang even o'er the cradled babe,
Stifling with rudest grasp all natural good.

*   *   *   *   *

Then grave and hoary-headed hypocrites,
Without a hope, a passion, or a love,
Who, through a life of luxury and lies,
Have crept by flattery to the seats of power,

*From Prometheus Unbound

Support the system whence their honors flow—
They have three words; well tyrants know their use,
Well pay them for the loan, with usury
Torn from a bleeding world!—*God, Hell* and *Heaven.*
A vengeful, pitiless, and almighty fiend,
Whose mercy is a nickname for the rage
Of tameless tigers hungering for blood.
Hell, a red gulf of everlasting fire,
Where poisonous and undying worms prolong
Eternal misery to the helpless slaves
Whose life has been a penance for its crimes.
And *Heaven,* a meed for those who dare belie
Their human nature, quake, believe and cringe
Before the mockeries of earthly power.

* * * * *

Fiend, I defy thee! with a calm, fixed mind,
 All that thou canst inflict I bid thee do;
Foul tyrant, both of Gods and Human-kind,
 One only being shall thou not subdue.
  Rain thy plagues upon me here,
  Ghastly disease, and frenzying fear;
   And let alternate frost and fire
   Eat into me, and be thine ire
Lightning, and cutting hail, and legioned forms
Of furies, driving by upon the wounding storms.

 Ay, do thy worst. Thou art omnipotent.
O'er all things but thyself I gave thee power
 And my own will. Be thy swift mischiefs sent
To blast mankind, from yon aetherial tower.
  Let thy malignant spirit move
  In darkness over those I love;
 On me and mine I imprecate
 The utmost torture of thy hate;
And thus devote to sleepless agony,
This undeclining head while thou must reign on high.

* * * * *

But thou, who art the God and Lord—O thou
 Who fillest with thy soul this world of woe,
To whom all things of Earth and Heaven do bow
 In fear and worship; all-prevailing foe!
  I curse thee! let a sufferer's curse
  Clasp thee, his torturer, like remorse;
   Till thine Infinity shall be
   A robe of envenomed agony;
And thine Omnipotence a crown of pain
To cling like burning gold around dissolving brain.

Heap on thy soul, by virtue of this Curse,
  Ill deeds, then be thou damned, beholding good;
Both infinite as is the universe,
  And thou, and thy self-torturing solitude.
    An awful image of calm power
    Though now thou sittest, let the hour
    Come when thou must appear to be
    That which thou art internally.
And after many a false and fruitless crime,
Scorn track thy lagging fall through boundless space and time.

*   *   *   *   *

WHEN THE TRINITY IS GONE

And behold, thrones were kingless and men walked
One with the other even as spirits do,
None fawned, none trampled; hate, disdain, or fear,
Self-love or self-contempt, on human brows
No more inscribed, as o'er the gate of hell,
"All hope abandon ye who enter here;"
None frowned, none trembled, none with eager fear
Gazed on another's eye of cold command,
Until the subject of a tyrant's will
Became, worse fate, the object of his own,
Which spurred him, like an outspent horse, to death.
None wrought his lips in truth-entangling lines
Which smiled the lie his tongue disdained to speak;
None, with firm sneer, trod out in his own heart
The sparks of love and hope till there remained
Those bitter ashes, a soul self-consumed,
And the wretch crept a vampire among men,
Infecting all with his own hideous ill.
None talked that common, false, cold, hollow talk,
Which makes the heart deny the *yes* it breathes,
Yet question that unmeant hypocrisy
With such a self-mistrust as has no name.
And women, too, frank, beautiful and kind
As the free heaven which rains fresh light and dew
On the wide earth, passed; gentle radiant forms,
From Custom's evil taint exempt and pure;
Speaking the wisdom once they could not think,
Looking emotions once they feared to feel,
And changed to all which once they dared not be,
Yet being now, made Earth like Heaven; nor pride,
Nor jealousy, nor envy, nor ill-shame,
The bitterest of those drops of treasured gall,
Spoilt the sweet taste of the nepenthe, love.

THE AIM

To suffer woes which Hope thinks infinite;
To forgive wrongs darker than death or night;
 To defy Power, which seems omnipotent;
To love, and bear; to hope till Hope creates
From its own wreck the thing it contemplates;
 Neither to change, nor falter, nor repent;
This, like thy glory, Titan! is to be
Good, great and joyous, beautiful and free;
This is alone Life, Joy, Empire and Victory.

Percy Bysshe Shelley
(1792-1822)

PURSERY RHYME

SING a song of Europe,
 Highly civilized.
Four and twenty nations
 Wholly hypnotized.

When the battles open
 The bullets start to sing;
Isn't that a silly way
 To act for any King?

The Kings are in the background
 Issuing commands;
The Queens are in the parlor,
 Per etiquette's demands.

The bankers in the counting house
 Are busy multiplying;
The common people at the front
 Are doing all the dying.

Gen. Isaac R. Sherwood
(1835-1925)

IN THE MARKET-PLACE

IN BABYLON, high Babylon,
 What gear is bought and sold?
All merchandise beneath the sun
 That bartered is for gold;
Amber and oils from far beyond
 The desert and the fen,
And wines whereof our throats are fond—
 Yea! and the souls of men! . . .

In Babylon, grey Babylon,
    What goods are sold and bought?
Vesture of linen subtly spun,
    And cups from agate wrought;
Raiment of many-colored silk
    For some fair denizen,
And ivory more white than milk—
    Yea! and the souls of men! . . .

In Babylon, sad Babylon,
    What chattels shall invite?
A wife whenas your youth is done,
    Or leman for a night.
Before Astarte's portico
    The torches flare again;
The shadows come, the shadows go—
    Yea! and the souls of men!

In Babylon, dark Babylon,
    Who take the wage of shame?
The scribe and singer, one by one,
    That toil for gold and fame.
They grovel to their masters' mood;
    The blood upon the pen
Assigns their souls to servitude—
    Yea! and the souls of men!

George Sterling

TO THE GODDESS OF LIBERTY

OH! is it bale-fire in thy brazen hand—
The traitor-light set on betraying coasts
To lure to doom the mariner? Art thou
Indeed that Freedom, gracious and supreme,
By France once sighted over seas of blood—
A beacon to the ages, and their hope,
A star against the midnight of the race,
A vision, an announcement? Art thou she
For whom our fathers fought at Lexington
And trod the ways of death at Gettysburg?
Thy torch is lit, thy steadfast hand upheld,
Before our ocean-portals. For a sign
Men set thee there to welcome—loving men,
With faith in man. Thou wast upraised to tell,
To simple souls that seek from over-seas
Our rumored liberty, that here no chains
Are on the people, here no kings can stand,

Nor the old tyranny confound mankind,
Sapping with craft the ramparts of the Law
For such, O high presentment of their dream!
Thy pathless sandals wait upon the stone,
Thy tranquil face looks evermore to sea:
Now turn, and know the treason at thy back!
Turn to the anarchs' turrets, and behold
The cunning ones that reap where others sow!

In those great strongholds lifted to the sun
They plot dominion. Throned greed conspire,
Half allied in a brotherhood malign,
Against the throneless many. . . .

Would One might pour within thy breast of bronze
Spirit and life! Then should thy loyal hand
Cast down its torch, and thy deep voice should cry:
"Turn back! Turn back, O liberative ships!
Be warned, ye voyagers! From tyranny
To vaster tyranny ye come! Ye come
From realms that in my morning twilight wait
My radiant invasion. But these shores
Have known me and renounced me. I am raised
In mockery, and here the forfeit day
Deepens to West, and my indignant Star
Would hide her shame with darkness and the sea—
A sun of doom forecasting on the Land
The shadow of the sceptre and the sword."

George Sterling
(1869-1926)

HAD I THE POWER THAT HAVE THE WILL

HAD I the power that have the will,
  The enfeebled will—a modern curse—
This book of mine should blossom still
  A perfect garden-ground of verse.

White placid marble gods should keep
  Good watch in every shadowy lawn;
And from clean, easy-breathing sleep
  The birds should waken me at dawn.

A fairy garden; none the less.
  Throughout these gracious paths of mine
All day there should be free access
  For stricken hearts and lives that pine;

And by the folded lawns all day—
No idle gods for such a land—
All active Love should take its way
With active Labor hand in hand.

Robert Louis Stevenson
(1850-1894)

THE FAITH-FIEND

BACK thro' the dim and silent ages;
  Back thro' the tombs of buried time;
Witness the blots on history's pages;
  Follow the track of my guilt and crime.
Down thro' the dismal, silent turnings—
  Corridors dark of the human mind—
See there the trace of my cruel burnings
  And the ghastly relics I've left behind!

See ye the ghastly and pale procession
  Gliding along thro' the centuries dim;
My martyred victims; death's expression
  Sits on their phantom faces grim.
Hark to their cries and shrieking,
  'Tis the music of old so sweet to me—
My priests on the heretic vengeance wreaking
  And I laugh again in my fiendish glee.

Millions of slaves have I bowed before me;
  States and nations have owned my sway.
Their monarchs have bade their serfs adore me;
  Yet, what is their glory worth today?
For I've cast my poisoning shadow o'er them,
  And silently killed with my sickly breath;
And like the empires that shone before them
  Their glory is lost in decay and death.

I delight in the smoke and blood of battle;
  'Tis sport for me and my priestly knaves;
I goad men to fight like maddened cattle,
  'Tis thus they become my blind, dumb slaves.
Wide o'er the world have I spread my pinions
  Whilst tyrants ever the weak oppress.
And wealth I bring to my pious minions
  Who only mock at the poor's distress.

I plunder and kill for the great God's glory;
  My hands are red with the children's blood.

And the streams that have flowed from my altars gory
  Would bathe the world in a crimson flood.
To my dungeon and rack has Truth been yielded;
  I have aided the sword of the coward strong;
With the name of Christ and his cross I have shielded
  The holy and sanctified the throne of Wrong.

I check the rippling of laughter;
  I chill the sunshine of youthful love;
I awe mankind with dread hereafter
  'Twixt the hell below and the heaven above;
Friendship's golden links I sever;
  I shackle the soul with a weary chain;
I crush and smother each brave endeavor;
  I load and fetter the human brain.

I enshroud and darken life's brief hist'ry,
  Around the cradle my gloom is spread.
I clothe the grave in an awful myst'ry,
  And fill the living with gruesome dread.
I guide the tongue in pious lying;
  I warp the mind with the curse of prayer;
I haunt the side of the sick and dying
  And, mockingly, point to my hell's red glare.

I poison the silvern stream of pleasure;
  I wither the flowers of the bright to-day;
I bribe men's minds with the phantom treasure
  Of the mystic realms of the far away.
I stifle the voice of inquiring Reason;
  I set my signet on Thought's pale brow;
I enslave the soul thro' life's long glad season
  And a prison make of the golden Now!

                              H. Gordon Swift

ON AN ILL-MANAGED HOUSE

LET ME thy properties explain:
A rotten cabin dropping rain:
Chimneys, with scorn rejecting smoke;
Stools, tables, chairs, and bedsteads broke.
Here elements have lost their uses,
Air ripens not, nor earth produces:
In vain we make poor Shellah toil,
Fire will not roast, nor water boil.

Through all the valleys, hills, and plains,
The Goddess Want in triumph reigns:
And her chief officers of state,
Sloth, Dirt, and Theft, around her wait.

Jonathan Swift
(1667-1745)

From A MARCHING SONG

WE MIX from many lands,
  We march for very far;
In our hearts and lips and hands
  Our staffs and weapons are;
The light we walk in darkens sun and moon and star.

It doth not flame and wane
  With years and spheres that roll,
Storms cannot shake nor stain
  The strength that makes it whole,
The fire that moulds and moves it of the sovereign soul.

From the edge of harsh derision,
  From discord and defeat,
From doubt and lame division
  We pluck the fruit and eat;
And the mouth finds it bitter, and the spirit sweet.

O nations undivided,
  O single people and free,
We dreamers, we derided,
  We mad, blind men that see,
We bear you witness ere ye come that ye shall be.

Ye sitting among tombs,
  Ye standing round the gate,
Whom fire-mouthed war consumes,
  Or cold-lipped peace bids wait,
All tombs and bars shall open, every grave and grate.

O sorrowing hearts of slaves,
  We heard you beat from far!
We bring the light that saves,
  We bring the morning star;
Freedom's good things we bring you, whence all good things are.

Rise, ere the dawn be risen;
Come, and be all souls fed;
From field and street and prison
Come, for the feast is spread;
Live, for the truth is living; wake, for night is dead.
Algernon Charles Swinburne
(1837-1909)

THESE THINGS SHALL BE

THESE things shall be! a loftier race
Than e'er the world hath known shall rise,
With flame of freedom in their souls,
And light of knowledge in their eyes.

They shall be gentle, brave and strong
To spill no drop of blood, but dare
All that may plant man's lordship firm
On earth, and fire, and sea and air.

Nation with nation, land with land,
Unarmed shall live as comrades free;
In every heart and brain shall throb
The pulse of one fraternity.

New arts shall bloom of loftier mould,
And mightier music fill the skies,
And every life shall be a song,
When all the earth is paradise.
John Addington Symonds
(1840-1893)

PRELUDE

STILL south I went and west and south again,
Through Wicklow from the morning till the night,
And far from cities and the sights of men,
Lived with the sunshine and the moon's delight.

I knew the stars, the flowers, and the birds,
The grey and wintry side of many glens,
And did but half remember human words,
In converse with the mountains, moors and fens.
J. M. Synge
(1871-1909)

THE UNEMPLOYED

O'ER OUR land Poor Men are walking,
  Walking one by one;
Numb with cold, and drenched by rain-fall,
  Blistered by the sun.
Worn and gaunt they stumble onward,
  Hunger drives the band;
Young men, old men, frail and burly,
  Walking through the land.

Through our land the Poor are seeking,
  Seeking work to do;
Work by which to earn a living,
  Any work would do.
Soldiers, sailors, men of learning,
  Seeking everywhere,
Cursed and damned, they beg for labor,
  Beggars in despair.

Every hand is turned against them,
  Branding each one thief;
Power and Greed are rich with grinding,
  Grinding gold from Grief!
Ah, but Strength like flame is leaping,
  Leaping through the land;
Right and might shall blast the grinders—
  Blast them from the land!

Stuart Stanton Taber

WHY NOT?

WHEN the schemes of all the systems, kingdoms and republics fall,
Something kindlier, higher, holier—all for one and one for all.

All the full-brain, half-brain races, led by Justice, Love and Truth;
All the millions one at last with all the visions of my youth.

All disease quenched by science, no man halt, or deaf or blind;
Stronger ever born of weaker, lustier body, larger mind.

Earth at last a warless world, a single race, a single tongue—
I have seen it far away—for is not earth as yet so young?

Every tiger madness muzzled, every serpent passion killed,
Every grim ravine a garden, every blazing earth tilled.

Robed in universal harvest up to either pole she smiles,
Universal ocean softly washing all the warless isles.

Alfred Tennyson
(1809-1892)

DEMOCRACY

DEMOCRACY! Democracy!
Word dear as life itself to me.
As sunlight shines on all alike,
As darkness falls on all by night,
As blow the winds over every sea,
As thought unchained will ever be,
So equal rights are thy demands
And for all freedom in all lands.

The stars of night ever declare
That each man is the rightful heir
To all that Nature holds to man
Of life, of death—of all he can.
Of pleasure, pain or woe control,
From East to West, from pole to pole,
From mountain heights to the gray sea—
Through all of life's mortality.

No law shall stay eternal right,
No statute old or new shall blight
Man's swelling hopes that come there may
The dream, the dawn of the full day
When scepters, thrones and tyrants all
Into oblivion's pit shall fall;
When each shall cast off love of pelf
And all shall be masters of self.

Then speed the day and haste the hour,
Break down the barriers, gain the power
To use the land and sail the sea,
To hold the tools, unchecked and free;
No tribute pay, but service give,
Let each man work that all may live.
Banish all bonds and usury,
Be free! Set free!
Democracy! Democracy!   *A. W. Thomas*

THE POWER OF THOUGHT

NOT BY cannon nor by saber,
  Not by flags unfurled,
Shall we win the rights of labor,
  Shall we free the world.
Thought is stronger far than weapons,
  Who shall stay its course?
It spreads in onward-circling waves
  And ever gathers force.

Hopes may fail us, clouds may lower,
   Comrades may betray,
Crushed beneath the heel of power
   Justice lies to-day!
But every strong and radiant soul,
   Whom once the truth makes free,
Shall send a deathless impulse forth
   To all eternity.

Words of insight, sympathetic,
   Flash from soul to soul,
Of the coming time prophetic,
   Freedom's distant goal.
Kindling with one's aspiration,
   Hearts will feel the thrill,
And iron ropes be bands of sand
   Before the people's will.

Right shall rule whene'er we will it,
   All the rest is naught;
"Every bullet has its billet,"
   So has every thought.
When the people wish for freedom,
   None can say them nay—
'Tis slavery of the darkened mind
   Alone which stops the way.

Phillips Thomson

TRUE FREEDOM

WAIT not till the slaves pronounce the word
   To set the captive free,—
Be free yourselves, be not deferred,
   And farewell, Slavery.

Ye all are slaves, ye have your price,
   And gang but cries to gang;
Then rise! the highest of ye rise!—
   I hear your fetters clang.

The warmest heart the North doth breed
   Is still too cold and far;
The colored man's release must come
   From outcast Africa.

What is your whole Republic worth?
    Ye hold out vulgar lures;
Why will you be disparting Earth
    When all Heaven is yours?

He's governed well who rules himself,—
    No despot vetoes him:
There's no defaulter steals his pelf,
    Nor Revolution grim.

'Tis easier to treat with kings
    And please our country's foes,
Than treat with Conscience of the things
    That only Conscience knows.

                Henry David Thoreau
                    (1817-1862)

I LOOK FAR DOWN THE REDDENED ROAD

I LOOK far down the reddened road that reaches 'round the earth
All strewn along with mangled men, and ask, "What is it worth?"
The ones that have been idolized as though surpassing great—
What are they worth—what glory marks their lauded lords of state?
What of the empires that are built on beds of dead men's bones—
What of the pile of princely pomp—the palaces and thrones—
What of the curse and infamy of war—the pageantry of kings?

Such stuff as this is worthless trash to build a better world—
Far wiser that from every throne the last damned king were hurled.
With none to blow the bugle blast to call the dogs of war,
Who, then, would march to murder those they never met before?
And all the retinue of priests that say that God ordains
The crown that rests upon the brow of every brute that reigns—
Let these go, too, and take their myths, their goblins and their hell,
And give this tortured world of ours a longed-for breathing spell!

One peasant lad that plows the field where grows the golden corn
Is nobler breed than all the whelps that wolves of war have born;
One song sung by some genial soul, along some sheltered glade,
Shall hush some day the savage shock that madmen's guns have made;
One gleam of love that suckling babe in mother's eye beheld
Shall silence all the threats of doom that insane priests have yelled,
One word of brotherhood and peace—one breath from fragrant flowers,
These be the only things of worth, in this old world of ours!

                    Henry M. Tichenor

LABOR

I saw that you fed the loom; but who fed you?
I saw that you fueled the fire; but who fueled you?
History put up big signs, but they never bore your name,
History set great feasts, but you were never invited.

You go to work in the morning with your dinner pail on your arm.
Does that pail contain your dinner alone and provide only for your
    simple day?
Millions of mouths to come hereafter are to be fed by that pail you
    carry on your arm.

When you go home at night after the day's work the universe goes
    home with you,
When you strike against the injustice of the master the sun strikes
    with you.

Horace Traubel
(1858-1919)

FOR THOSE WHO GIVE THANKS

For laughter that never graces,
    For song that is ever still,
There where those pallid faces
    Bow in the toil of the mill,
For baby hands at the spindle,
    For baby hands at the loom,
While childhood calls and the sunlight falls
    Out in the springtime of bloom—
Wealth extols and might decrees—
Shall we give thanks for these?

For life in the crowded city,
    The stretch of its friendless ways,
Its children of wrong and pity,
    Its weary round of days,
The tramp of the morning army,
    Embattled for daily bread,
The ceaseless moil of those who toil,
    The sound of their homeward trend,
And all the sorrow the city sees,
Shall we give thanks for these?

For hands that are mangled and broken,
    For limbs that are tattered and scarred,
For every salient token
    Of greed in the guise of a God,

For bodies stunted and wasted,
　　Knowing too well health's dearth,
And all of the throng who are bonded to Wrong—
　　Bonded and sold at birth.
The faithful march of the poor's disease—
Shall we give thanks for these?

For those that the system tosses
　　Aside like useless waste,
For those unnumbered forces,
　　By younger hands displaced,
For morgue and almshouse welcome,
　　The pauper's nameless grave,
The prisoner's sigh, the harlot's cry—
　　(Who talks of serf and slave?)—
Yet, thank your god on bended knees,
And give him thanks for these.

Bert Ullad

THE GENIUS OF REVOLUTION

REVOLUTION am I.
Red, grim, and grisly.
Aroused from my sleep
In the cave of the Ages,
I come!

Dream-haunted I come!
With the cries of the wretched—
The Strong, the Decrepit—
The greed-poisoned infant
That writhed out its life.

Unnoticed I stalk
Through the maze of the frenzied,
Urging them on in their hellish carouse—
There, 'midst the scenes of bloodshed and terror,
August, magnificent—
I rule Alone.

When ambition is stripped of its pomp,
And Folly is wholly rebuked;
When man is man—
No more, nor less—
I return to my sleep and my dreams.

John Francis Valter

A SONG OF ACADEMIC LIBERTY

ARISE! who bend o'er song and story,
    Who search for truth in her retreat;
What profits all your learned glory
    If freedom suffer a defeat?
Arise and listen! Down the ages
    The shackles on the thinker ring;
And what ye read on placid pages
    Was once condemned by priest and king.

O ye who guard the sacred portals
    With vigilance of heart and brain,
Through which the troop of the immortals
    Comes over with their glistering train—
O thinker, teacher, seer, bestowing
    Guardian service, shall ye be
The slaves of tyrants, all unknowing
    The highest gifts are from the free?

Shall ye not see a Hamlet's passion
    Portrayed upon a tragic stage?
Must truth be right to you in fashion
    When it is duly stamped with age?
Shall ye not dare condemn the writer
    Who writes from vanity and greed?
And dare to be the public smiter
    Of men who mount by evil deed?

Of old did Galileo mutter
    As he recanted "Yet it moves"?
Ye, too, below your breath must utter
    What blinded custom disapproves.
O ye for truth who groan in travail,
    Shall ye be driven to obey
The barren slaves who basely cavil
    Or live life's imperious way?

For you no sword that cleaves asunder,
    And not for you the piercing ball;
But eloquence has still her thunder—
    The people are the open hall.

Ida Ahlborn Weeks

FIGHT? WHAT FOR?

I AM "wanted to go in the army."
Well, what would they give me to do?
"You'll have to be killing your brothers
If one of them doesn't kill you."

I am "wanted to go in the army."
Say, what is there in it for me?
"You'd help to be saving your country
From brother-men over the sea."

My country? Who says I've a country?
I live in another man's flat
That hasn't as much as a door yard—
And why should I battle for that?

I haven't a lot nor a building,
No flower, no garden, nor tree.
The landlords have gobbled the country—
Let *them* do the fighting, not me.

Celia Baldwin Whitehead

EUROPE*

SUDDENLY, out of its stale and drowsy air, the lair of slaves,
Like lightning it leapt forth half startled at itself,
Its feet upon the ashes and the rags, its hands tight to the throats of
    kings.

O hope and faith!
O aching close of exiled patriots' lives!
Of many a sicken'd heart!
Turn back unto this day and make yourselves afresh.

And you, paid to defile the People—you liars, mark!
Not for the numberless agonies, murder, lusts,
For court thieving in its manifold forms, worming from his simplic-
    ity the poor man's wages,
For many a promise sworn by royal lips and broken and laugh'd at in
    the breaking,
Then in their power not for all these did the blows strike revenge, or
    the heads of the noble fall;
The People scorn'd the ferocity of kings.

But the sweetness of mercy brew'd bitter destruction, and the fright-
    en'd monarchs come back,
Each comes in state with his train, hangman, priest, tax-gatherer,
Soldier, lawyer, lord, jailer, and sycophant.

*1848-1849

Yet behind all, lowering, stealing, lo, a Shape,
Vague as the night, draped interminably, head, front and form, in
    scarlet folds,
Whose face and eyes none may see,
Out of its robes only this, the red robes lifted by the arm,
One finger crook'd, pointed high over the top, like the head of a snake
    appears.

Meanwhile corpses lie in new-made graves, bloody corpses of young
    men,
The rope of the gibbet hangs heavily, the bullets of princes are flying,
    the creatures of power laugh aloud,
And all these things bear fruits, and they are good.

Those corpses of young men,
Those martyrs that hang from the gibbet, those hearts pierc'd by the
    gray lead,
Cold and motionless as they seem, live elsewhere with unslaughter'd
    vitality.

They live in other young men, O kings!
They live in brothers again ready to defy you,
They were purified by death, they were taught and exalted.

Not a grave of the murder'd for freedom but grows seed for freedom,
    in its turn to bear seed,
Which the winds carry afar and re-sow, and the rains and the snows
    nourish.
Not a disembodied spirit can the weapons of tyrants let loose,
But it stalks invisible over the earth, whispering, counseling, caution-
    ing.

Liberty, let others despair of you—I never despair of you.

Is the house shut? is the master away?
Nevertheless, be ready, be not weary of watching,
He will soon return, his messengers come anon.

Walt Whitman

From SONG OF THE OPEN ROAD

Afoot and light-hearted, I take to the open road,
Healthy, free, the world before me,
The long brown path before me, leading wherever I choose.

Henceforth I ask not good-fortune, I myself am good-fortune,
Henceforth I whimper no more, postpone no more, need nothing,
Done with indoor complaints, libraries, querulous criticisms,
Strong and content I travel the open road.

The earth, that is sufficient;
I do not want the constellations any nearer;
I know they are very well where they are;
I know they suffice for those who belong to them.

Yon road I enter upon and look around, I believe you are not all that
  is there,
I believe that much unseen is also here.

From this hour, freedom!
From this hour I ordain myself loosed of limits and imaginary lines,
Going where I list, my own master, total and absolute,
Listening to others, and considering well what they say,
Pausing, searching, receiving, contemplating,
Gently, but with undeniable will, divesting myself of the holds that
  would hold me.

I inhale great draughts of space;
The east and the west are mine, and the north and the south are mine.

I am larger, better than I thought;
I did not know I held so much goodness.

All seems beautiful to me;
I can repeat over to men and women: "You have done such good to me
  I would do the same to you."
I will recruit for myself and you as I go;
I will scatter myself among men and women as I go;
I will toss the new gladness and roughness among them;
Whoever denies me, it shall not trouble me;
Whoever accepts me, he or she shall be blessed, and shall bless me.

Now I see the secret of the making of the best of persons,
It is to grow in the open air, and to sleep with the earth.

Allons! whoever you are, come travel with me!
Traveling with me, you find what never tires.

The earth never tires,
The earth is rude, silent, incomprehensible at first,
Nature is rude and incomprehensible at first,

Be not discouraged, keep on, there are divine things well envelop'd,
I swear to you there are divine things more beautiful than words can
  tell.

Listen! I will be honest with you;
I do not offer the old smooth prizes, but offer rough new prizes.

These are the days that must happen to you:
You shall not heap up what is called riches,
You shall scatter with lavish hand all that you achieve.

Allons, through struggles and wars!
The goal that was named cannot be countermanded.

Have the past struggles succeeded?
What has succeeded? Yourself? Your Nation? Nature,
Now understand me well—it is provided in the essence of things that
        from any fruition of success, no matter what, shall come forth
        something to make a greater struggle necessary.

My call is the call of the battle, I nourish active rebellion,
He going with me must go well arm'd,
He going with me goes often with spare diet, poverty, angry enemies,
        desertions.

Allons! the road is before us!
It is safe—I have tried it—my own feet have tried it well—
Allons! be not detain'd!

Let the paper remain on the desk unwritten, and the book on the shelf
        unopen'd!
Let the tools remain in the workshop! let the money remain unearn'd!
Let the school stand! mind not the cry of the teacher!
Let the preacher preach in his pulpit! let the lawyer plead in the court,
        and the judges expound the law!

Mon enfant! I give you my hand!
I give you my love more precious than money,
I give you myself before preaching or law;
Will you give me yourself? will you come travel with me?
Shall we stick by each other as long as we live?

Walt Whitman
(1819-1892)

From STANZAS FOR THE TIMES

Is THIS the land our fathers loved,
    The freedom which they toiled to win?
Is this the soil whereon they moved?
    Are these the graves they slumber in?
Are we the sons whom are borne
To mantles which the dead have worn?

And shall we crouch above the graves
    With craven soul and fettered lip?

Yoke in with marked and branded slaves,
　　And tremble at the driver's whip?
Bend to the earth our pliant knees,
　　And speak but as our masters please?

No; by each spot of haunted ground,
　　Where Freedom weeps her children's fall:
By Plymouth's rock and Bunker's mound,
　　By Griswold's stained and shattered wall;
By Warren's ghost, by Langdon's shade,
By all the memories of our dead!

　　　*　　*　　*　　*　　*

By all above, around, below,
Be our indignant answer: No!
　　　　　　　John Greenleaf Whittier
　　　　　　　　(1807-1892)

THE DISAPPOINTED

THERE are songs enough for the hero
　　Who dwells on the heights of fame;
I sing for the disappointed—
　　For those who have missed their aim.

I sing with a tearful cadence
　　For one who stands in the dark,
And knows that his last best arrow
　　Has bounded back from the mark.

I sing for the breathless runner,
　　The eager, anxious soul,
Who falls with his strength exhausted,
　　Almost in sight of the goal.

For the hearts that break in silence,
　　With a sorrow all unknown;
For those who need companions,
　　Yet walk their way alone.

There are songs enough for the lovers,
　　Who share life's tender pain;
I sing for the one whose passion
　　Is given all in vain.

For those whose spirit-comrades
    Have missed them on the way;
I sing, with a heart o'erflowing,
    This minor strain to-day.

And I know the solar system
    Must somewhere keep in space
A prize for that spent runner
    Who barely lost the race.

For the plan would be imperfect
    Unless it held some sphere
That paid for the toil and talent
    And love that are wasted here.

              Ella Wheeler Wilcox
                 (1855-1919)

AFTER A HANGING*

I NEVER saw sad men who looked
    With such a wistful eye
Upon that little tent of blue
    We prisoners call the sky,
And at every careless cloud that passed
    In happy freedom by. . . .

The Warders strutted up and down,
    And kept their herd of brutes,
Their uniforms were spick and span,
    And they wore their Sunday suits,
But we knew the work they had been at
    By the quicklime on their boots.

For where a grave had opened wide
    There was no grave at all:
Only a stretch of mud and sand
    By the hideous prison-wall,
And a little heap of burning lime,
    That the man should have his pall.

For he has a pall, this wretched man,
    Such as few men can claim;
Deep down below a prison-yard,
    Naked, for greater shame,
He lies, with fetters on each foot,
    Wrapt in a sheet of flame! . . .

*From *The Ballad of Reading Gaol*

I know not whether Laws be right,
  Or whether Laws be wrong;
All that we know who lie in jail
  Is that the wall is strong;
And that each day is like a year,
  A year whose days are long.

But this I know, that every Law
  That men have made for Man,
Since first Man took his brother's life,
  And the sad world began,
But straws the wheat and saves the chaff
  With a most evil fan.

This too I know—and wise it were
  If each could know the same—
That every prison that men build
  Is built with bricks of shame,
And bound with bars lest Christ should see
  How men their brothers maim.

With bars they blur the gracious moon,
  And blind the goodly sun:
And they do well to hide their Hell,
  For in it things are done
That son of God nor son of Man
  Ever should look upon.

The vilest deeds like poison weeds
  Bloom well in prison-air:
It is only what is good in Man
  That wastes and withers there:
Pale Anguish keeps the heavy gate,
  And the Warder is Despair.

For they starve the little frightened child
  Till it weeps both night and day:
And they scourge the weak, and flog the fool,
  And gibe the old and grey,
And some grow mad, and all grow bad,
  And none a word may say.

Oscar Wilde
(1856-1900)

WHY IS THIS?

WHEN the land is full of workers,
  Busy hands and active brains,
When the craftsmen and the thinkers
  Feel about them bonding chains;
When the laborer is cheated
  Of the worth his hands have wrought,
And the thinker, vain of logic,
  Sees that reason comes to naught;
When the forces men have harnessed
  And have trained to do their will,
Ought to leave no homeless people,
  And no hungry mouths to fill,
Have but proved themselves the servants
  Of the shrewd and selfish few,
And the many have but little
  For the work they find to do;
When the labor of a million
  Goes to swell the gains of one,
As the serfs of ancient Egypt
  Starved beneath the burning sun;
When the schemer and the sharper
  Hold the wealth and rule the land,
Using up the thinker's brain and force,
  Mortgaging the craftsman's hand;
When the many shear the sheep,
  And the few secure the wool,
And the gallows claims its victims,
  And your costly jails are full—
Then the men who dreamed of progress
  And the hopes of peace and bliss,
While they weep and wonder vainly
  Ask each other: "Why is this?"
Then the thinker, while confessing
  That his vision yet is dim,
Says that one thing very clearly
  Is apparent unto him,
That the people, blind or heedless,
  Place themselves beneath the rule,
Either of the fiendish knave, or
  Worse, perhaps, the sodden fool.

                              N. P. Willis
                              (1806-1867)

THE MODERNS

CUT LOOSE

IT COMES prancing over pavements,
We shall be struck in the forehead sometimes,
The Great Parade, the Great Celebration,
The Declaration of Independence.
And you will cut loose from the factory machines,
Fling down the bolts and nuts, the hammers and saws,
Shout your anathema on the horizon.

I shall break every pen in the penholder, write sacrilege on the face of
   the company's paper.
Cut loose, all of us!
Cut loose, with our timid, time-clock ways and our afraid-of-losing-a-
   job faces!
We shall make a hullabaloo—a giant parade for the stars to blink at.

Loureine A. Aber

VICARIOUS ATONEMENT

THIS is an old and very cruel god . . .

We will endure;
We will try not to wince
When he crushes and rends us.

If indeed it is for your sakes,
If we perish or moan in torture,
Or stagger under sordid burdens
That you may live—
Then we can endure.

If our wasted blood
Makes bright the page
Of poets yet to be;
If this our tortured life
Save from destruction's nails
Gold words of a Greek long dead;
Then we can endure,
Then hope,
Then watch the sun rise
Without utter bitterness.

But O thou old and very cruel god,
Take if thou canst this bitter cup from us.

Richard Aldington
(1892—   )

THE QUEEN'S CORONATION ROBE

*"Greppo is a weaver. It was he
who while in exile in England
wove the coronation robe of Queen
Victoria."—Victor Hugo:
"The History of a Crime."*

I

In a gloomy attic in Spitalfields,
A weaver is plying his loom;
With work-worn hands the shuttle he wields,
But the woof and the warp through the gloom
Are tinctured with purple and crimson and gold;
With heaven's deep blue and with sunset red,
Like a rainbow-hued wave in a bright river rolled,
Quivers and glistens each silken thread:
But the weaver is poor and his face it is white,
And the weaver's attic is empty and bare;
What means all that golden-wrought vesture so bright
'Mid the want and the hunger and suffering there?
The weaver is weaving the robe of a queen,
But he weaves in his blood and his tears in between.

II

Westminster Abbey's nave and aisles
Teem with a courtly crowd:
The Queen with her maids of honor files
Through an ocean of heads low bowed;
She walks—and with rich iridescent sheen
Her robe glistens rich in each fold,
The gem-laden robe of a maiden queen
Resplendent with crimson and gold.
Bow!—but draw back as the pageant nears,
Draw back in horror and dread;
The crimson is blood and the diamonds are tears
By millions of laborers shed—
A rebel hath woven the robe of his queen,
But he wove in his blood and his tears in between.

James Allman
(1864—   )

A SLAVE PRAYS TO THE WIND

Fling me back from this mother of wrath, O hurtling
Rush of spirit between the sea and dawn,
Between the wash of darkness and the hard cusps
Of mountain barriers against which the day

Breaks into shattered light. Strike, and instill
The fury of this unappeasable flood,
The pagan envy, and the eating fire
That burns life down to the quick. O make me mad
With all the ancient winging sons of the sun-rise
Whose dreams were smoldering to set a world in flames,
Who spoke the lightning, and whose passing drew
A little whirl of dust to rise in storms
And shake the granite bastions of years.
Come to my lips and hands, spray-laden and swift,
Fill me once more with the long-remembered, delirious
Wine of the visions of men, visions that flare
In quick white levin over the midnight skies
Of war and darkening tumult. For bitter death,
Death and despairing grief have dulled us all,
And the many bodies that sleep so easily
Weigh on us heavily, till our spirits sleep
Sunk in a field of tombs, and drugged with blood,
Doubting the end. . . . Marked cards again, cogged dice;
And men go down and the mocking mountain tops
Shake with laughter of masters, as in old days.
Is there any winning the game?   Will they shift forever
Flying before us unseen from form to form
Invulnerable as air?
My mouth and hands are a little shaken dust,
My eyes and ears are dust, and I am dumb.

But lift me, and hold me free, O piercing clarion
Clamor of challenge from the abyss that lies
About us and beyond, unknown. Brine cold,
Stinging and pure, cleanse my dim mind of clinging
Webs of doubt, lend me a breath from the gulfs
To fan these ash-filmed embers. Out of the drift
Of forces incommunicable and wild
That besiege our lives, blow through these inert cells
New courage from the outer rim of stars.
For their tricks are done; we shall play them one for the last;
We shall upset their game; even yet the pawns
Shall ride the wild horses of these rebel winds
And seas, compact in a tempest of men's lives
Rising white-angered from oblivion;
And sweeping salt and stern across the waste
Pitch the whole checker-board to the night of time.

Maxwell Anderson
(1888—   )

THE CAGE

MAN, afraid to be alive,
Shuts his soul in senses five;
From fields of Uncreated Light
Into the crystal tower of Sight;
And from the roaring Songs of Space
Into the small, flesh-carven place
Of the Ear whose cave impounds
Only small and broken sounds;
And to his narrow sense of Touch
From Strength that held the stars in clutch;
And from the warm ambrosial Spice
Of flowers and fruits of Paradise
To the frail and fitful power
Of Tongue's and Nose's sweet and sour.
And toiling for a sordid wage
There in his self-created Cage,
Ah, how safely barred is he
From menace of Eternity.

Martin Armstrong
(1882-   )

EVERETT, NOVEMBER FIFTH*

*". . . and then the Fellow Worker
died, singing "Hold the Fort." . . .
—From the report of a witness.*

SONG on his lips he came;
    Song on his lips he went;—
This be the token we bear of him,—
    Soldier of Discontent!

Out of the dark they came; out of the night
    Of poverty, injury and woe—
With flaming hope, their vision thrilled to light,—
    Song on their lips and every heart aglow;

They came, that none should trample Labor's right
    To speak, and voice her centuries of pain.
Bare hands against the master's armored might!—
    A dream to match the tolls of sordid gain!

*On November 5, 1915, hundreds of I. W. W. members who boarded the passenger boat Verona bound for Everett, Wash., to defy the authorities' suppression of free speech, were upon arrival attacked by "citizens." Five I. W. W. were murdered and many more wounded. In addition to this loss, five were jailed and tried on murder charges, but were acquitted.—M. G.

And then the decks went red; and the green sea
  Was written crimsonly with ebbing life.
The barricades spewed shots and mockery
  And curses, and the drunken lust of strife.

Yet, the mad chorus from that devil's host,—
  Yea, all the tumult of that butcher throng,—
Compound of bullets, booze and coward boast,—
  Could not out-shriek one dying worker's song!

    Song on his lips he came;
      Song on his lips he went;—
    This be the token we bear of him,—
      Soldier of Discontent!

                Charles Ashleigh

OUT OF WORK

ALONE at the shut of day was I,
With a star or two in a frost-clear sky,
And the byre smell in the air.

I'd tramped the length and breadth o' the fen;
But never a farmer wanted men;
Naught doing anywhere.

A great calm moon rose back o' the mill,
And I told myself it was God's will
Who went hungry and who went fed.

I tried to whistle, I tried to be brave;
But the new ploughed fields smelt dank as the grave;
And I wished I were dead.

                Kenneth H. Ashley

THE RIVETER

THE steam-shovels had sunk their teeth
  Through earth and rock until a hole
Yawned like a black hell underneath,
  Like a coal-crater with all the coal
Torn out of her: the shovels bit
The stinking stony broth—and spit.

The Wops went up and down; they spilled
  Cement like a groggy soup in chutes;

They mixed the mortar and they filled
    The gash with it. . . . Short, swarthy brutes
They were, who reeked of rock and wet
Lime and accumulated sweat.

At first the work was tame enough:
    Only another foundation like
Hundreds before and just as tough
    To stand under a ten-ton spike.
But it was different when a whir
Of steel announced the riveter.

One long lad of them took the crowd
    As he straddled the girders and hooked the nuts
Livid-white hot: and we allowed
    He was the lunatic for guts;
The sidewalk bleachers yelled as he
Speared a sizzler dizzily.

They got to call him the "Rivet Ruth"*
    That crisp corn shock of gusty hair,
That blue hawk-eye and devil of youth
    Juggling with death on a treacherous stair,
Tipping his heart on a beam of steel
That made his pavement audience reel.

The riveting hammers stuttered and kicked;
    The ten-ton trestles whined in the winch;
And still this golden Icarus picked
    The hissing rivets by half an inch,
Twirled and nailed them on the spin
Out of the air and rocked them in.

And one fine sun-splashed noon he lunged
    Over the stark deadline—and missed!
Swung for an instant and then plunged
    While the lone insane rivet hissed
Him all the way down from truss to truss
And dropped beside its Icarus!

The old strap-hanger thumbed his paper;
    Feet shuffled sidewalks; traffic roared. . . .
Icarus had performed his caper—
    Little New York minced by bored;
Leave the lads with the broken backs,
Soiled feathers and some melted wax!

Joseph Auslander
(1897—   )

*The "Ruth" referred to is a well-known baseball player of this country.—M. G.

EVIDENCE

DAY after day she stands
With aching back, her busy hands
Smoothing the silks and laces fair
She does not wear.
Night after night she climbs up to her barren cell,
Whose dingy walls foretell
The drawn-out torture of the future years.
She shudders and her frightened tears,
Flooding the roses of her skin,
Turn it to parchment, wan and thin.
And then—
We call together sleek and prosperous men,
Fat jowled and double-chinned,
To find out why the girl has sinned!

Ralph Bacon

THE GODS

THE Gods are dead!
Dead lies their Heaven, their Hell.
The Gods are dead,
With all their terrors! Well!
Man now unmakes them,
Who made them in his youth;
He boldly breaks them
With shattering blows of Truth!

Well that each Idol
Has fallen where it lies.
Man is man's highest,
With grandeur in his eyes!
But hear, ye Humans!
Give Man no crowns or rods:
Men are your fellows;
Nay, raise not up new Gods!

William Francis Barnard
(1872-   )

THE REAPERS

I HAVE dreamed the dreams of the lowly,
And garnered the scattered grain,
Where the reapers have toiled before me—
My harvest was tears and pain.

But I said: Tomorrow—season
  Will ripen the unshorn field;
I will girdle my loins in the morning
  And gather the dew-fresh yield.

And the season brought forth its reapers
  Who garnered the golden grain
While the dew was fresh on the grasses—
  And the dew was my tears of pain.

But I smothered my sorrow within me,
  Awaiting the season again;
The reapers I saw in the meadows,
  And the toilers were sowing the grain.

And I swore to my soul: Not the morrow,
  But today, unmindful of yield
I would sow the grain I would gather
  Tho' I got not an ear from the field.

And lo! from my broadcast sowing
  On the bounteous breast of the field
Amazing rich was the harvest,
  And children were fed from the yield.

And I care not to garner while others
  Know only to harvest and reap,
For mine is the reaping of sowing
  Till the spirit of rest gives me sleep!

                Ralcey Husted Bell
                (1869—   )

THE REBEL

THERE is a wall of which the stones
Are lies and bribes and dead men's bones.
And wrongfully this evil wall
Denies what all men made for all,
And shamelessly this wall surrounds
Our homestead and our native grounds.

But I will gather and I will ride,
And I will summon a countryside,
And many a man shall hear my halloa
Who never had thought the horn to follow:
And many a man shall ride with me
Who never had thought on earth to see
High Justice in her armory.

When we find them where they stand,
A mile of men on either hand,
I mean to charge from right away,
And force the flanks of their array,
And press them inward from the plains,
And drive them clamoring down the lanes,
And gallop and harry and have them down,
And carry the gates and hold the town.
Then shall I rest me from my ride
With my great anger satisfied.

Only, before I eat and drink,
When I have killed them all, I think
That I will batter their carven names,
And slit their pictures in their frames,
And burn for scent their cedar door,
And melt the gold their women wore,
And hack their horses at their knees,
And hew to death their timber trees,
And plough their gardens deep and through—
And all these things I mean to do
For fear perhaps my little son
Should break his hands, as I have done.

Hilaire Belloc
(1870—   )

"POOR GIRL"

THERE was an earthquake in my heart, and I
  Have been what I have been,
Now there's the long street and the bitter sky
  Crying "Unclean! Unclean!"

But you're more swine—you—you who have withstood,—
  So smug, so self-sufficed!
Oh, there's a thing called "frenzy" in my blood;
  Snarls at your frock-coat Christ!

"Seduction," "the starvation wage"? Not me!
  I seemed to flower in flame.
And so my "soul is lost eternally,"
  You say. You "view my shame."

Oh, can that guff! If I'm no startled hare,
  I'm caught. I know your traps.
I took my chance. You've got me in the snare,
  Society—*perhaps!*

Call me "poor girl," and psalm-sing through your nose
   The harlot she gets hers.
Think I should fawn on God then, I suppose,
   You whited sepulchres.

Some poet will even put me in a song
   And sell it, just to live.
People buy books to read why I "go wrong."
   I gave, and I forgive.

                          William Rose Benét
                          (1886—   )

THE BUILDERS

Staggering slowly, and swaying
Heavily at each slow foot's lift and drag,
With tense eyes careless of the roar and throng,
That under jut and jag
Of half-built wall and scaffold streaming along,
Six bowed men straining strong
Bear, hardly lifted, a huge lintel stone.
This ignorant thing and prone,
Mere dumbness, blindly weighing,
A brute piece of blank death, a bone
Of the stark mountain, helpless and inert,
Yet draws each sinew till the hot veins swell
And sweat-drops upon hand and forehead start,
Till with short pants the suffering heart
Throbs to the throat, where fiercely hurt
Crushed shoulders cannot heave; till thought and sense
Are nerved and narrowed to one aim intense,
One effort scarce to be supported longer!
What tyrant will in man or God were stronger
To summon thrall and seize
The exaction of life's uttermost resource
That from the down-weighed breast and aching knees
To arms lifted in pain
And hands that grapple and strain
Up surges, thrusting desperate to repel
The pressure and the force
Of this, which neither feels, nor hears, nor sees?

                          Laurence Binyon
                          (1869—   )

From A GREAT INDUSTRIAL CENTRE

SQUALID street after squalid street,
  Endless rows of them, each the same,
Black dust under your weary feet,
Dust upon every face you meet,
Dust in their hearts, too—or so it seems—
  Dust in the place of dreams.

Spring in her beauty thrills and thrives,
  Here men hardly have heard her name.
Work is the end and aim of their lives—
Work, work, work! for their children and wives;
Work for a life which, when it is won,
  Is the saddest thing 'neath the sun!

Work—one dark and incessant round
  In black, dull workshops out of the light;
Work that others' ease may abound,
Work that delight for them may be found,
Work without hope, without pause, without peace,
  That only in death can ease.

Brothers, who live glad lives in the sun,
  What of these men, at work in the night?
You who were glad and who liked life well
  While they did your work in hell!

E. (*Nesbit*) *Bland*
(1858—   )

SENTIMENTALITY

SENTIMENTALITY,
You win the love of men
Who look upon you as a soft
And indiscreetly reassuring minx.
You stand upon the street corner
Of their trysts and felonies.
Underneath your glance
Their disappointments grow less harsh
And assume a charmed, theatrical pose,
While their momentary victories
Feel an ardent ownership of life.
Again, to other men you seem
Obnoxious, cloying and replete
With remedies that merely drug the wound.
To them you wander through the sharp

And carnal vagaries of life,
And make the faces of men and women
Blind beneath your perfumed handkerchief.
Yet, you are none of the figures
Engraved upon you by the needs of men.
You stand, invincibly compassionate;
Disguised by frail, poetic mockeries;
Held up by an ephemeral erectness:
Whose finely knitted lies
Are often better than the stripped
And grossly stooping honesties of life.
You wait for men to corrupt you
With their snivelings and heavy smiles,
But at your best you add
A quickly graceful, valiant compensation
To the underpaid and slowly wilting
Slaveries of minds and hearts.

Maxwell Bodenheim
(1893—   )

THE COUNTY JAIL

THE jail was built by workers for their friends
Who, sickened by the thought of work in shops,
Might take to jobs annoying to the cops.
Brick-layers built the stairway that descends
To dungeons, built the doorway that portends
Of bugs or floggings. Hunkies, Yankees, Wops,
Whose widows someday will be pushing mops,
May see their own sons here before life ends.

So old among us here this jail has grown
That even now there in the cells, in gray,
May be a man whose father built with stone
The high walls; one whose father hauled clay
For those dark bricks that close him in; or one
Whose father wired the gong that marks his day.

Stanley Boone

CAGES

FOUR walls enclose men, yet how calm they are!
They hang up pictures that they may forget
What walls are for in part, forget how far
They may not run and riotously let
Their laughter taunt the never-changing stars.

In circus cages wolves and tigers pace
Forever to and fro. They do not rest,
But seek nervously the longed-for place.
Our picture-jungles would not end their quest,
Or pictures of another tiger's face.

On four square walls men have their world, their strife,
Their painted, framed endeavors, joys and pain;
And two curators known as man and wife
Hang up the sunrise, wipe the dust from rain
And gaze excitedly on painted life.

Stirling Bowen

DECLARATION

OUT with the rims of the world,
    Shave the horizon out;
Go then with flag unfurled,
    With song and solemn shout.

Break all boundaries down,
    Untrack the bordered way,
Against the charted town
    Arise, invoke, inveigh.

Rid the world of its gods:—
    Yea, man is god enough
If he break the ruler's rods
    And march with perfect love.

Deny the Christian name
    Employed for pelf and strife,
And in its stead proclaim
    Man, that is lord of life!

Then out on the coasts of the world
    With eyeballs taut and grim,
Where the uttermost wind is hurled
    Across the uttermost rim.

Peer till darkness gives,
    And light unblurs the sky,
Fight till the unborn lives
    And the dying die!

Bayard Boyesen

LABOR

OUT of chaos, out of murk
I arose and did my work;
While the ages changed and sped,
I was toiling for my bread.
Underneath my sturdy blows
Forests fell and cities rose,
And the hard reluctant soil
Blossomed richly from my toil.
Palaces and temples grand
Wrought I with my cunning hand.
Rich indeed was my reward—
Stunted soul and body scarred
With the marks of scourge and rod.
I, the tiller of the sod,
From the cradle to the grave
Shambled through the world—a slave.
Crushed and trampled, beaten, cursed,
Serving best, but served the worst,
Starved and cheated, gouged and spoiled.
Still I builded, still I toiled,
Undernourished, underpaid,
In the world myself had made.
Up from slavery I rise,
Dreams and wonder in my eyes.
After brutal ages past
Coming to my own at last.
I was slave—but I am free!
I was blind—but I can see!
I, the builder, I, the maker,
I, the calm tradition breaker,
Slave and serf and clod no longer,
Know my strength—and who is stronger?
I am done with ancient frauds,
Ancient lies and ancient gods—
All that sham is overthrown.
I shall take and keep my own.
Unimpassioned, unafraid.
Master of the world I've made!

Berton Braley
(1882—   )

THE HARP NOTE

THEY tell the hoary legend still
  Of that glad night of old,
When the angel throng burst into song,
  And struck their harps of gold:
And the starry hosts on heaven's plains
  The flag of peace unfurled,
And the message ran: good will to man,
  O'er all the weary world.

The angels throng the skies no more—
  Their harps are silent now;
Still toiling man bends pale and wan,
  With the blood sweat on his brow.
O well the angels struck the note
  Of our Christian age of gold—
Of soulless greed in its fight with need
  In the mart where men are sold.

Ay, now it is men that must strike the note,
  And, it may be, with harps of steel,
When they sound the lay of the dawning day
  Of the happy commonweal.
Then, comrades, fight, through the storm and the night,
  Till the reign of wrong shall cease,
For beyond the field, where the foe must yield,
  There lies the land of peace.

Haldane Burgess

A BALLAD OF DEAD GIRLS

SCARCE had they brought the bodies down
  Across the withered floor
Than Max Rogosky thundered at
  The District Leader's door.

Scarce had the white-lipped mothers come
  To search the fearful noon,
Than little Max stood shivering
  In Tom McTodd's saloon!

In Tom McTodd's saloon he stood,
  Beside the silver bar,
Where any honest lad may stand,
  And sell his vote at par.

"Ten years I've paid the System's tax,"
  The words fell quivering, raw;
"And now I want the thing I bought—
  Protection from the law!"

The Leader smiled a twisted smile:
  "Your doors were locked," he said.
"You've overstepped the limit, Max—
  A hundred women . . . dead!"

Then Max Rogosky gripped the bar
  And shivered where he stood.
"You listen now to me," he cried,
  "Like business fellers should!"

"I've paid for all my hundred dead,
  I've paid, I've paid, I've paid."
His ragged laughter rang, and died—
  For he was sore afraid.

"I've paid for wooden hall and stair,
  I've paid to strain my floors,
I've paid for rotten fire-escapes,
  For all my bolted doors.

"Your fat inspectors came and came—
  I crossed their hands with gold.
And now I want the thing I bought,
  The thing the System sold."

The District Leader filled a glass
  With whiskey from the bar
(The little silver counter where
  He bought men's souls at par).

And well he knew that he must give
  The thing that he had sold,
Else men should doubt the System's word,
  Keep back the System's gold.

The whiskey burned beneath his tongue:
  "A hundred women dead.
I guess the boss can fix it up,
  Go home—and hide," he said.

*   *   *   *   *   *

All day they brought the bodies down
  From Max Rogosky's place—
And oh, the fearful touch of flame
  On hand and breast and face!

All day the white-lipped mothers came
  To search the sheeted dead;
And horror strode the blackened walls,
  Where Death had walked in red.

But Max Rogosky did not weep.
  (He knew the tears were vain)
He paid the System's price, and lived
  To block his doors again.

Dana Burnet
(1888—   )

FACTORY CHILDREN

HERE toil the striplings, who should be a-swarm
In open sun-kissed meadows; and each day,
Amid the monstrous murmur of the looms
That still their treble voices, they become
Tiny automata, mockeries of youth:
To her that suckled them, to him whose name
They bear, mere fellow-earners of Life's bread;
No time for tenderness, no place for smiles—
These be the world's wee workers, by your leave!

Naught is more piteous underneath the sky
Than at the scant noon hour to see them play
Feebly, without abandon or delight
At some poor game; so grave they seem and crushed!
The young! and foulness sucks them in once more.

Yet still the message wonderful rings clear
Above all clang of commerce and of mart:
"Suffer the little children," and again:
"My Kingdom is made up of such as these."

Richard Burton
(1861—   )

LOOPING SILK STOCKINGS

ROW UPON row of workers' houses
Stretch at the foot of the factory.
Company houses, dingy and gray,
Each with a high pointed roof
And a puny red spike of chimney,
Narrow and gray, like our lives,
From the factory window I see them.

And yonder on the hill, a jewel in the sunlight,
The house of our boss.
Slender columns rising white from the blossoming shrubbery,
Rosy roof all aglow, great glimmering windows.

I look down the long room, like a vast whitewashed jungle,
With its row upon row of machines, all clicking and turning.
Heads of workers bent low, great vistas of columns and drop-lights.
Two hundred and fifty girls I see, young and old, looping silk stockings,
Even the little hunchback, with her back like a question mark,
And her face like a poor hunted rabbit's
. . . But the daughter of our boss I do not see.

Where is she this spring day, the rich man's daughter?
Is she playing her piano there in the palace-like mansion?
Is she driving her car in the sweet air, breathing the scent of blossoms?
Or is she dawdling in Europe, seeing the wonders
We never shall see? . . . She is not here, the rich man's daughter.

All day I have sat here, looping silk stockings,
Heel and toe, heel and toe, each mesh precisely
Impaled upon its sharp needle.
Numb is my brain with the tiny monotonous meshes,
Drowsy my thoughts with the tireless trumping machinery.

Yonder the lazy sun gilds the palace-home
With a distant, dream-like splendor.
Was it a dream that I heard that some day
I shall play with the boss' daughter there and she
Work with me here, some day, looping silk stockings?

Vera Bush

THE DAY

NOT AS they planned it or will plan again,
Those captains whose command was forged in hell,
Not as they promised for their terrible
Obedient horde, Teuton and Saracen,
Bulgar and Slav, not as they dreamed it then,
Masters of might with sobs for pæans to swell
Their darkening sway, but like a far-off bell
Undoing night, the day has come for men.

The people's day has dawned, a deeper sky
Than any day that ever rose from sea,
And more than any captain dared is won,

And this great light that opens carries high
More justice than we dreamed of, even we
Who still are blind awhile, facing the sun.

Witter Bynner
(1881—   )

JUSTICE IS DEAD

> *"Judge Thayer boasted of what he would do to the 'anarchistic bastards.' "*—From an affidavit alleging prejudice of trial judge in Sacco and Vanzetti case.

TOLL the bells for Justice. . . .
   Justice is dead!
Cowards hold the scepter
   Over her head;
Hatred holds the balance,
   Vengeance is the cry:
"Kill them without mercy;
   Let the bastards die!"

Toll the bells: the judgment's
   Cruelty stands;
Pilate, blind and groping,
   Washes his hands.
Prejudice has triumphed,
   Triumphed in its lust;
Hope is bruised and bleeding,
   Trampled in the dust.

Ring the bells for Freedom!
   Truth is not dead:
Love still weaves its garland
   Over her head.
Legal crucifixion
   Done by little men
Cannot vanquish Justice—
   It shall rise again!

Harold D. Carew

THE ROUGH RIDER

TAKE UP, who will, the challenge;
   Stand pat on graft and greed;
Grow sleek on others' labor,
   Surfeit on others' need;

Let paid and bloodless tricksters
   Devise a legal way
Our common right and justice
   "To sell, deny, delay."

Not yesterday nor lightly
   We came to know that breed;
Our quarrel with that cunning
   Is old as Runnymede.
We saw enfranchised insult
   Deploy in kingly line,
When broke our sullen fury
   On Rupert of the Rhine. . . .

Now, masking raid and rapine
   In debonair disguise,
The foe we thought defeated
   Deludes our careless eyes,
Entrenched in law and largess
   And the vested wrong of things,
Cloaking a fouler treason
   Than any faithless king's.

He takes our life for wages,
   He holds our land for rent,
He sweats our little children
   To swell his cent per cent;
With secret grip and levy
   On every crumb we eat,
He drives our sons to thieving,
   Our daughters to the street. . . .

Against the grim defenses
   Where might and murrain hide,
Unswerving to the issue
   Loose-reined and rough we ride
Full tardily, to rescue
   Our heritage from wrong,
And establish it on manhood,
   A thousand times more strong.

            Bliss Carman
            (1861—   )

THE CITY OF THE SUN

ALL DOWN the ages comes a cry of anguish,
  Where workers toil and sweat without release,
That others may grow rich the while they languish
  In poverty and pain till life shall cease.
Always a cry of men in desperation,
  Of women, ay, and children, stung beneath
The slaver's whip—the chain, the scanty ration,
  The goad of hunger, and the fear of death.

Always the Land, the one means of existence,
  Snatched from the peasant-folk by guile and force;
Always brave hearts of manhood and resistance
  Crushed by machine-like Law without remorse;
Always the seamstress in her attic dreary,
  The miner in his murky tomb immured,
The factory hand, the clerk—ill, worn and weary—
  By those for whom they toil, unknown, ignored.

Ah yes! and always through the strife and tangle,
  Through all the cries and counsels of despair,
A music heard that silences the jangle,
  A rising chord of Hope that fills the air.
Always the song—despite the world's derision
  Of suffering hearts that welded into one,
In dream prophetic, self-fulfilling vision,
  Of days to be—the City of the Sun.

Always of things unseen one surest token—
  Their deep foundation in the human breast;
The words, now dark within, that shall be spoken—
  Freedom and Comradeship from East to West.
Always from weakness a new strength emerging,
  From sorrow shared a greater ecstasy;
Always the common soul and purpose urging
  To Life and Love and Power and Victory.

Edward Carpenter
(1844—   )

PORTRAIT OF A PALTRY POLITICIAN

MAN OF THE people, everybody's friend,
  As faithful to the false as to the right,
  Parroting speeches morning, noon, and night,
Reckoned to sway the multitude, to bend

The unthinking to your cause (itself a blend
   Of half truths, sophistries—a mildewed blight
   Of buds rhetorical)—stark black is white
Compared in hue to your soul's paltry trend;
Votes! Votes! and Votes! What is there more to life
   Than ballots angled for by sham and guile?
   At journey's end the devil, with a smile,
Grasps your hand warmly (even the one with knife
   Concealed) and cries: "I love your every wile!
Were you but woman I should seek a wife!"

Robert Cary
(1882—   )

THE WARRIOR-WIND

ONCE more the wind leaps from the sullen land
With his old battle-cry.
A tree bends darkly where the wall looms high;
Its tortured branches, like a grisly hand,
Clutch at the sky.

Gray towers rise from the gloom and underneath—
Black-barred and strong—
The snarling windows guard their ancient wrong;
But the mad wind shakes them, hissing through his teeth
A battle song.

O bitter is the challenge that he flings
At bars and bolts and keys,
Torn with the cries of vanished centuries
And curses hurled at long-forgotten kings
Beyond dim seas.

The wind alone, of all the gods of old,
Men could not chain.
O wild wind, brother to my wrath and pain,
Like you, within a restless heart, I hold
A hurricane.

The wind has known the dungeons of the past,
Knows all that are;
And in due time will strew the dust afar,
And, singing, he will shout their doom at last
To a laughing star.

O cleansing warrior wind, stronger than death,
Wiser than he may know;
O smite these stubborn walls and lay them low,
Uproot and rend them with your mighty breath—
Blow, wind, blow, blow!

Ralph Chaplin
(1887—   )

WHAT WILL THERE BE TO REMEMBER*

WHAT will there be to remember
Of us in the days to be—
Whose fate was a trodden ember
And even our doubt not free?
Parliaments built of paper,
And the soft swords of gold
That twist like a waxen taper
In the weak aggressor's hold.
A hush around Hunger slaying,
A city of serfs unfed—
What shall we leave for saying
To praise us when we are dead?

Gilbert K. Chesterton
(1874—   )

*From *The March of the Black Mountain*

RED FLAG

THIS is no time for tears, no place for mournful poses;
We have a trust to fill before our brief day closes.

A hundred thousand Saccos and Vanzettis starkly die
Whose agonizing arms accuse the stormy, bloodied sky.

On battlefields, in dismal mills and dank, dark mines;
In fetid tenements and on brave, far-flung picket-lines.

Whence comes the hue that stains the workers' flag so red?
The rich have dyed it deep with the blood of our slaughtered dead;

It is they who have sown the tempest, they who have made it war.
Our children shall win to freedom; theirs shall pay the score.

Ralph Cheyney
(1896—   )

PARDONED

CONVENTION shut him close inside
    A narrow, four-walled cell;
Civilization held the key,
    And he was guarded well.

He never tried to break lock-step,
    He kept a steady pace;
No signs of wrath or mutiny
    Were ever on his face.

He set a good example, too,
    Before imprisoned men,
And so one day the pardoning board
    Said, "Let him out again."

And now he is as free as clouds
    That drift above my head;
No regulations bind his soul—
    But men say, "He is dead!"

Helene Claiborne

GOLF LINKS

THE GOLF LINKS lie so near the mill
    That almost every day
The laboring children can look out
    And see the men at play.

Sarah N. Cleghorn
(1876—   )

I AM

MY FODDER is the metal
of a machine sprouting work,
my days are the soul
of a dirty factory.
Those slapping belts above my head
are the song
of dead cattle chaining live men,
For I am a cog
of universal toil.
I am a tree
cut into firewood,
I am a spike
of a broken wheel;
I am all the things
that Wealth says I am not.

For I was born
 in Poverty's stinking stable
 and rented to Capital;
 and Capital
 pays me wages
 that shrink in an envelope
 of futility.

                    Albert Edward Clements
                       (1906—   )

FACTORY SMOKE

SEE how the smoke attacks the sunset sky!
A smudge of factory fumes against the west,
It oozes through the red clouds' glowing breast,
Until their beauty, poisoned, droops to die.
Higher the murk ascends, and still more high,
And gnaws the pink and gold with evil zest,
Until the peak of heaven seems oppressed,
And only grayness spreads before the eye.

And still the smoke is rising! In the night,
Starless and dense, I know it soars and soars,
With snaky folds and vapors blackly curled
To quench all gleam of magic in the world;
To drown all wonder, coloring and light,
Till round the very hearts of men it pours!

                    Stanton A. Coblentz
                       (1896—   )

EMPLOYMENT

WEAVER am I—of tapestries;
Weaving from the tangled threads
Of other men—
Abandoned certainties
Which I must tear to shreds
And weave again.

                    Julia Walcott Cockcroft

From THE FIRE-BRINGER

WHO will bring the red fire
Unto a new hearth?
Who will lay the wide stone
On the waste of the earth?

Who is fain to begin
To build day by day?
To raise up his house
Of the moist yellow clay?

There's clay for the making,
Moist in the pit,
There are horses to trample
The rushes thro' it.

Padraic Colum
(1881—   )

FROM THE DARK TOWER

WE SHALL not always plant while others reap
The golden increment of bursting fruit,
Not always countenance, abject and mute,
That lesser men should hold their brothers cheap;
Not everlastingly while others sleep
Shall we beguile their limbs with mellow flute,
Not always bend to some more subtle brute;
We were not made eternally to weep.

The night whose sable breast relieves the stark
White stars is no less lovely, being dark;
And there are buds that cannot bloom at all
In light, but crumple, piteous, and fall;
So in the dark we hide the heart that bleeds,
And wait, and tend our agonizing seeds.

Countee Cullen
(1903—   )

IMPRESSIONS

the hours rise up putting off stars and it is
dawn
into the street of the sky light walks scattering poems

on earth a candle is
extinguished   the city
wakes
with a song upon her
mouth having death in her eyes

and it is dawn
the world
goes forth to murder dreams . . . .

i see in the street where strong
men are digging bread
and i see the brutal faces of
people contented hideous hopeless cruel happy

and it is day,

in the mirror
i see a frail
man
dreaming
dreams
dreams in the mirror

and it
is dusk   on earth

a candle is lighted
and it is dark.
the people are in their houses
the frail man is in his bed
the city
sleeps with death upon her mouth having a song in her eyes
the hours descend
putting on stars. . . . .

in the street of the sky night walks scattering poems.

E. E. Cummings
(1896—   )

LA DAME REVOLUTION

RED was the Might that sired thee,
   White was the Hope that bore thee,
Heaven and Earth desired thee,
   And Hell from thy lovers tore thee;
But barren to the ravisher,
   Thou bearest Love thy child,
Immortal daughter, Peace; for her
   Waits Man, the Undefiled.

Olive Tilford Dargan

THE DEAD MAKE RULES

THE DEAD make rules, and I obey.
I too shall be dead some day.

Youth and maid who, past my death,
Have within your nostrils breath,

I pray you, for my own pain's sake,
Break the rules that I shall make!
Mary Carolyn Davies

LEISURE

WHAT is this life if, full of care,
We have no time to stand and stare?

No time to stand beneath the boughs
And stare as long as sheep or cows.

No time to see, when woods we pass,
Where squirrels hide their nuts in grass.

No time to see, in broad daylight,
Streams full of stars, like skies at night.

No time to turn at Beauty's glance,
And watch her feet, how they can dance.

No time to wait till her mouth can
Enrich the smile her eyes began.

A poor life this if, full of care,
We have no time to stand and stare.
William Henry Davies
(1871—)

From SOLIDARITY

THE WORLD is mine, to toil in and enjoy,
 Is mine to love in and to weep.
Is mine to build upon but not destroy,
 Is mine to labor in and sleep.
The world is mine, my heritage it is;
 It is not mine alone;
Who 's born of woman, it is also his;
 His title is my own.

'Tis more my own than were it given me
 To hold in undisturbed repose.
For me alone, a desert it would be;
 Men make it blossom like the rose.
And whoso will not for my title fight,
 Must likewise his resign;
And whoso tramples on another's right,
 Abridges also mine.

We stand together; neither can escape
 Our joint responsibility.
The injuries we do each other, shape
 The common, racial destiny.

Miles Menander Dawson
(1863—)

RUSSIA

THAT smooth tree-trunk glistening in the rain,
Like the bronze wet skin of a swimmer fighting the waves,
Lightens the cloud behind it, proclaiming a sign of birth.
Alive and big with its prophetic sap,
It stands against the drab and dying winter . . . .
So, against this dingy life,
Stands Russia.

 Rain, O feed the roots of that tree!
 Clouds, spill your nourishing wine upon it!
 Under it, as under the living sun,
 Gather men who know the meaning of manhood.

*All over the menacing, terrified earth, see how the Possessors have
  gathered,*
*How they have driven before them their bondservants armed and
  enrolled!*
*Lo, the axe that is laid to the root of that tree turns liquid and bathes
  it with silver;*
*And the sword that is lifted to slash it melts, powerless, and laves
  it in gold!*
*And the haughty Possessors grow pallid with terror, and cry to their
  bondsmen—*
*But the bondsmen are dumb, for their hearts are aflame and their
  arms are afold!*

From her far casement, withdrawn from the fumy earth,
The Future, waiting, gazes out with her serene vision.
Many centuries has she sat, lighting her window with candles,

And always, sighing, she has averted her clear gaze.
Below her, like sparks that war in the seething flame,
Fret th' uneasy worlds, and when sometimes,
Over the streaked smoke, that which she waits for has mounted,—
That plant whose roots are of earth, but its leaves sun-fed,—
Instant as risen it vanishes, sucked again into the turmoil;
And only welters beneath her the steamy furnace of battle.

But now! ah, once more its fresh leaves push sunward!
Once again rises its golden crest to the Maker of Gold!
Eager the Future gazes—and up, and up—
The Tree of Freedom is grown, whose fruits are ordained to the
        Future!

Think you, O Possessors, that bondsmen shall serve the Future?
Think you there shall be heard in her time the wail of the slave?

    Under the snows of Russia, how many a young heart lay,
        Slain for the love of freedom, whose blood has warmed that soil!
    Meetly, O land of Russia, from consecrated clay
        Burgeoned that tree of dreams, haven of men who toil!

    Limitless plains of Russia, how often the young feet trod,
        Wearily marching to exile, for the vision of truth they saw!
    Fitly, O men of Russia, in dedicated sod
        Have you planted your tree of hope and mercy and righteous law!

That tree fears not the rain that beats its flanks:
Rain shall make rich the sap within its veins!
It shivers not before the blade that hacks its branches:
Molten by truth, the guilty steel pours down upon it!
The placid Future smiles, within her windowed chamber.
She shall see ripe fruits put forth, out of the chilling rain,
And shall partake of one of them, whose name is Wisdom;
And of another, Justice;
And of another, shining and splendid, that shall be called Liberty.

Lo, each leaf of that tree is a song of its growth; the Possessors have
    trembled to hear it:
    And its buds are a promise of fire that scorches the wrongs of the
        earth:
And the bondsmen are come to the boughs of that tree and a-sudden
    their souls are awakened;
    And they that were sent to deal death taste the perilous sweetness
        of birth!
Yea, they have stood to destroy in its shade, and have heard how its
    branches have whispered
    Into their acolyte spirits the secret of man and his worth!

Men have prayed, O rain, that you might drown that tree!
Men have longed, O clouds, for lightning from you!
And their curse has become a blessing,
Because the tree has been guarded by truth.

Singing in the rain,
The dull rain of grey and dying winter,—
Tending the blossomy Tree of Freedom,—
O light of the lowering sky—
Russia!

Miriam Allen de Ford
(1888—   )

HURRICANE

HURRICANE, hurricane . . . brutal boor!
Why are you razing the huts of the poor?

"I am sent by God on a scouring tour . . .
He hates the meek, and he hates the poor. . . .

Last night he called on me by name . . .
I feared his wrath. I quickly came . . .
His face was a mask of blistering flame.

His eyes were two black-anger pools.
'Go out,' he said, 'and crush these fools;
Hie to the tarn and over the town;
Seek out the hovels and flatten them down;
Scourge like a cossack; pound like a boor . . .
I'm wearied with pity . . . . I'm sick of the Poor. . . .,

He spoke and I answered . . . . 'Your will be done. . . .
I shut up the heavens and doused the sun;

And now I am out on a scourging tour . . . .
And now you know why I punish the poor. . . ."

S. A. deWitt
(1891—   )

IRONIC

YOU are hungry for bread,
You are cold as the dead,
You, the fireless poor.
Yet you

Who stare ahead
Envisaging bleak toil,
Hard and unsure,
Are crying for beauty too.
Life gives you one thing, one thing only:
War.
Your weapons are despair
And hate,
And the irons you wore so long,
And famine to share.
You are strong with all that you bore.
You can strike. Strike!
What do you ask for more?

Babette Deutsch
(1895—   )

WHITE HYACINTHS

IF ALL my loaves of bread were two,
I would divide my store
And buy me fragrant hyacinths
To glad the grated door
Of some one hedged in and confined;
Of one whose bolts and bars
Have shut out almost everything
But friendship, love and stars.

Margarette Ball Dickson

From MY WORDS

MY TEXT is not taken from ballroom
    Or palace of those who are gay;
I'd rather these lines were a heart-throb
    To echo the life of today . . .

To echo the lives of the toilers
    Who carry the burdens of earth;
While those whom they love are ill-nourished
    And curse the sad day of their birth.

I've toiled since the days of my childhood
    In shops and in factory hells;
And the sorry result of my labor
    My careworn countenance tells.

I have lived in the midst of the lowly,
  Where sunshine is awfully rare;
Where babes in their cradles must perish
  Because of the pestilent air.

I have lived and hoped and struggled
  For freedom that seemed so remote;—
And when I was weary and downcast
  I stayed in my hallroom and wrote.

David Irving Dobson

THE COMRADE

CALL me friend or foe
  Little I care!
I go with all who go
  Daring to dare.

I am the force,
  I am the fire,
I am the secret source
  Of desire.

I am the urge,
  The spur and throng:
Moon of the tides that surge
  Into song.

Call me friend or foe,
  Little care I!
I go with all who go
  Singing to die.

Call me friend or foe. . . .
  Taking to give,
I go with all who go
  Dying to live.

Lee Wilson Dodd
(1879—   )

GEDDO STREET

BLEARY dwellings,
Dreary dwellings—
Mansions remodelled into tawdry shops;
And flaming posters on vacant lots

Telling of dubious attractions
Or impossible delights—
For these.
And open saloon doors at every corner,
And girls and children
Plodding home through the wet wintry streets,
Or, in summer,
Idling in hallways
Or doors, or windows,
Or slipping away to the gaieties of a trumpery beach
Or a park,
And dreaming rag dreams
Of happiness in rags.

    *   *   *   *   *

Yet the flash of splendid machines,
Speeding to the west,
Which never pause.
And the looks of eyes
That know not this,
Nor vice defiant,
Nor poverty equally so,

Nor aught of rags
That make all riches interesting.

    *   *   *   *   *

Yet Geddo Street,
It knows—
It knows its worth
(This dirty street,
This meanest street
This beaten street)
It knows that *it* it is,
Antithesis of that—
That makes that other
Interesting.

Theodore Dreiser

THE FACTORY

UNAPPREHENDED, the stealing dawn,
And now, the grinding cars,
Bearing their human loads
Cityward or out.
Cars full of men and girls,
Their shabby clothes speaking work,
Their deepest, darkest moods repressed,
Their paling faces

Speaking the needs they feel.
Yet here is one who dreams a dream,
And here is one who laughs,
And here is one who sings a song,
Or moans,
Or scowls;
Old blood a-chill,
Young blood at play,
Or fearsome youth,
Or gloom, or need upon the march,
The while they dodge the trucks and cars.

But hark you—the great whistle there
About the corner, over the shoe factory,
Under the tall chimney that belches smoke,
Against a leaden sky,
It shrieks and bellows its fierce warning,
It yells, it yells:
"Haste ye, haste ye, haste ye,
"Lest poverty o'ertake ye,
"Lest ye may not eat,
"Lest the respect of men fall from ye"—
And it they believe.

Like a flood that feeds a chasm—
Like the grain that fills a hopper.
Oh, clattering feet
Oh, whirring, murmuring wheels,
Oh, trembling, fleeing thoughts that run
Before the giant whistles you believe.

Theodore Dreiser
(1871—   )

HOLINESS

IF ALL the carts were painted gay,
   And all the streets swept clean,
And all the children came to play
    By hollyhocks, with green
    Grasses to grow between,

If all the houses looked as though
   Some heart were in their stones,
If all the people that we know
    Were dressed in scarlet gowns,
    With feathers in their crowns,

I think this gaiety would make
A spiritual land.
I think that holiness would take
This laughter by the hand,
Till both should understand.

John Drinkwater
(1882—   )

WHY?*

THERE is no wrath in the stars,
They do not rage in the sky;
I look from the evil wood
And find myself wondering why.

Why do they not scream out
And grapple star against star,
Seeking for blood in the wood
As all things around me are?

Lord Dunsany
(1878—   )

*From *Songs From An Evil Wood*

DIOGENES

A HUT, and a tree,
And a hill for me,
And a piece of a weedy meadow.

I'll ask no thing,
Of God or King,
But to clear away his shadow.

Max Eastman
(1883—   )

HANDS WANTED

HANDS wanted, says an "ad,"
And nothing, nothing more.
Some girls read it
And they come to the master's door;
And he hires only hands,
And nothing, nothing more.

The hands weave, spin and sew,
And he thinks they do nothing more,
But they love and dream, hope and sigh,
Though he hears only the loom's creaking cry
And nothing, nothing more.

He sees not the brutality suppressed,
He sees only that hands shall not rest
And nothing, nothing more.

So they come in their youthful bloom
To pale and wither before the loom,
And when they have seen a better day
The master spurns these jaded hands away
And hangs a sign outside the door.
"Hands wanted," it says,
And nothing, nothing more.

Isaac Einsein

RESIST ALL EVIL

"RESIST not evil!"
How well indeed for scoundrels!
Slaves, your backs shall bend beneath their whip in joy,
And pray the fist be mightier and the blow more sharp,
To prove you worthy martyrs to a tyrant's adage!

O glittering words!
O bitter warfare clad in peace!
O Satan-smile beneath a god's decree!

"Resist not evil!"
That evil grow luxuriant,
And they who perpetrate it grow rich and strong,
Till changed shall be the dictum—
"Fools, you can't resist the evil!"

I say—"Resist all evil!"
Your cheek unturned, strike back the blow,
The sword with sword shall answer!
"Resist all evil!"
Till evil hands fall leaden,
And evil hearts turn dust!

Paul Eldridge
(1888—   )

THE HOLLOW MEN

A PENNY FOR THE OLD GUY

WE ARE the hollow men,
We are the stuffed men
Leaning together
Headpiece filled with straw. Alas!
Our dried voices, when

We whisper together
Are quiet and meaningless
As wind in dry grass
Or rats' feet over broken glass
In our dry cellar.

Shape without form, shade without color,
Paralyzed force, gesture without motion.

Those who have crossed
With direct eyes, to death's other kingdom
Remember us—if at all—not as lost
Violent souls, but only
As the hollow men
The stuffed men.

T. S. Eliot
(1882—   )

ONWARD, BROTHERS

ONWARD, brothers, march still onward,
 Side by side and hand in hand;
We are bound for man's true kingdom,
 We are an increasing band.
Though the way seems often doubtful,
 Hard the toil which we endure,
Though at times our courage falter,
 Yet the promised land is sure.

Olden ages saw it dimly,
 And their joy to madness wrought;
Living men have gazed upon it,
 Standing on the hills of thought.
All the past has done and suffered,
 All the daring and the strife,
All has helped to mould the future,
 Make man master of his life.

Still brave deeds and kind are needed,
 Noble thoughts and feeling fair;
Ye too must be strong and suffer,
 Ye too have to do and dare.
Onward, brothers, march still onward,
 March still onward hand in hand;
Till ye see at last man's kingdom,
 Till ye reach the Promised Land.

Havelock Ellis
(1859—   )

MY HEROINES

O, WHAT sing I? Blood-lusting men who climb,
Mad with false lures, behind a flag that whips
Its riddled tatters o'er the crimson shine
Of the red rampart?

           Nay, nor on the ships
That plunging die, I sing not those who stand
Watching the boats, calm while fears foam up
In strangling brine about them, stay the hand,
Nor put from writhing lips the numbing cup
Of Death. . . .

       I sing not martyrs known to men
(As these are known): such have their certain meed,
Rather sing I the humble, those whose need
Unsatisfied, ever re-born again
With the sad travail of each aching day,
Torments them with a woe that never dies,
Transmutes life's meaning to a gasp of pain!

Sing I the heroines of store, of mill!
The unsung victims of greed-tyranny,
The sweatshop legion, in whose breasts the still
Insistent call of motherhood must die;
Who must not harken the insistent cry
Of the Unborn, nor with the Springtide thrill!

Sing I the silent and the all-obscure,
Unheralded in dull, drab lives of toil;
Dogg'd by the lean, gray wolves of Greed, of Lust,
Patiently wise, they cheat the glistening lure,
Fight the long fight and keep the sacred trust,
Blossoming wanly, blooms o'erchoked with dust!

These be the brave, dumb in the dragon-coil!
These I salute, invincible and pure!
              George Allen England
              (1877—   )

"GENTLEMEN"

GOD placed the Russian peasant
Under the Great White Czar;
God put the Prussian worker
Beneath the Lord of War.
But he sent the English gentleman,
The perfect English gentleman,
God's own good English gentleman,
To make us what we are.

Our fathers once were freemen,
And as freemen wont to toil,
To reap the fruitful harvest,
And to gather golden spoil.
But the greedy, grasping gentlemen,
The land-engrossing gentlemen,
The honest English gentlemen,
They stole away the soil.

They drove us from our villages
By force and fraud and stealth,
They drove us into factories,
They robbed us of our health.
But the cotton-spinning gentlemen,
The coal-mine, shipyard gentlemen,
Stock-broking, banking gentlemen,
They gathered wondrous wealth.

We toil to make them prosperous,
We fight to make them great;
But we know how they have robbed us,
We bide our time and wait:
While the fat, well-living gentlemen,
The easy, well-bred gentlemen,
The thoughtless, careless gentlemen,
Forget that slaves can hate.

The patient Russian peasant
Has overthrown his Czar;
The patient Prussian worker
Has smashed his Lord of War.
And soon—ah! soon, our gentlemen,
Our proud, all-powerful gentlemen,
Our God-damned English gentlemen,
Shall find out what we are.

W. N. Ewer
(1885—   )

THE SCAR

I GO through city streets and hear
The clamorous cry of childhood
And the gray, grim sigh of age,
Wrought in our human tapestry,
Welded in one great protest,
Shaped in one horrid scar.

James Waldo Fawcett

SOVEREIGNTY

Who shall be sovereign? Not the titled bones
Of salvaged indiscretions, nor the kings
Who sit beside the banquet, where the groans
Of proletarians are food for jovial flings.

They are in the shadows, and their pet
Drooling debaucheries stare, panic-stricken,
At every rumor in the winds that set
With thunder-showers and shouts that quicken

Twilight into morning, night into the red
Salute of gladness. We shall be sovereign, we
Who shaped the harrowing bed
Of sovereignty.

Out of the cold grimaces of the rain,
Unwelcomed tourists in the land of pain.

Martin Feinstein
(1892—   )

PRAYER IN MASSACHUSETTS*

Upon this soil may no tree ever grow.
   In this land may no lips ever again
Speak the word justice, now that all men know
   Those lips have long boasted and in vain.
May never young men hither come to learn
   What cruel elders have no power to teach.
May no lights burn here save witch fires that burn
   Along some desolate and abandoned beach.
May this dour land go back now whence it came—
   To early granite, to implacable sea.
May there descend on it the cleansing flame
   Of some supreme remote catastrophe
Divorcing it forever with its shame
   From men who would be generous, wise and free.

Arthur Davison Ficke
(1883—   )

*Written before the execution of Nicola Sacco and Bartolomeo Vanzetti, Boston, August 22, 1927.—M. G.

CONTEMPORARY

Then to Emmaus with him, I too walked,
No mark of nails in hand or feet I traced.
So quietly of star-wise dream he talked,

I did not know a savior with me paced
The dripping city street; that by my side,
In the familiar clothes of modern men,
There lived again the tale of one who died
"To make earth good"—the thorns, the scourge again.

At lunch he told in simple phrases to me
The story of the strike and his arrest,
Charged with inciting murder. A near tree
Bent while he told of prison, Death, his guest,
And when he spoke of rising from that tomb,
It threw a cross of shadow on the room.

Sara Bard Field
(1882—   )

A REBEL

TIE a bandage over his eyes,
And at his feet
Let rifles drearily patter
Their death-prayers of defeat.

Throw a blanket over his body,
It need no longer stir;
Truth will but stand the stronger
For all who died for her.

Now he has broken through
To his own secret place;
Which, if we dared to do,
We would have no more power left to look on that dead face.

John Gould Fletcher
(1886—   )

A SONG OF MEN

WE SING the songs that we make,
    Naked, stark and true;
Songs that are red with our blood,
    Stained with our tears right through.

We sing of the men who gather
    In factory, forge and mill;
And warm their hands at the fire
    In the cold, gray morning chill.

Warming their hands for a little time,
    Strong hands at the Fire of Life;
Living and working and hoping,
    'Midst the din, the stress and the strife.

We sing of the cold and dark,
    The fog and the damp and the gloom;
Of the road that the worker journeys on
    That ends for him, ever in doom.

And whatever the road we travel,
    In our search for life and bread;
We see the sun in the evening
    As it dyes the sky blue-red.

And over the hill in the morning
    We see the golden glow,
Giving us hope and courage
    To strive for the things we know.

Out of the dark to the sunlight,
    Forth from the slum to the glen;
We are the Sons of the Future,
    Men and the Children of Men.

Forward! We press, ever forward!
    Over the ground we pass;
We are the men who matter,
    We are the Working Class.
             R. M. Fox

THE GIRL STRIKE-LEADER

A WHITE-FACED, stubborn little thing
Whose years are not quite twenty years,
Eyes steely now and done with tears,
Mouth scornful of its suffering—

The young mouth!—body virginal
Beneath the cheap, ill-fitting suit,
A bearing quaintly resolute,
A flowering hat, satirical.

A soul that steps to the sound of the fife
And banners waving red to war,
Mystical, knowing scarce wherefore—
A Joan in a modern strife.
            Florence Kiper Frank

CHANGE

I AM that creature and creator who
Loosens and reins the waters of the sea,
Forming the rocky marge anon anew.
I stir the old breasts of antiquity,
And in the soft stone of the pyramid
Move wormlike; and I flutter all those sands
Whereunder lost and soundless time is hid.
I shape the hills and valleys with these hands,
And darken forests on their naked sides,
And call the rivers from the vexing springs,
And lead the blind winds into deserts strange,
And in firm human bones the ill that hides
Is mine, the fear that cries, the hope that sings.
I am that creature and creator, Change.

John Freeman
(1885—   )

FOR POETS

THE ANCIENT tyranny is with us still,
With duller costume but with stronger hands;
A newer jargon masks the old commands;
The Bastille looms no more—but there's the mill.
Shelley abhorred the priests; the priests are dead,
But journals lie to us of other things,
And merchants rule as certainly as kings,
Drinking sweet wine, throwing us crumbs of bread.

Then what have we, however words may shift—
Lovers of light and freedom, what have we
To do with lords, whatever lords they be,
Crowned or uncrowned, when we have still to lift
On high the golden banners of romance,
And wake the world to freedom with our chants!

Joseph Freeman
(1897—   )

FIRE AND ICE

SOME say the world will end in fire,
Some say in ice.
From what I've tasted of desire
I hold with those who favor fire.
But if it had to perish twice,

I think I know enough of hate
To say that for destruction ice
Is also great
And would suffice.

Robert Frost
(1875—   )

THE ETERNAL REBEL

SALT of the earth am I,
Sullen and prideful, careless, mocking, strong.
So? Do you hate my laughter, little man?
　　Not as I hate the things at which I laugh!

　　Who is the better man, then,—you or I?
I, who can hate,—and laugh,—and make you hate
Just by the laughing at your trifles-heap?
I, who can fight your love, your hate, your fear,
Knowing I lose before I start, and yet
Laugh at your win, and make your winning damn you?
I, who can hate,—but still can laugh?—or you!
　　You, who can hate but as your pride is touched,
　　Your maxims jeered, your fears which riders roused?
　　You, who can only fight for what had died!
Not that I look for truth from you,—but, say!
　　Who is the better man?

　　Salt of the earth am I,
Bloody and mirthful, hurling your idols down.
Slay me! Your son shall speak my words, and you
Shall pride in mine, that you believe are his!
While I, re-born, will rasp his tender skin,—
Too soft like yours, to wear a rebel's cloak
Until a generation's use has smothered
The harshness of its fire—

　　Laugh with me!

　　Ah, no, you cannot. But I still will laugh,—
Rasp you,—and damn your *winning*. Who am I?
　　Salt of the earth am I,
　　Sullen and prideful, careless, mocking, strong.
Look at your law, and perfume its decay.
Sputter your curses! Mouth your maxims! Slay!
Build your arch of triumph! But beneath,
I am the first to walk. It is for that,
　　I am the Rebel!

Rex G. Fuller

COURAGE

COURAGE is but a word, and yet, of words,
The only sentinel of permanence;
The ruddy watch-fire of cold winter days,
We steal its comfort, lift our weary swords,
And on.   For faith—without it—has no sense;
And love to wind of doubt and tremors sways;
And life forever quaking marsh must tread.

Laws give it not; before it prayers will blush;
Hope has it not; nor pride being true;
'Tis the mysterious soul which never yields,
But hales us on to breast the rush
Of all the fortunes we shall happen thro';
And when Death calls across his shadowy fields—
Dying, it answers: "Here! I am not dead!"

John Galsworthy
(1867—   )

CHILDREN OF KINGS

THE DRY leaf blown along the dusty street
Is not so soon forgot as one of these—
The children learning prayers at Mammon's knees,
Whose small starved bodies and whose weary feet
A million and a million times repeat
The short same way that the machine decrees.
Treaders of wine, their portion is the lees
Weavers of cushions for old Mammon's seat.

The daylight is more weary than the dark—
The dark more weary than the daylight was—
Why wait ye? Ah—how long before the spark
Shall light the kindling that shall burn the throne?
A million and a million times ye pause
While Mammon claims your children for his own.

Lydia Gibson

THE DISASTER

AGAINST the sunset's rose
Purple the pit-head glows—
The mound of slate and slack
That all day long gloomed black:

And the gaunt shaft-wheel seems
Hub to a wheel of dreams,
With flaming spokes that whirl
In a celestial swirl

Of hues beneath whose fire,
With patience naught can tire,
Quiet, with close-shawled head,
Each woman 'waits her dead.

Wilfred Wilson Gibson
(1878—   )

TO LABOR

SHALL you complain who feed the world?
　　Who clothe the world,
　　Who house the world?
Shall you complain, who are the world,
Of what the world may do?
　　As from this hour
　　You use your power,
The world must follow you!

The world's life hangs on your right hand,
　　Your strong right hand,
　　Your skilled right hand,
You hold the whole world in your hand—
See to it what you do!
　　Or dark or bright
　　Or wrong or right
The world is made by you!

Then rise, as you never rose before,
　　Nor hoped before,
　　Nor dared before,
And show, as you never showed before,
The power that lies in you.
　　Stand all as one!
　　See justice done!
Believe, and dare, and do!

Charlotte Perkins Gilman
(1860—   )

THE CITY AT MIDNIGHT

AT MIDNIGHT I look o'er the city,
　That is sleeping and resting from toil,
And I think Life himself must needs pity
　His creatures that endlessly moil.

I hark to the multitude moaning—
　　They are stirring with sorrow I know—
I hark to the multitude groaning
　　In darkest abysses of Woe.

They are trampled upon by the ages
　　That, wrapped in their cynical years,
Have rendered them prey to the rages
　　Of custom and doubts and fears.

Ah, I hear them wearily weeping,
　　As in darkness of sorrow they grope;
For o'er their dim souls there is creeping
　　No redolent zephyrs of hope!

As hushed, I look o'er the city
　　That's darkening and trembling with woe,
My soul is now stirred—not with pity—
　　But with hope (which is truth-born, I know).

O why must they ever be haunted
　　And goaded by sorrow and care?
O why must they ever be taunted
　　And tortured by grief and despair?

See, above the stars are all surging
　　And panting with hope and desire—
I hear well their shouting—their urging
　　As brighter they burn with faith's fire.

O, out of the city of sorrow!
　　O, out of the hills of pain!
Come forth to the land of Tomorrow,
　　Where right shall eternally reign!

Louis Ginsberg
(1896—　　)

From **WHEN THE COCK CROWS***

SIX MEN drove up to his house at midnight, and woke the poor woman
　　who kept it,
And asked her: "Where is the man who spoke against war and insulted
　　the army?"
And the old woman took fear of the men and the hour, and showed
　　them the room where he slept,

*Poem written upon the lynching of Frank Little, active speaker of the In-
dustrial Workers of the World in the year 1917.—M. G.

And when they made sure it was he whom they wanted, they dragged
 him out of his bed with blows, tho' he was willing to walk,
And they fastened his hands on his back, and they drove him across the
 black night,
And there was no moon and no star and not any visible thing, and
 even the faces of the men were eaten with leprosy of the dark,
 for they were masked with black shame,
And nothing showed in the gloom save the glow of his eyes and the
 flame of his soul that scorched the face of Death.

*   *   *   *   *

Now he is dead, but now that he is dead is the door of your dungeon
 faster, O money changers and scribes, and priests, and masters
 of slaves?
Are men now readier to die for you without asking the wherefore of
 the slaughter?
Shall now the pent-up spirit no longer connive with the sun against
 your midnight?
And are we now all reconciled to your rule, and are you safer and we
 humbler, and is the night eternal and the day forever blotted
 out of the skies,
And all blind yesterdays risen, and all tomorrows entombed,
And listen forever to one word of shame and subjection,
And leave the plough in the furrow, the trowel on the wall, the hammer on the anvil, and the heart of the race on the knees of
 screaming women, and the future of the race in the hands of
 babbling children,
And yoke on your shoulders the halter of hatred and fury,
And dash head-down against the bastions of folly,
Because a colored cloth waves in the air, because a drum beats in the
 street,
Because six men have promised you a piece of ribbon on your coat,
 a carved tablet on a wall and your name in a list bordered with
 black?
Shall you, then, be forever the stewards of death, when life waits for
 you like a bride?
Ah, no, brothers, not for this did our mothers shriek with pain and
 delight when we tore their flanks with our first cry;
Not for this were we given command of the beasts,
Not with blood but with sweat were we bidden to achieve our salvation.
Behold! I announce now to you great tidings of joy,
For if your hands that are gathered in sheaves for the sickle of war
 unite as a bouquet of flowers between the warm breasts of
 peace,
Because of six faceless men and ten feet of rope and one corpse dangling
 unseen in the blackness under a railroad trestle?

No, I say, no! It swings like a terrible pendulum that shall soon ring
out a mad tocsin and call the red cock to the crowing.
No, I say, no, for someone will bear witness of this to the dawn,
Someone will stand straight and fearless tomorrow between the armed
hosts of your slaves, and shout to them the challenge of that
silence you could not break.

*   *   *   *   *

"Brothers"—he will shout to them—"are you then, the God-born,
reduced to a mute of dogs,
That you will rush to the hunt of your kin at the blowing of a horn?
Brothers, have then the centuries that created new suns in the heavens
gouged out the eyes of your soul,
That you should wallow in your blood like swine,
That you should squirm like rats in carrion,
That you, who astonished the eagles, should beat blindly about the
night of murder like bats?
Are you, brothers, who were meant to scale the stars, forever to crouch
before a footstool,
Freedom will come without any blows save the hammers on the chains
of your wrist, and the picks on the walls of your jails!

Arise, and against every hand jeweled with the rubies of murder,
Against every foul smell of the earth,
Against every mouth that sneers at the tears of mercy,
Against every head that a footstool raises over your head,
Against every word that was written before this was said,
Against every happiness that never knew sorrow,
And every glory that never knew love and sweat,
Against silence and death, and fear,
Arise with a mighty roar!
Arise and declare your war;
For the world of dawn is blowing,
For the eyes of the East are glowing,
For the lark is up and the cock is crowing,
And the day of judgment is here!"

Arturo Giovannitti
(1884—   )

From A STRANGE FUNERAL IN BRADDOCK

LISTEN to the mournful drums of a strange funeral.
Listen to the story of a strange American funeral.

In the town of Braddock, Pennsylvania,
Where steel-mills live like foul dragons burning, devouring man and
earth and sky,

It is spring. Now the spring has wandered in, a frightened child in
    the land of the steel ogres,
And Jan Clepak, the great grinning Bohemian on his way to work
    at six in the morning,
Sees buttons of bright grass on the hills across the river, and plum
    trees hung with wild, white blossoms,
And as he sweats half-naked at his puddling trough, a fiend by the
    lake of brimstone,
The plum trees soften his heart,
The green grass-memories return and soften his heart,
And he forgets to be hard as steel and remembers only his wife's
    breasts, his baby's little laughter, and the way men sing when
    they are drunk and happy,
He remembers cows and sheep, and the grinning peasants, and the
    villages and fields of sunny Bohemia.

     *   *   *   *   *   *   *   *   *

Wake up, wake up! Jan Clepak, the furnaces are roaring like tigers,
The flames are flinging themselves at the high roof, like mad, yellow
    tigers at their cage.
Wake up! it is ten o'clock, and the next batch of mad, flowing steel
    is to be poured into your puddling trough,
Wake up! wake up! for a flawed lever is cracking in one of those
    fiendish cauldrons,
Wake up! and wake up! for now the lever has cracked, and the steel
    is raging and running down the floor like an escaped madman,
Wake up! O, the dream is ended, and the steel has swallowed you
    forever, Jan Clepak!

     *   *   *   *   *   *   *   *   *

Now three tons of hard steel hold at their heart, the bones, flesh,
    nerves, the muscles, brains and heart of Jan Clepak,
They hold the memories of green grass and sheep, the plum-trees, the
    baby-laughter, and the sunny Bohemian villages.
And the directors of the steel-mill present the great coffin of steel and
    man-memories to the widow of Jan Clepak,
And on a great truck it is borne now to the great trench in the
    graveyard,
And Jan Clepak's widow and two friends ride in a carriage behind
    the block of steel that holds Jan Clepak,
And they weep behind the carriage blinds, and mourn the soft man
    who was killed by hard steel.

                                                         Michael Gold
                                                  (1893—   )

A CHANGE OF VIEW

THEY cut the trees, they dug the mains,
They trampled all the meadow way;
Left not a blade of daisied grass
To lay cool hands upon the day.

A cry floats in the stifled air,
The anguish of some wild, dumb thing;
In muted misery caged and caught,
While the green earth yet glows with Spring.

Now red bricks flaunt their insolence
Like tawdry women of the town;
Leering with cheap impertinence,
Tricked out to please in garish gown.

And where was once blue space of Heaven,
New painted, horrid windows glare;
Marking a mock of beauty gone,
Like empty eyes, that stare and stare.

S. Marguerite Goode

THE LITTLE THINGS

THE LITTLE things, the little restless things,
The base and barren things, the things that spite
The day, and trail processions through the night
Of sad remembrances and questionings;
The poverties, stupidities and stings,
The silted misery, the hovering blight;
The things that block the paths of sound and sight;
The things that snare one's thought and break its wings—

How shall we bear these? we who suffer so
The shattering sacrifice, the huge despair,
The terrors loosed like lightnings on the air
To leave all nature blackened from that curse!
The big things are the enemies we know,
The little things the traitors. Which are worse?

Gerald Gould
(1885—)

THIRD DEGREE*

BECAUSE
I dared to question
By the written word
Wrongs that made

*A personal experience—February 21, 1921.—M. G.

Of man
A slave,
They placed me
Under arrest.

Two protectors of
Everything unjust
Suddenly encircled me—
As I arose to leave the
Public Library.

Without even a
Legal formality they
Rushed me off—
Into the secret chambers of
New York's Bomb Squad.

Upholders of "justice"
Began swarming
Around me,
As I looked on—
Defiantly.

Soon
I found myself
Thrown about and
Trodden upon.
Hands raised
Me up, as
Fists, blackjacks, and feet
Hurled me down again
Into
Unconsciousness!

Bleeding,
Battered and almost
Stupefied—
I was led out
Of the
Torture room and
Thrown into a
Cell.

As
I turned
On the iron cot—
Every part
Of the body
Aching in pain—

The story of the
Martyrs
Of ancient days
Reappeared.

Then,
As somewhat
In a dream,
I beheld
Mephistopheles
Mockingly
Laughing.

My
Mind
Was stumbling
Over
Two
Words:
Civilization and
Progress.

Marcus Graham
(1893—   )

CHILDREN OF DARKNESS

IN THEIR GENERATION WISER THAN THE CHILDREN OF LIGHT

WE SPURRED our parents to the kiss
Though doubtfully they shrank from this—
Day had no courage to review
What lusty dark alone might do—
Then we were joined from their caress
In the heat of midnight, one from two.

This night-seed knew no discontent,
In certitude his changings went;
Though there were veils about his face,
With forethought, even in that pent place,
Down towards the light his way he bent
To kingdoms of more ample space.

Was day prime error, that regret
For darkness roars unstifled yet?
That in this freedom, by faith won,
Only acts of doubt are done?
That unveiled eyes with tears are wet
They loathe to gaze upon the sun?

Robert Graves
(1895—   )

MEN

FACTORY whistles blow Dawn
  From reverberant throats.
Hollow and mournfully drawn
  Are the answering notes
Chorused from harbor and shore
  Through the fog-wreaths, and then
Cityward ceaselessly pour
  Inundations of Men.
East from the Jerseys, and West
  From the sea-girded plains,
South from the hills is the quest
  Of the sinuous trains;
Thronged is each wave-spanning arc,
  And again and again
Shuttle the ferry-craft dark
  With their burthen of Men.
  Men! Men! Men!
Heavy-browed, eager-eyed,
Tremulous, resolute
        Men.

Torrents and billows of life—
  And alas for the spray!
Highway and house-top are rife
  With the turbulent clay.
Men! in the rush and the stir
  And the roar of the street.
Men! in the factory's whirr
  And the furnace's heat.
Men! at the forges that ring
  And the shuttles that fly.
Men! on the girders that swing
  In the vault of the sky.
Swift through its underground lane
  Like a snake to its den
Burrows the glowering train
  With its burthen of Men.
    Men! Men! Men!
  Pitiful, glorious,
  Conquering, desperate
        Men.

Arthur Guiterman
(1871—   )

LAUGH IT OFF

HAVE the Trusts devoured your pay?
    Laugh it off.
Do they cheat you night and day?
    Laugh it off.
Don't make tragedies of trifles,
Don't shoot butterflies with rifles—
    Laugh it off.
Has the Landlord raised your rent?
    Laugh it off.
Have you spent your bottom cent?
    Laugh it off.
If it's sanity you're after,
There's no recipe like laughter—
    Laugh it off.

Bolton Hall
(1854—   )

US, THE HOBOES AND DREAMERS

WE SHALL laugh to scorn your power that now holds the world in awe,
We shall trample on your customs and shall spit upon your law;
We shall come up from life's desert to your burdened banquet hall,
We shall turn your wine to wormwood, your honey into gall.

We shall go where wail the children, where from your race killing mills
Flows a bloody stream of profit to your cursed insatiate tills;
We shall tear from your drivers in our shame and angered pride,
With the fury and the fierceness of a fatherhood denied.

We shall set our sisters on you, those you trapped in your hells,
Where the mother instinct's stifled and no earthly beauty dwells;
We shall call them from the living death, the death in life you gave,
To sing our class's triumph o'er your cruel system's grave.

We shall strip them of their epaulets, the panderers who fight
Your wars against the workers from a bone on which to bite;
We shall batter down your prisons, we shall set your chain-gangs free,
We shall drive you from the mountainside, the valley, plain and the sea.

We shall hunt around the fences where your ox-men sweat and gape
Till they stampede down your stockades in the panic to escape;
We shall steal up through the darkness, we shall prowl to wood and
        town
Till they waken to their power and arise and ride you *down*.

We shall send a message to them on a whisper down the night,
And shall cheer the warrior women drive the ox-men to fight;
We shall use your guile against you—all the cunning you have taught,
All the wisdom of the serpent to attain the ending sought.

We shall come as comes the cyclone—in the stillness we shall form,
From the calm your terror fashioned, we shall hurl on your storm;
We shall strike when least expected, when you deem toil's rout
        complete,
And crush you and your Hessians 'neath our brogan-shodded feet.

We shall laugh to scorn your power that now holds the world in awe,
We shall trample on your customs, we shall spit upon your law,
We shall outrage all your temples, we shall blaspheme all your gods,—
We shall turn the Slave World over as a plowman turns the clods!

Covington Hall

ONE HUNDRED DEAD*

One hundred dead in a hideous pile;
One hundred dead and they talk of a trial!
Murder and greed and the iron of fate—
One hundred dead and they ask us to wait!

One hundred dead by the hand of a scab;
One hundred dead for the feast of their grab;
Coffins of wood and the sham of the laws—
One hundred dead and they ask for the cause!

One hundred dead and they're hunting for more;
One hundred victims to fatten the score;
Master and slave in the annals of time—
One hundred dead and they're seeking the crime!

One hundred dead and the slaughter goes on,
Hearings and quibbles and charges anon,
Graft and collusion in city and state—
One hundred dead and they wipe off the slate!

One hundred dead in their money-mad game;
One hundred dead and they're shifting the blame,
The motorman green and the platforms jammed—
One hundred dead and the public be damned!

*Written upon hearing of the Brooklyn Rapid Transit tragedy, Nov. 1, 1918.

One hundred dead in a murderous race,
Arms without body and heads without face,
Women and children and dreams of the brain—
One hundred dead in the lust for gain!

Laughter and sneers, but the blackguards shall pay
For that hundred dead in the dawn of the day.

Robert S. Hanna

OUR PURPOSE

WE COME not with the blaring of trumpet,
  To herald the birth of a king;
We come not with traditional story,
  The life of a savior to sing.

We come not with jests for the silly,
  We come, not to worship the strong,
But to question the powers that govern,
  To point out a world-old wrong.

To kiss from the starved lips of childhood
  The lies that are sapping its breath,
And brighten the brief cheerless valley
  That leads to the darkness of death;

With reason and sympathy blended,
  And a hope that all mankind shall see,
Untrammeled by Creed, Law or Custom—
  The Attainable Goal of the Free.

Mary Hansen
(1874—   )

MADONNA IN FLANDERS

DRUNK as the glamour of disgrace
A torpid shadow scars her face;
Golgotha seems her star-veiled skull:
Her eyes glow dull and pitiful,

As like the ghoul of God she picks
From tumid fields bouquets of sticks,
And mourns that such blooms leaped from seeds
Too rich for these trite pæans of weeds.

Alas that Lust had crucified
New gods in every man who died,
And made the cross the signpost of
The street to Hate, not the road to Love.

Sad Mother of immortal sons,
No wonder your quaint weeping runs
Like laughter of infernal nuns
In convents of oblivions;

No wonder Hell delights to hear
Opposing prayers for vengeance rear
Their hydra heads in pious guise
To the sad Monarch of the skies.

There is more pleasure stirred in Hell
For each fair youth the Christians fell
Than for a million men who sin
Against a moral discipline.

It is not strange, it is not queer
That Hell is quenched with Heaven's tear;
It is not strange, it is not odd
That Satan's laughs are the groans of God.

It is to mourn, it is to weep
That God gives His beloved sleep;
It is to smile, it is to laugh:
Hell's joke is Heaven's epitaph.

Ernest Hartsock
(1903—   )

IS FREEDOM BUT A NAME?

Is FREEDOM but a name to please the ear,
Spilled from the two-edged tongue of orators,
Who, for their hire, plead peace or rant for wars,
Whom gullibility delights to hear?

Is it the "presto" term of those who rule,
Who say they give, but with their hands behind them,
Whose very acts are fingered but to blind them
Who look with awe and play the part of fool?

No, it is a title from a sturdy age;
It is for one to cherish and defend;
It is for those whose nature will not bend;
It is for us our dearest heritage.

Then let whoever worthy is possess it:
Not having, we profane if we profess it.

Walter Hendricks
(1892—   )

THE WORKERS

THE DAY is gray, not shifting gray
   Of wind-blown fog and shining sea,
But steel-like, still, with that grim chill
   Of barren, dead monotony!

No colors gleam, no banners fly,
   No laughter rests the tired brain,
The old, grim drill, the money-mill;
   And in the street the beat of rain.

Tame faces all about the room,
   And tame the day, its dull routine:
Gay Youth seems but a mockery,
   Trapped, helpless in the vast machine.

And yet, last night, high in the sky
   The bright stars sang, the white moon shone,
While Beauty's self, that mystic elf,
   Sat like a queen upon her throne!

Today the City's noise and dust,
   Its heat and crowds and senseless speed,
Seem only selfishness and lust,
   A cynical and cruel greed.

Men work in cages, like tamed beasts,
   For shelter, children, daily bread—
Not just for gold—while young and old
   Are haunted by one common dread. . . .

Not dread of pestilences, wars,
   Not dread that Death may come too soon,
But fear of uselessness, lest they
   May lose their work, that priceless boon!

And yet tonight, high in the sky,
   The pale stars sing, the frail moon gleams,
As on our housetop you and I
   Dream once again Love's fragile dreams. . . .

Elizabeth Newport Hepburn

WELFARE SONG

SING a song of "Welfare,"
  A pocket full of tricks
To soothe the weary worker
  When he groans or kicks.
If he asks for shorter hours
  Or for better pay,
Little stunts of "Welfare"
  Turn his thoughts away.

Sing a song of "Welfare,"
  Sound the horn and drum,
Anything to keep the mind
  Fixed on Kingdom Come.
"Welfare" loots your pocket
  While you dream and sing,
"Welfare" to your paycheck
  Doesn't do a thing.

Sing a song of "Welfare,"
  Forty 'leven kinds,
Elevate your morals,
  Cultivate your minds.
Kindergartens, nurses,
  Bathtubs, books and flowers,
Anything but better pay
  Or shorter working hours.

Will Herford
(1863—   )

THE RAILROAD ATTORNEYS

THE MEN sat about the room chatting in a cloud of smoke,
Discussing coldly the case of a woman killed by a car.
I listened.
So these were the lawyers of the company,
Slim men behind glaring, black-rimmed glasses.
They were seeking some loophole by which they could cheat
The family of the indemnity,
And somehow when I got up to leave
I felt half ashamed of being there. . . .
To be rich and influential
One must do so many dirty things.

Harold Hersey
(1893—   )

THE HAMMERS

NOISE of hammers once I heard
Many hammers, busy hammers,
Beating, shaping, night and day,
Shaping, beating dust and clay
To a palace; saw it reared;
Saw the hammers laid away.

And I listened, and I heard
Hammers beating, night and day,
In the palace newly reared,
Beating it to dust and clay:
Other hammers, muffled hammers,
Silent hammers of decay.

Ralph Hodgson
(1871—   )

From THE QUESTION

I DO NOT grope in mystic dusks
    For glimmers of a great Design
That casts to epicures dry husks
    And pearls to swine—

That cheats the strong, the daring still,
    And mocks them with the bitter need—
The spark to forge the iron Will
    Into the deed.

Yet grants what precious talents are
    To stragglers on the phantom ways
To spend at Dream's grotesque bazaar
    For painted days.

I do not ask some bolt of Thought
    To open wide the veiling sky
And show the purpose subtly wrought
    And planned on high.

I simply ponder, night or day,
    A question quite beyond my ken—
The strange, inscrutable, blind way
    Of fate with men.

I simply know that right or wrong
    Are aspects of my mortal mind;
That faith is frail, that doubt is strong,
    And tears are kind.

Samuel Hoffenstein
(1890—   )

THE CITY OF SLEEP

MANIKIN, maker of dreams,
  Came to the city of sleep:
The watch was on guard, and the gates were barred
  And the moat was deep.

"Who is on my side, who?"
  Moonbeams rose in a row:
He tuned them loud betwixt town and cloud,
  But his voice was low.

He sang a song of the moon
  For loan of her silver beams;
Misty and fair, and afloat in air,
  Lay the ladder of dreams.

He harped by river and hill;
  And the river forgot to flow,
And the wind in the grass forgot to pass,
  And the grass to grow.

He harped to the heart of earth,
  Where honey in hive lies sweet:
And that sound leapt through the gates, and crept
  Through the silent street.

Manikin, maker of dreams,
  He pursed his lips to pipe:
And the strange and the new grew near and true,
  For the time was ripe.

He piped to the hearts of men:
  And dreamers rose up straight,
To drift unbarred by the drowsy guard,
  And beyond the gate.

He piped the dream of the maid:
  And her heart was up and away;
And fast it beat and hurried her feet
  To the gates of day.

He piped the dream of the mother,
  The cry of her babe for food:
And she rose from rest to give it the breast
  And that was good!

He piped the dream of the child:
    And into its hands and feet
Came tunes to play of the live-long day;
    And that was sweet!

He piped to the heart of youth:
    And the heart of youth had sight
Of love to be won, and a race to be run;
    And that was right!

He piped the song of age:
    And that was a far-off song—
When life made haste and the mouth could taste:—
    But that was wrong!

Manikin, maker of dreams,
    Had piped himself to sleep:
The watch was on guard, and the gates were barred,
    And the moat was deep!

Laurence Housman
(1865—   )

SILHOUETTES

GRANT PARK

THE haunting face of poverty,
The hands of pain,
The rough, gargantuan feet of fate,
The nails of conscience in a soul
That didn't want to do wrong—
You can see what they've done
To brothers of mine
In one back-yard of Fifth Avenue.
You can see what they've done
To brothers of mine—
Sleepers on iron benches
Behind the library in Grant Park.

STEEL MILLS

THE mills
That grind and grind,
That grind out new steel
And grind away the lives
Of men,—
In the sunset
Their stacks

Are great black silhouettes
Against the sky.
In the dawn
They belch red fire.
The mills,—
Grinding out new steel,
Old men.

PRAYER FOR A WINTER NIGHT

O GREAT GOD of Cold and Winter,
Wrap the earth about in an icy blanket
And freeze the poor in their beds!
All those who haven't enough coal
To keep them warm,
Nor food enough to keep them strong—
Freeze, dear God!
Let their limbs grow stiff
And their hearts cease to beat,
Then tomorrow
They'll wake up in some rich kingdom of nowhere
Where nothingness is everything
And everything is nothingness.

GODS

THE IVORY gods,
And the ebony gods,
And the gods of diamond and jade,
Sit silently on their temple shelves
While the people are afraid.
Yet the ivory gods,
And the ebony gods,
And the gods of diamond and jade,
Are only silly puppet gods
That the people themselves
Have made.

Langston Hughes
(1902—   )

TIRED

I AM tired of work; I am tired of building up somebody else's
     civilization.
Let us take a rest, M'lissy Jane.
I will go down to the Last Chance Saloon, drink a gallon or two of gin,
     shoot a game or two of dice, and sleep the rest of the night on
     one of Mike's barrels.

You will let the old shanty go to rot, the white people's clothes
    turn to dust, and the Calvary Baptist Church sink to the
    bottomless pit.
You will spend your days forgetting you married me and your nights
    hunting the warm gin Mike serves the ladies in the rear of the
    Last Chance Saloon.
Throw the children into the river; civilization has given us too many.
    It is better to die than it is to grow up and find out that you
    are colored.
Pluck the stars out of heaven. The stars mark our destiny. The
    stars marked my destiny.
I am tired of civilization.

Fenton Johnson
(1888—   )

HOPE

FRAIL children of sorrow, dethroned by a hue,
The shadows are flecked by the rose sifting through,
The world has its motion, all things pass away;
No night is omnipotent, there must be day!

The oak tarries long in the depths of the seed
But swift is the season of nettle and weed,
Abide yet awhile in the mellowing shade
And rise with the hour for which you were made.

The cycle of seasons, the tidals of man,
Revolve in the orb of an infinite plan;
We move to the rhythm of ages long done,
And each has his hour—to dwell in the sun!

Georgia Douglas Johnson
(1886—   )

MAY THE FIRST

INTERNATIONAL LABOR DAY

LOUD are the voices and thrilling the cheers
Claiming this day for the people who toil;
Sons of the fact'ries and sons of the mines,
Sons of the railroads, the woods and the soil:
All *one* class with *one* object in view
(That with the spirit and courage to do),
Labor to battle the profiteer-foe,
Onward to conquer upon the word Go!

Labor of nations who speak not our tongue,
Labor, great Labor, the old and the young;

Men of all trades and all nations—and true,
All of *one* class with *one* object in view;
Stand in your strength and now reckon your aim,
None be divided—your cause is the same.
Spirit! and Courage! and Power! to be
Master and Owner of world-industry!

Greater no power than yours of today—
This be the song of your triumph in May!

Harold Roland Johnson
(1898—   )

From FIFTY YEARS

THE land is ours by right of birth,
   This land is ours by right of toil;
We helped to turn its virgin earth,
   Our sweat is in its fruitful soil. . . .

And yet, my brothers, well I know
   The tethered feet, the pinioned wings,
The spirit bowed beneath the blow,
   The heart grown faint from wounds and stings;

The staggering force of brutish might,
   That strikes and leaves us stunned and dazed;
The long vain waiting through the night
   To hear some voice for justice raised.

James Weldon Johnson
(1871—   )

From TO E . . . .

(A VERY YOUNG GIRL, ABOUT TO BEGIN OFFICE WORK)

GOODBY, dreaming girl.
Goodby, gray eyes, set in a rosy face;
Aureole of golden hair,
Goodby.

Goodby, slim hands,
Forever busy, though the gray eyes dreamed.
What cunning frailties and what towers of strength
Those slender fingers wrought!

Goodby, singing voice,
That spun a silver thread of tuneful sound
Round every household task, that heightened joy
And tempered grief.

O dreaming girl,
Your slim young loveliness was made for love,
Love passionate and deep!
What cosmic "inefficiency" is this—
To dim those eyes and blanch that sweet flushed face,
Fret it with lines, and dull the radiant hair!
To take those skillful hands
From their accustomed tasks and grime them over
With ink and dust, till they are rough and stiff.
To hush
The day-long music of that singing voice
And let old songs make way
For "vouchers," "contracts," "F. O. B. Detroit."

Josephine Johnson

THE MARCH OF THE HUNGRY MEN

IN THE dream of your downy couches, through the shades of your
    pampered sleep,
Give ear, you can hear it coming, the tide that is steady and deep—
Give ear, for the sound is growing, from the desert and dungeon
    and den:
The tramp of the marching millions, the March of the Hungry Men.

As once the lean-limbed Spartans at Locris' last ascent,
As William's Norman Legions through the Sussex meadows went,
As Wolfe assailed the mountain, as Sherman led the way
From Fulton to Savannah; as they and more than they;

So comes another army your wit cannot compute;
The man-at-arms self-fashioned, the man you made the brute,
From farm and sweatshop gathered, from factory, mine and mill,
With lever and shears and auger, dibble, drift and drill.

They bear not sword or rifle, yet their ladders are on your walls;
Though the break is turned to a jumper, the jumper to overalls;
They come from the locomotive, the cab and the cobbler's bench;
They are armed with the pick and the jack-plane, the sledge and the
    ax and the wrench.

And some come empty-handed, with fingers gnarled and strong,
And some come bent with sorrow, and some sway drunk with song,
But all that you thought were buried are stirring and lithe and quick,
And they carry a brass-band scepter: the brass composing stick.

Through the depths of the devil's darkness, with the distant stars
    for light,
They are coming, the while you slumber, and they come with the
    might of Right.
On a morrow—perhaps tomorrow—you will waken and see, and then
You will hand the keys of the cities to the ranks of the Hungry Men.

Reginald Wright Kaufman
(1877—   )

I SING THE BATTLE

I SING the song of the great clean guns that belch forth death at will.
Ah, but the wailing mothers, the lifeless forms and still!

I sing the songs of the billowing flags, the bugles that cry before.
Ah, but the skeletons flapping rags, the lips that speak no more!

I sing the clash of bayonets and sabres that flash and cleave.
And wilt thou sing the maimed ones, too, that go with pinned-up
    sleeve?

I sing acclaimed generals that bring the victory home.
Ah, but the broken bodies that drip like honey-comb!

I sing the hearts triumphant, long ranks of marching men.
And wilt thou sing the shadowy hosts that never march again?

Harry Kemp
(1883—   )

STRIKE

IN THE tunnels of the earth
A great wind is blowing:
There is the sound of galloping horses,
There is the sound of men riding into battle—
The clatter and iron hoofs,
The cry of men swinging in their stirrups,
Riding into battle.

Hungry men are mightier than kings;
Hungry men overthrow empires;
Hungry men ride fearless.

Stanley Kimmel

THE OATH

HEAR US, ye Damned!
By the starved child's
Pitiful cry, the sunken
Eyes, the pale and hollow
Cheeks, robbed of
The glowing rose;
By the short and labored
Breath, the racking pain,
The body's slow decay;
By all the agony
Brooding in the mother's
Heart, the muttered
Curses on the lips of men
Tortured by their helplessness,

Hear us, ye Damned!
By these, by these
We swear that we
Who have the power
Will use it
To bring about
The REVOLUTION!

Hear us, ye Damned!
By the strain of man's
Upward striving, the sweat,
The long nights and days,
Of his unfulfilled desire;
By the sword that slays,
The faggot's burning breath,
The dungeon's bitter walls
Of loneliness, the frenzied
Shriek, mocked even as it
Rises in the shuddering air;
By the weary sighs of men
Spent in the fight
For Freedom's crown;
By the lost hopes, yea,
By all the patient efforts
That have failed,
By the hearts, the sorrow
Hidden in the night,

Hear us, ye Damned!
By these, by these

We swear that we
Who have the power
Will use it
To bring about
The REVOLUTION!

Louise W. Kneeland

THE DAY

I

O YOU rulers and princes of kingdoms,
　You have prayed—and for what have you prayed?
Your wildest ambitions have brought you
　But a trust and people betrayed.
Hark! Hark! to the feet of stern thousands
　As they tramp, bloody-shod, on the way,
And they march in the splendor of dawning—
　In the soul-searching light of THE DAY!

II

You have sinned in the court of Belshazzar,
　O you tyrants, all deaf to the storm;
You have drunk from the courtesan's wine-cup
　While the soul of the people took form;
Like swine you have fed from the vessels
　That were blessed in the blood of the fray,
And now you stand trembling and fearful—
　In the soul-searching light of THE DAY!

III

O you cravens, you sent them to slaughter,
　And they died as they always die—
Like men, as they fought for their hearthstones,
　Not knowing your cheat and your lie;
But they'll strip you now in the market-place,
　And all naked they'll make you pay;
And naked you'll give them your reckoning—
　In the soul-searching light of THE DAY!

Edgar Daniel Kramer

ADVERTISEMENT

WE WANT a man of forty for the job.
One who has enjoyed his little fill of romance.
And suffered intermittent indigestion ever since.

One whose memories are sufficiently cold
     successfully to resist the embraces of truancy.
To whom a mountain
     no longer looms an ideal
     to scramble up and tumble down,
     but is an actual thing made of stone
     bristling with multitudinous edges
     to bark one's shins or break one's neck upon.
To whom a lake or river
     or other body of water
     no longer entices the search for one's likeness
     (we only ask a man to be himself
     and not go diving after phantoms),
     but is a place one might easily drown in,
     one's muscles no longer quite what they were.
Who has achieved
     that ultimate disillusionment:
     not to be able to differentiate
     the respective features, limbs or what not
     of his whilom Graces and Gwendolyns,
     and if he could wouldn't want to,
     would devote the rest of his days to a desk
     piled sky-high with ledgers and cash-books:
Such a man would be certain to stick.
We want such a man for the job.

Alfred Kreymborg
(1883—   )

AGAINST DESTRUCTION

BESIDE the throbbing beasts, the strong machines,
That crouch, tight-muscled, in the angry dark,
A file of mannikins now lifts, now beams,
Forgetful of the sun, the field, the lark.
Man serves his own inventions, that transform
Him to themselves: this lathe, this gyroscope,
Was sinuous of body as the worm
And had the grace of deer and antelope.
A heavy soot is falling in the air
Like ash of doom: it rots the human skin,
It falls upon the mouth, the eyes, the hair,
Entombing the clean core of flame within.

I rise out of my sleep, I cry, O soul,
Be vehement and bright, thou fierce red coal!

Stanley J. Kunitz

ON THE PICKET LINE

ON THE picket line
The morning starts with
A flaming mass of scorn and
Endurance;
With the parade of the humble and
Cops
With judicial assurance to
The big
Cheap buyers of life.

On the picket line
Peddlers sell red, ripe, sliced watermelon
And workers give their red blood free.
On the picket line policemen chew fleshy desires for live human steak.
On the picket line we can detect the buzzing of a bee and
The sneering of
A snake.

On the picket line
Flaming contempt threatens the mild, sleepy eyes of
Early rising girls—on the early rushing picket line—
Where live governors keep guard on skins of dead squirrels.

On the picket line the city is being trimmed with
The mass of
Ripening colors of the meek.

On the red, stretched, early-morning picket line
The coarse world is at war with its toilers,
Who rise in the morning to decorate the earth.

Aron Kurtz
(1892—   )

FREEDOM OF SPEECH

I SHALL speak out!
Like the roar of the sea, I have a message.
There is danger ahead and I would give warning.
The greater the danger the louder the roar,
And my foghorn voice is pitched deep and strong.
I am the spirit of Discontent.
I chafe under the galling collar of wrathful restraint,
And Nature has conferred upon me the power of insight, of foresight.
The things I see I shall tell,
And the world shall judge be they true or false.
I shall speak out!

Who art thou that says me nay?
Whence comes thy right to stopple my mouth
And barricade the free flow of words to willing listeners?
Who appointed thee guardian of speech?
Who made thee custodian of ideas?
Who commissioned thee jailor of progress?
Thou art usurper and I flout thy authority!
I shall speak out!
My words shall sting thee, shall cut thy hide, shall drive thee to shame,
      shall whelm thee with remorse!
Fool! thou standest in the light of thine own good,
Casting a blighting shadow on thine own soul!
I come with the blaze of the sun on my face,
And thou canst not gaze with candor on my eyes.
I shall speak out!
Thy criminal purpose would blow out the lights that guide the
      mariners to ports of safety;
Would ruthlessly take the breast from hungry infants;
Would blot out the sign-boards on the road to knowledge;
Would fasten cords across the pathway to the spring of righteousness
To trip the unwary and impede the watchful.
I shall speak out!

Joseph A. Labadie
(1850—   )

THE MAN FROM THE MOORS

OUT where the stars are shining,
Out on the misty lea,
Out where the winds are pining;
There's where I long to be.

Far away from the city,
Its toil and moil and care,
Away from fear and pity,
Confusion, noise and glare.

Far from your civilization,
Back where my heart was free.
Out of this desolation
Of fettered misery.

Far away from this city;
Into the cool, keen air,
Singing a careless ditty
To challenge my despair.

Louise Burton Laidlaw

THE ILLUSION OF WAR

WAR
I abhor,
And yet how sweet
The sound along the marching street
Of drum and fife, and I forget
Wet eyes of widows, and forget
Broken old mothers, and the whole
Dark butchery without a soul.

Without a soul, save this bright drink
Of heady music, sweet as hell;
And even my peace-abiding feet
Go marching with the marching street—
For yonder, yonder goes the fife,
And what care I for human life!
The tears fill my astonished eyes,
  And my full heart is like to break;
And yet 'tis all embannered lies,
  A dream those little drummers make.

O, it is wickedness to clothe
  Yon hideous grinning thing that stalks,
Hidden in music, like a queen,
  That in a garden of glory walks,
Till good men love the thing they loathe.
Art, thou hast many infamies,
  But not an infamy like this.
Oh, snap the fife, and still thy drum,
  And show the monster as she is!

            Richard Le Gallienne
            (1866—   )

THE PROPHET

A PROPHECY

INTO a world of Blood and Flame
The Prophet with his Voices came.

And the Battle stopped and the People said:
"For ourselves, our children, and our dead!"

And he journeyed by sea in times of awe
To write in a Temple the Book of the Law.

But (housed with Greed, and Feud, and Wit)
New worlds of Blood and Flame he writ. . . .

With the Prophets' Voices the People in wrath
Scourged the Prophet from their Path.

With the Prophet's Voices themselves they wrought
The Book of Law whereof he taught.

For out of the People, blind and dumb,
The Prophet's Voices, unknown, had come.

William Ellery Leonard
(1876—   )

THE ARMY OF FREEDOM

THERE's a call in every village—there's a stir in every street,
There's a murmur in the distance as of countless marching feet;
On the highway sounds the echo of that voice uprisen high—
As it rings with quick rejoinder from the earth unto the sky;
There's a song flung to the breezes and a thousand men uprise;
To the ranks they add their numbers, sending up their eager cries;
There's a movement stealing forward; there's a quickening abroad—
Look and listen, feel it thrill you, humble children of the sod!

There's rebellion in the hovel, and the hunted look is gone—
There's a hope sprung in the shadow—there's a glimpse of coming
    dawn;
And the gloomy eyes have wakened and the soul once more is free;
There's a sweet song in each being in that mighty human sea;
And the waves are speeding shoreward to the goal of brotherhood,
There's a roar of many voices in the tempest of their mood,
They can feel it deep within them—they can hear it in the street.
They can sense it rolling forward—they can hear its steady beat.

They can see the vision dawning, daily growing more replete—
For a murmur in the distance tells of marchers' counting feet;
In the coal mines grim and soddy, there's an answer to the foe;
Where the forges shriek and glimmer, where the slaves move to and fro.
There's a reason why these shoulders, once so narrow and so bent,
Now are straightened, now unburdened in the prison they are pent—
Once the eye looked outward hopeless, now the light is calm and clear;
There's an impulse in each body—there's a slowing of all fear.

There's an army in the battle—there are recruits falling in,
Not a day ebbs softly by us, but some soul steps forth to win;
From Atlantic to Pacific, o'er the seas in foreign lands—
Out of every nook and corner, brave toilers emerge in marching bands.

Would you help us, then be with us, up with courage in your face—
Throw aside your coward feeling—step not idly into place;
Lend your heart to our endeavor and we'll greet you as a friend,
We will fight if need be, and our hand we here extend.

Robert Page Lincoln

THE LEADEN-EYED

LET NOT young souls be smothered out before
They do quaint deeds and fully flaunt their pride.
It is the world's one crime its babes grow dull,
Its poor are ox-like, limp and leaden-eyed.

Not that they starve, but starve so dreamlessly,
Not that they sow, but that they seldom reap,
Not that they serve, but have no gods to serve,
Not that they die, but that they die like sheep.

Vachel Lindsay

MICE

HERE'S to the mice that scare the lions,
Creeping into their cages.
Here's to the fairy mice that bite
The elephants fat and wise:
Hidden in the hay-pile while the elephant-thunder rages;
Here's to the scurrying timid mice,
Through whom the proud cause dies.

Here's to the seeming accident
When all is planned and working,
All the wheels a-turning,
Not one serf a-shirking.
Here's to the hidden tunneling thing
That brings the mountain's groans.
Here's to the midnight scamps that gnaw;
Gnawing away the thrones.

Vachel Lindsay
(1879—   )

"LIBERTY ENLIGHTENING THE WORLD"

HARD by the ferry's rail I stood, one night,
And saw the beacon gleam across the bay,
Of that fair statue bravely raised to say:—
O Brain and Hand be free!—in words of light;

But as I looked, no statue met my sight,
Only a shapeless shade that seemed to stay
Atween the glorious torch-star, sweet as day,
And where the pedestal shone palely white.

A symbol this, it seemed to me; forsooth
The world lies wan beneath high Freedom's flame,
And, dazzled, knows not yet her form, nor grace;
Her torch to men is but a torch in truth,
Few read as yet her lines of healing fame—
Too dark! Too soon!—the morrow sees her face.

J. William Lloyd
(1857—   )

FREEDOM

WITH head uplifted,
Saying my prayers unto the stars,
That I may advance into a new life,
Waking with flowers at dawn
Passing through the path of knowledge,
I make myself known unto myself,
A grafted branch of a storm-lashed tree,
Leaping with the growth of life,
Free from the brutal clasp of regret,
Through a forest of beauty,
Blazed with the stars of Hope,
Belted with a girdle of abundance,
The green lit grass spreading a carpet of silence,
As love trips down the world-wide street,
Letting down the everlasting bars of darkness,
Breaking the bonds of convention,
Blazing the trail of freedom,
I return to my task.
No longer shall I wear the garments of heaviness,
Dwelling in the imprisoned future,
Drinking from the black spring of death,
But breaking, restive, striving—
For the path of joy and song,
I march with the multitude
In search of understanding
Where the words Justice and Freedom
Are graven by the hand of time
On the heart of brotherhood.

Isobel Luke

From SERFS

THESE are our serfs and our bondmen, slighted, forsaken, outcast,
Hewing the path of the future, heirs of the wrongs of the past,
Forespent in the vanguard of progress, vagrant, untutored, unskilled,
Laboring forever and ever, so that our bellies be filled.
Building the homes of the haughty, rearing the mansions of worth—
Wanderers lost to the wide world, hell-harried slaves of the earth,
Visionless, dreamless, and voiceless children of worry and care,
Sweltering, straining and striving under the burdens they bear—
Stretches the future before them clouded and bleak as their past;
They are our serfs and our brothers, slighted, forsaken, outcast.

Patrick MacGill
(1890—   )

RUSSIA, 1917

No MONARCH's hand can stay the morning star
  Of Liberty. Though, like a miner's lamp
  Long years her light burned swart with dungeon damp,
Yet Liberty above the fallen czar
Now flames electric, etching vast and far
  Her radiant image on the darkling camp
  Of mazed Russia, healing the old cramp
Of tyranny and superstition's scar.
No gulf of earth or tide can stay the increase
  Of freedom's lovers. Russia, not our meed
  Of tears for your long anguish, nor indeed
Our happy tears for your divine release
  Shall speak our love, but this: with souls alive
  To war with you on czars who still survive.

Percy MacKaye
(1875—   )

HOTEVILLA

THE INDIANS dance for tourist trade
  And speak an alien tongue,
But dream of years and years ago
  When their tribe was young.
With stolid pride and bitter heart
  They know the race is dying—
Religion, a commercial right
  Gods are exercising.

Norman Macleod
(1906—   )

IF WE MUST DIE

IF WE must die—let it not be like hogs
Hunted and penned in an inglorious spot,
While round us bark the mad and hungry dogs,

Making their mock at our accursed lot.
If we must die, O let us nobly die,
So that our precious blood may not be shed
In vain; then even the monsters we defy
Shall be constrained to honor us though dead!
Oh, kinsmen! We must meet the common foe!
Though far outnumbered let us still be brave,
And for their thousand blows deal one death-blow!
What though before us lies the open grave?
Like men we'll face the murderous, cowardly pack,
Pressed to the wall, dying, but—fighting back!

Claude McKay
(1890—   )

CIVILIZATION

WHY do I sing a civilization that martyrs singers?
Think you I am a traitor to the queen of song, a spy within the realm
    of poetry?

No.
'Tis because its hands, gnarled with toil, have bandaged with a bloody
    rag the wounds of many;
Because its face, sotted and seamed, offers still some kindling for the
    dying soul;
Because its breath, thick with discord, is also hot with wrath over the
    murdered beauty of the world;
Because its shoulders, knotted and bowed down, hold yet the strength
    to lift the world up;
Because its breasts, shriveled and shrunk to a scar, still have milk roots
    that can swell with joy;
Because its smile, crucified within the heart, lies waiting for the resur-
    rection day:—
That's why I sing of a civilization that martyrs singers.
Oh, I am no traitor to the queen of song.

Edmond McKenna

JOHNNY MADEIROS IS DEAD*

OUT OF the water they took him, smoothed the tangled hair,
Carried him home to his mother, laid him on the bed.
Dark hot words and wailing hung in the frightened air:
Johnny Madeiros is dead!

---

*Johnny Madeiros, six-year-old son of a Fall River textile striker, was chased
by a mounted policeman into the river, where he was drowned.

Dead now. Quiet.

"They have taken our terrible toil," said one,
"They have taken the years of our youth and the filthy crusts of our
    bread;
They have taken the clothes from our backs and out of our sky the
    sun—
They have given us our dead.

"But the dead shall make us stronger; our picketlines shall be
Like a great sweeping tide with a little boy at the head.
Masters, O bloody masters, rejoice in your victory:
Johnny Madeiros is dead!"

A. B. Magil
(1905—   )

THAT WOULD—

ANTS covering a sterile nut shell,
A quivering, shifting mass of lives . . .
Don't step on it!
That would make a god of you. . . .

Rosa Zagnoni Marinoni

ARMAGEDDON

WE SIT there and whisper and wonder
    Of the woes that are coming on earth,
When the stooped, silent toilers in thunder
    Shall ask what the ages are worth.

There'll be curses and cries for the reasons,
    And a tempest of feet on the stairs;
And kings will turn white in their treasons,
    And prelates grow pale at their prayers.

There'll be cries—there'll be beating of hammers,
    For the anarchs will gather again!
There'll be knocking at gates—there'll be clamors
    By night—there'll be whirlwinds of men.

Edwin Markham

THE PERIL OF EASE

ARE you sheltered, curled up and content by the world's warm fire?
    Then I say that your soul is in danger!
The sons of the Light, they are down with God in the mire,
    God in the manger.

The old-time heroes you honor, whose banners you bear,
　The world no longer prohibits:
But if you peer into the past you will find them there,
　Swinging from gibbets.

So, rouse from your perilous ease to your sword and your shield!
Your ease is the ease of the cattle,
Hark, hark, where the bugles are calling: Out to some field—
　Out to some battle!

Edwin Markham

THE MAN WITH THE HOE*

God made man in his own image;
In the Image of God made He him.—Genesis.

BOWED by the weight of centuries he leans
Upon his hoe and gazes on the ground,
The emptiness of ages in his face,
And on his back the burden of the world.
Who made him dead to rapture and despair,
A thing that grieves not and that never hopes,
Stolid and stunned, a brother to the ox?
Who loosened and let down this brutal jaw?
Whose was the hand that slanted back this brow?
Whose breath blew out the light within this brain?

Is this the Thing the Lord God made and gave
To have dominion over sea and land;
To trace the stars and search the heavens for power;
To feel the passion of Eternity?
Is this the dream He dreamed who shaped the suns
And markt their ways upon the ancient deep?
Down all the caverns of Hell to their last gulf
There is no shape more terrible than this—
More tongued with cries against the world's blind greed—
More filled with signs and portents of the soul—
More packt with danger to the universe.

What gulfs between him and the seraphim!
Slave of the wheel of labor, what to him
Are Plato and the swing of Pleiades?
What the long reaches of the peaks of song,
The rift of dawn, the reddening of the rose?
Through this dread shape the suffering ages look;
Time's tragedy is in that aching stoop;

*Written after seeing Millet's painting of a brutalized toiler in the deep abyss
of labor.

Through this dread shape humanity betrayed,
Plundered, profaned and disinherited,
Cries protest to the Powers that made the world,
A protest that is also prophecy.

O masters, lords and rulers in all lands,
Is this the handiwork you give to God,
This monstrous thing distorted and soul-quenched?
How will you ever straighten up this shape;
Touch it again with immortality;
Give back the upward looking and the light;
Rebuild in it the music and the dream;
Make right the immemorial infamies,
Perfidious wrongs, immedicable woes?

O masters, lords and rulers in all lands,
How will the Future reckon with this Man?
How answer his brute question in that hour
When whirlwinds of rebellion shake all shores?
How will it be with kingdoms and with kings—
With those who shaped him to the thing he is—
When the dumb Terror shall rise to judge the world,
After the silence of the centuries?

Edwin Markham
(1852—   )

JESUS THE CARPENTER

Jesus the Carpenter
Shifted his load,
Smiled on the multitude
Coming down the road.

Jesus the Carpenter
Set down his tools,
Called to the little ones,
Questioned the fools.

Jesus the Carpenter
Held out his hand,
Blessing the fishermen
Who came from the sand.

Now in the churches,
One day in seven,
Bishops and rich men
Talk about heaven!

Jeannette Marks

UNREST

A FIERCE unrest seethes at the core
　Of all existing things:
It was the eager wish to soar
　That gave the gods their wings.

From what flat wastes of cosmic slime,
　And stung by what quick fire,
Sunward the restless races climb!—
　Men rise out of mire!

There throbs through all the worlds that are
　This heart-beat hot and strong,
And shaken systems, star by star,
　Awake and glow in song.

But for the urge of this unrest
　These joyous spheres were mute;
But for the rebel in his breast
　Had man remained a brute.

When baffled lips demanded speech,
　Speech trembled into birth—
(One day the lyric world shall reach
　From earth to laughing earth.)—

When man's dim eyes demanded light,
　The light he sought was born—
His wish, a Titan, scaled the height
　And flung him back the morn!

From deed to dream, from dream to deed,
　From daring hope to hope,
The restless wish, the instant need,
　Still lashed him up the slope!

　　　*　　*　　*　　*　　*

I sing no governed firmament,
　Cold, ordered, regular—
I sing the stinging discontent
That leaps from star to star.

Don Marquis
(1878—　)

A CONSECRATION

Not of the princes and prelates with periwigged charioteers
Riding triumphantly laurelled to lap the fat of the years;
Rather the scorned—the rejected—the men hemmed in with the
  spears;

The men of the battered battalion which fights till it dies,
Dazed with the dust of the battle, the din of the cries,
The men with the broken heads and the blood running into their eyes.

Not the be-medalled Commander, beloved of the throne,
Riding cock-horse to parade when the bugles are blown,
But the lads who carried the koppie and cannot be known.

Not the ruler for me, but the ranker, the tramp of the road,
The slave with the sack on his shoulders pricked on with the goad,
The man with too weighty a burden, too weary a load.

The sailor, the stoker of steamers, the man with the clout,
The chantyman bent at the halliards putting a tune to the shout,
The drowsy man at the wheel and the tired look-out.

Others may sing of the wine and the wealth and the mirth,
The portly presence of potentates, goodly in girth;
Mine be the dearth and the dross, the dust and scum of the earth!

Theirs be the music, the color, the glory, the gold;
Mine be a handful of ashes, a mouthful of mould;
Of the maimed, of the halt and the blind, in the rain and the cold—
Of these shall my song be fashioned, my tale be told. *Amen.*

John Masefield
(1874—   )

From BALLAD OF DEAD REPUBLICS

Tell me, ye King-craft of to-day,
  Where is Athens, who made men free;
Then sank into stupor by the way,
  Subdued by the Spartan tyranny?
And Rome that staggered to death, perdie,
  Stabbed by the sword of Hannibal,
And bled by patrician infamy—
  The Dragon of Greed destroyed them all!

Cleon and Pericles held sway
  O'er the foes of Greek Democracy,

The Gracchi brothers struggled to stay
    The stress of the Caesars' stern decree.
And look at Rienzi's passion, he
    Who strove the republic to recall!
Slain at last for his perfidy—
    The Dragon of Greed destroyed them all!

What of Florence and Venice, say?
    And the Netherlands that ruled the sea?
And Cromwell's England more strong than they
    Which banished the throne and the bended knee?
Yes, and Savonarola's plea,
    And William of Orange's rise and fall?
Yea, though they labored for you and me—
    The Dragon of Greed destroyed them all!

Dexter Wallace (Edgar Lee Masters)
(1868—   )

THOUGHTS OF A BOOKKEEPER

LEDGER, ledger, let me be!
Past my window winds the sea!

    Morn is a moth wing, silver frail;
    Puff, tall wind, in my tipsy sail!
    Spread is the spray like a peacock tail.

Two times four times three—

    Sinks the sun through the froth and fire,
    Pricked to the heart by a pinnacled spire;
    Flaked are the faggots, cold the pyre.

Two times four times three—

    Waves begin their sobbing croon;
    Night, the reaper, up the dune
    Swings a silent, sickle moon.

Ledger, ledger, let me be!
Past my window winds the sea!

Mildred Plew Merryman
(1892—   )

TO THE LIBERTY BELL

TOLL, toll,
O cracked and venerable!
Start swinging suddenly
And speak
Upon this jigging air.

Tell us of a day when men stood up in meeting
And spoke of God,
And nobody laughed.

Toll, toll.

They say we have no leader now. It may be.
I know
We have no cause.

America!—Beautiful Nowhere in the hearts of a few
Periwigged men
Sitting about a table.

Toll, toll.

Yet toll not,
Lest to our shame we learn how few to-day
Would stand in the street and listen.
Only some lean, half-hearted anarchist
Who happened to be out;
And the children,
That shout at air-planes.

Edna St. Vincent Millay
(1892—   )

SACCO AND VANZETTI

WAKE

I AM ashamed of weeping and of words,
They are the little way
For little woes
To swagger for a while and find their ease;
They are the empty way
For frightened souls
To clamor and be still.

DIRGE

It is too much to know a million men
Can make no footprint on the bleeding world,

It is too hard for humankind to learn
A million million cries can but return
Into the emptiness whence they were hurled—
And wait a little while and cry again.

ELEGY

If in the past at times I have forgotten,
If I have hoped the world was such a place
That men might live and laugh beneath the sun
And lay them down to rest when day was done—
If in the past at times I have forgotten,
Now nevermore again shall I forget.

Kathleen Millay

OUR DEFENCE

IN THE END the loss or triumph of the case shall not be hung
On the golden ease and smoothness of a hired lawyer's tongue,
Nor how ably or how bungling every man shall plead his cause,
It's something beyond the courtroom that makes judge and jury pause.
For they sense the mighty forces in the mutterings of unrest
And the songs of hope and freedom rising in the Worker's breast,
And wherever men are willing for their beliefs to do and dare,
There's a cause that stands behind them and they feel its power there.
Over treachery and cunning, through all darkness and suspense,
'Tis the cause itself shall triumph and in that is our defence.

Vera Moller

IMPRESSION

HE'S SOMETHING in the city. Who shall say
  His fortune was not honorably won?
Few people can afford to give away
  As he, or help the poor as he has done.

Neat in his habits, temperate in his life;
  Oh, who shall dare his character besmirch?
He hardly ever quarrels with his wife,
  And every Sabbath carefully goes to church.

He helps the village club, and in the town
  Attends parochial meetings once a week,
Pays for each purchase ready-money down.
  Is anyone against him? Who will speak?

There is a widow somewhere in the north
  On whom slow ruin gradually fell,
While she, believing that her God was wroth,
  Suffered without a word—or she might tell.

And there's a beggar somewhere in the west,
  Whose fortune vanished gradually away:
Now he but drags his limbs in horror lest
  Starvation feed on them—or he might say.

And there are children stricken with disease,
  Too ignorant to curse him, or too weak.
In a true portrait of him all of these
  Must figure in the background—they shall speak.

Harold Monro
(1879—   )

MAKE OF MAN THE STATUE

MAKE of man the statue, the priceless piece of art.
All that Greece has given,
All that time has striven
For ages to impart,
Weld it in his sinews, mold it in his thought,
Till the humblest scavenger is gloriously wrought.
Shame upon the galleries, filled with treasures fine
While the work of Heaven — *man,* who is divine, —
Shivers in the hallway, shuffles through the street,
Shambles down the alley, with weak and ragged feet.

Make of man the statue, make of man the building.
What avails the gilding
Of Altar or of dome,
What the gorgeous tapestries blooming in the home,
What avails the splendor where stately mansions stand
If men who made the mansions are homeless in the land?
Shame upon the church spires climbing to the sky,
While the drudging millions suffer, starve and die.

Make of *man* the poem, make of *man* the theme;
Fruiting of the vision, flowering of the dream.
All that Rome has given,
All that art has striven
For centuries to say,
Breathe it in his spirit, coin it in his heart,
Till the poorest laborer can share the loveliest part.
Make of man the shining, pure and perfect thing:
Give him room to grow in;

Give him fields to sow in,
Teach his lips to sing.
Shame upon the white streets, brilliant with display,
While the hungry people struggle on their way.

Make of *man* the towering, the beautiful emprise,
Great as any temple that reaches to the skies.
Take your "worthless derelict, ignorant and vile,"
Give him skies to dream in,
Love and chance to gleam in,
Teach his soul to smile.
Give his toil its payment;
Clothe him sweet with raiment,
Give him food to nourish,
Help his thought to flourish.
Proudly lift his head, then
Freely let him stand. . . .
All the rest is said, then;
Clasp his godly hand.

Angela Morgan

AWAY TO THE MOUNTAINS

Away with the time-tested wrongs of the ages;
   Out from the error-worn ruts of the past;
Out upon custom's law! Burn the old pages,
   Light on the mountains is sighted at last.

Too long in the ruts of the ancients we have slumbered,
   With eye-crumbling guide posts to mark out the way,
Too long in the halls of our fathers we have slumbered,
   Inhaling the poisonous breath of decay.

Too long we have followed with custom before us,
   Aping old errors forever in sight.
Too long has the spell of the fathers been over us,
   Veiling our greed-darkened minds from the light.

Traditions and customs, inhuman, invade us.
   Away with the Mammon-wrought fetters we have worn;
Behold on the mountains the light that shall save us,
   Gilding the crests with the rays of the morn.

Away, then, away with our face to the mountains;
   Fast fades the darkness in Reason's bright ray.
Loose we the chain from the soul's hidden fountains,
   Go forward, rejoice and forever be free.

J. E. Morgan

THANKSGIVING UP TO DATE

I THANK THEE, Lord, that I have got
Those things which other men have not;
That I have better clothes and looks
And better meals from better cooks;
That thou hast dowered me with the will
And hast acknowledged, though I rob,
To snatch the good from others' ill
That I am better than the mob.
I thank thee that I've never had
To hustle like a sordid cad;
That thou hast known how much I need
The luxuries of my higher creed;
Hast given me leisure and the wealth
To guard my comfort and my health,
And cast my lot in places where
No squalid traffic taunts the air.
I thank thee for exclusive friends
Who keep the pace where pleasure wends,
Who ask no pledge of books or brains
But base their favor on one's gains.
Bored by the drama, music—and
Keen only with the poker hand,
Polite at bridge, or swift to rip
The landscape with an auto trip;
With now a cocktail, now a smoke,
And ne'er the levity of a joke.

And last, O Lord, thy Church I owe
Thanks for the good it doth bestow
In social prestige, nodding friends,
And advantageous business ends.
Without thy altar where to kneel
How could I make a prosperous deal;
How could I drive against the wall
The enemies who plan my fall;
How could I keep my favored place
As one elect among the race?

In gratitude for this rich year
I kneel (but still the ticker hear)
And offer thanks that thou hast blest
The unearned funds I could invest.
That thou hast made the market see
I am thy chosen devotee,
And from thy bounty thou hast given
Thy servant shrewdness born in heaven.

Harrison S. Morris
(1856—   )

LEST WE FORGET

TO THE CHICAGO MARTYRS, NOVEMBER 11, 1887

FORGET THEM, our comrades, the true and the noble,
  Who marched with the foremost in liberty's van,
Who pled for the cause of the weak and downtrodden,
  Who spoke the great word of the freedom of man?

Forget them, our brothers, the sweet and the tender,
  Who lived for the sake of a world that was blind,
Who recked not the slander, nor heeded the peril,
  Secure in the truth, and the love of their kind?

Forget them, our heroes, the strong and the fearless,
  Who faced the wild beast in its innermost lair,
Who blenched not, though lashed by the rage of the tempest,
  Who taught slaves and tyrants what freemen can dare?

Forget them, our martyrs, the grand and the peerless,
  Who mastered the scaffold, and conquered the grave,
Who murdered are living, and dying are deathless,
  Whose memory lives in the hearts of the brave?

Forget them? When hopeless and shrouded in darkness,
  When heavy the burden and long the delay,
They brighten the blackness, and speak from the silence,
  And point through the clouds to the dawn of the day.

Forget them? By liberty scorned and dishonored,
  By justice entangled in sophistry's net,
By truth doomed to drudge in the service of falsehood,
  By love turned to hatred—*we will not forget!*

Forget them? When lost to the meaning of manhood,
  And deaf to the cause which inspired us of yore,
We crouch with the craven or turn with the traitor,
  Then we may forget—for they know us no more!

Forget them? Humanity's triumph approaches;
  The harvest is white from the seed they have sown.
Forget them? Ye cannot, ye sons of the future;
  When freedom is victor, they come to their own!

                                    James F. Morton
                                      (1870—   )

RHAPSODY

MORNINGS, ungreeted, enter the cities
seeking a way thru the narrow streets,

there already men curse
the heavily moving hours;
a hoarse voice
modulates a song
to restore
the spent energy
of a moving arm;
amidst the echoes
of machines
men look upward

night is a long way, yet,

though dreams find
an expression
in every thought,
in every phrase.

*   *   *   *

When laughter would greet
the unmarred blue of the sky,
men bury their dead.

And night comes, welcomed
by the thumping beats of homegoing men—

and sleep comes.

*   *   *   *

When men will welcome mornings,
ushering them thru the streets,
dawn will paint the day
red with awakening,

to the accompaniment of hammer-beats
their hymn will rise.

Then will come the afternoon,
the many patterned sundown
will glow above the houses,
then night will descend, unseen,

and the moon shall glitter.

Nicholas Moskowitz
(1902—   )

CONTRASTS IN FUTILITY

CONSCRIPTS on a battle-field
Crying out in pain—
Cattle in a slaughter-pen
Bellowing in vain.

William Kenneth Moyer
(1892—   )

THE SONG OF REBELLION

Le couteau entre les dents!—HENRI BARBUSSE.

I AM THE Song of Rebellion.
Murmuring in breasts of Grecian galley slaves,
Sobbing in parched throats of pyramid hewers and builders,
Rankling in dark hearts of the chosen in segregated Ghettos,
I was their song unsung, their hymn unlearned.
Silent, to me they turned.

Silent, they turned. Into their spiritless being,
Into their eyes unseeing,
I gave them vision, insight, self-respect;
Into their voiceless agony, their mute dread,
Little by little through the centuries
I poured them breath and utterance and words;
I goaded them even because I loved them,
Made them suffer till they learn to cry,
Until their crying become an eloquent flood of righteous wrath,
Until the flood engulf the hand that smote them;
I was in their suffering, their cry,
Their unleashed flood,—I! I!
Moses besought me, and I led him forth;
Spartacus sang my prologue, Plato my aria.
I thundered, and a myriad empires fell,
And the powerful gates of hell
Crashed upon Rome.
Out of the feuds of Guelf and Ghibelline, of Moor and the Cid, of
        Lancaster and York,
Of chieftain and hy-king in Eire, of prince and belted knight in
        Britain,
Sons rose against oppressing sires, serfs against tyrants, the people
        against unfeeling power, right against might;
Calling my call, crying my cry, invoking my name,
Stronger through years they came.

Gautama the Buddha swept hearts to my trust
Away from material lust;
Jesus sang me, scourging money-changers in the temple;

Hermits glorified me in desert places;
Francis and Clare turned poverty into a vale of thornless roses;
Galahad the Spotless waved my oriflamme;
Bayard sans peur et sans reproche exulted in my song,
And the night was not long
Until my million sons of today
Broke plutocratic sway.

Down vistaed years I hear my echo slip
From war-rebelling lip—
Armies of peace, who dared to love the foe
And to all war say No!
Followers of Menno Simons and of Fox
Adamant against war with non-resistance but a will of steel
For God and for commonweal—
Mennonites, Quakers, Shakers, Dukhobortsi,
And other blessed heretics, each bringing
On wings of my singing
Something out of tyranny, ignorance, hate,
Something bigger and cleaner than had been
Sung in the song of sin.

I drove into the Babylonian captivity of Avignon
Inheritors of the poverty of a fisherman,
Monarchs reeking with the fat of sacrilege.
I whispered to a Florentine, and he stirred the Arno and the Tiber with
        his pen, ruffled their waters with his thundering voice.
I breathed upon a monk of Wittenburg, and he turned half a world
        to freedom.
I roared through Anglia, and Stuart fell and the common man lived.
I rustled in New England fields, and Cornwallis yielded up his sword.
I sang the Marseillaise, and laughed to count royal ringlets feed the
        trough.
I laid aside my banjo, and unwound your slaves from their cotton and
        stood them upon their feet.
I called for unity, and the red shirts flew on red wind through Porta Pia.
I whistled like the sound of many bullets, and Romanovs lay among
        their ikons.
My song is not hushed: my song is for brother, for friend
Till the end of the final end.

Well do I know
Discords have torn my heart and hurt my ears;
For through the years
Not in united voice has the song lilted;
Yet in disharmony is beauty of individuality,
And crash and cry of staccato shall in my song as truly belong

As the slow, measured beat.
Well do I know
My very sons have drowned each with his own
A brother's hymn to me.
This is not weakness; it may even be
Out of the shattering clash, the lyric tone, and the plaintive note, my
      truth we shall sing
With unmistakable ring.

Hear them, you who command perilous thrones;
You who drive youth into old men's wars for aggrandizement;
You who pass judgment upon your peers and dare to murder them by
      judicial act;
Hear them, you who trod upon whitened knuckles of women as they
      slowly climbed the crags to recognition of their equality
      with man.
Hear them, you who reel under opulence wrenched from the poor;
You who ease your elastic conscience by giving libraries and asylums
      to those who have earned your all.
Hear them, you, swine grubbing in the mire of poverty you have
      created, grubbing to wrench the last apple from starve-
      lings you have brought to desperation.
Hear them who hear me, and in their rebel cry
Know at last it is I.
I am the Song of Rebellion. . . .
Yet in my song is hope and pity, and courage and faith.
I am the Song of Social Vision, of Rebirth, of Brotherhood;
Be this understood.

Comrades, take up the strain, the cry of right and of truth,
Until in all the world,
Wherever is man,
Until the vision has been seen and the song heard,
And one has voiced my word,—
Wherever peace has trod, and brothers have embraced,
Wherever courage has faced
Brute strength, and justice has triumphed, and love has entered,
Until in all the world the song of revolt become the song of love,—
Comrades, until an angel be born of a hellion,
I am the Song of Rebellion!

                          Benjamin Musser
                          (1891—   )

THE CRY OF THE PEOPLE

TREMBLE before your chattels,
  Lords of the scheme of things!
Fighters of all earth's battles,
  Ours is the might of kings!
Guided by seers and sages,
  The world's heart-beat for a drum,
Snapping the chains of ages,
  Out of the night we come!

Lend us no ear that pities!
  Offer no almoner's hand!
Alms for the builders of cities!
  When will you understand?
Down with your pride of birth
  And your golden gods of trade!
A man is worth to his mother, Earth,
  All that a man has made!

We are the workers and makers!
  We are no longer dumb!
Tremble, O Shirkers and Takers!
  Sweeping the earth—we come!
Ranked in the world-wide dawn,
  Marching into the day!
The night is gone and the sword is drawn
  And the scabbard is thrown away!

John G. Neihardt
(1881—   )

HOBO

LITTLE WE KNOW how it is, nothing we know of the why,
  Simply we shuffle, the road leads to the end of the earth.
Everything kicks us. We learn, and those who quit learning must die,
  But the learning is all of the road and unriddles no riddle of birth.

The stars in their courses may set, the stars in their courses may rise,
  We look at them and say nothing, not knowing their why or ours;
Only sometimes we feel there is beauty in all those eyes
  Whether that beauty mocks or blesses our ways and hours.

But the wisdom we learn of the road, of folks that take and that give,
  The virtue of defiance or love, though its cry be a mortal cry,
In this alone we find faith and by this alone we can live
  Till the unquiet stars quit trooping the twilit road of the sky.

Robert Nichols
(1893—   )

OF PRISONERS

MY HEART is breaking. O why can I not break yours?
My heart is breaking because of prisoners.
O the terrible walls of stone!
O the hours and the months and the days
And Despair !
We laugh; we go our ways,
And they wait in their cells alone.
The cells are of steel and stone.
They sit and stare,
They curse, they weep,
And their souls die.
(O ask not a soul to live without light!)
And we go our ways and work and sleep
And sing, and we see the sky
And count it little thing and cry
"Keep them from our sight!"
For we deem they have done us a wrong.
For a wrong, O what is the price?
Alas, alas, what anguish will suffice?
And how long lasts the payment, how long?
O I dream at night of the iron doors
And my heart is breaking. Why can I not break yours?

Grace Fallow Norton
(1876—   )

PEACE?*

I

PEACE? when have we prayed for peace?
    Over us burns a star
Bright, beautiful, red for strife!
Yours are only the drum and the fife
And the golden braid and the surface of life.
    Ours is the white-hot war.

II

Peace? when have we prayed for peace?
    Ours are the weapons of men.
Time changes the face of the world.
Your swords are rust! Your flags are furled,
And ours are the unseen legions hurled
    Up to the heights again.

*This is but the "Dedication" to the remarkable war poem "The Wine-Press,"
first published in 1912.—M. G.

III

Peace? when have we prayed for peace?
    Is there no wrong to right?
Wrong crying to God on high
Here, where the weak and the helpless die,
And the homeless hordes of the city go by,
    The ranks are rallied to-night.

IV

Peace? when have we prayed for peace?
    Are ye so dazed with words?
Earth, heaven, shall pass away
Ere for your passionless peace we pray.
Are ye deaf to the trumpets that call us to-day,
    Blind to the blazing swords?

Alfred Noyes
(1880—   )

From PROLETARIA

THE SUNNY rounds of Earth contain
    An obverse to its Day,
Our fertile Vagrancy's domain,
    Wan Proletaria.

From pole to pole of Poverty
    We stumble through the years,
With hazy-lanterned Memory
    And hope that never nears.

Wherever Plenty's crop invites
    Our pitiful brigades
Lurk cannoneers of Vested Rights,
    Juristic ambuscades;

And here hangs Rent, that squalid cage
    Within which Mammon thrusts,
Bound with the fetter of a wage,
    The helots of his lusts.

With palsied Doubt as guide, we wind
    Among the lanes of Need,
Where meagre Hungers scouting find
    But slavered baits of Greed.

What wonder sometimes if in stealth
    Our starker outposts wait,
And, in the prowling eyes of Wealth,
    Dash vitriol of Hate;

Or if our Samsons, ere too late,
    Their treasons should make good
By whelming in the temple's fate
    Their viper owner's brood!

Tho' blind and dull, 'tis we supply
    The Painter's dazzling dreams;
The rolling flood of Poetry
    From our dumb chaos streams.

Nay, when your world is over-tired,
    And Genius comatose,
Our race, by Nemesis inspired,
    Old order overthrows:

With earthquake-life we thrill your land,
    Refill the cruse of Art,
Revitalize spent Wisdom, and—
    Resume our weary part.

The palace of successful Guilt
    Is mortared with our shame;
On hecatombs of Us are built
    The soaring towers of Fame.

Religion's dolmens, Sphinxes, spires,
    Her biblic armories;
The helot lightning of the wires
    That mesh your lands and seas;

The viaducts 'tween Near and Far,
    Whereon, o'er range and mead,
Bacchantic Trade's triumphant car
    And iron tigers speed;

The modern steely crops that rise
    Where technic Jasons sow:
All these but feebly symbolize
    The largesse we bestow.

And our reward? In this wan land,
    In clientage of Greed,
Despised, polluted, maimed and banned,
    To wander and—to breed.

                      Bernard O'Dowd
                    (1866—   )

SONS OF ADAM

ADAM, wrestler with storms,
Lusted and walked like a man;
Over the wilderness ways
The feet of his questing ran.

He knew how the north rains slash,
The teeth of the winds bite deep,
Knew how the forests war
Over a world asleep.

Swarthy and lean and hard,
Savage as wind and rain,
He knew how the gaunt wolf feels
Gnawed by the hunger pain.

Adam, wrestler with storms,
Battled and laughed and died,
And still to the savage joust
The rains and the lean winds ride.

But the sons of Adam wax fat;
Flaccid and fearful they drowse,
And count their beads in the dark
When the lean hosts rouse;

Mumble fat prayers in their fear,
Then turn their face to the wall;
ADAM walked like a man;
But the sons of Adam crawl!

Wade Oliver
(1890—   )

ZERO HOUR IN THE FACTORY

THERE'S a hissing and panting of steam
And a throbbing everywhere,
As I hang for a breath of air
Over a dusty window-sill
Out of a room that is never still
From whir of wheel and thump of press.

The whole thing seems so meaningless. . . .
Below me on the railroad track
An engine tries to move a train,

But groans and coughs and pulls in vain,
The hot smoke spouting from its stack.
There seems no sense to life at all—
Work and heat and smoke and sound. . . .

I am one of the sparks that pour
From a belching stack, to glow and soar
For a moment, only to die and fall,
A cinder-speck on the sooty ground.

Charles Oluf Olsen

THE SLAVE

THEY set the slave free, striking off his chains . . .
Then he was as much of a slave as ever.

He was still chained to servility,
He was still manacled to indolence and sloth,
He was still bound by fear and superstition,
By ignorance, suspicion, and savagery . . .
His slavery was not in the chains,
But in himself. . . .

They can only set free men free . . .
And there is no need of that;
Free men set themselves free.

James Oppenheim
(1882—   )

WOMEN WITH SHAWLS

BY MY windows which look out
On a polite and pleasant street,
There often pass
Women of the squalid quarter down the hill:
Creatures of timid faith and querulous doubt,
Brief love and little song and small deceit,
Brief sleep, long toil, a roof, a rag, and meat—
Patience behind unrealized defeat,
Mortgaged too deep to fate, alas!
To leave much scope for will.
And they are slow and large and ponderous,
And are not beautiful as all women should be,
For under life's incessant mockery
Those things that most make woman beauteous,
Serenity, wonder, gentleness, have quite gone.
Dull as a burdened river they go on,
With no complaint, no choice, no change, no thrill,

Brown clods with so much muscle, so much nerve,
A womb and two breasts each, who still must serve
As fate directs, until
Fate bids them be quite still.
I fancy they are quiet when they go.
And so
They pass, each folded in a sullen shawl,
Death's froward symbol, Life's ironic pall.

Shaemas O'Sheel

HE WHOM A DREAM HATH POSSESSED

HE WHOM a dream hath possessed knoweth no more of doubting,
For mist and the blowing of . winds and the mouthing of words he
scorns.
No sinuous speech and smooth he hears, but a knightly shouting,
And never comes darkness down, yet he greeteth a million morns.

He whom a dream hath possessed knoweth no more of roaming.
All roads and the flowing of waves and the speediest flight he knows,
But wherever his feet are set his soul is forever homing,
And going he comes, and coming he heareth a call and goes.

He whom a dream hath possessed knoweth no more of sorrow.
At the death and the dropping of leaves and the fading of suns he
smiles,
For a dream remembers no past and takes no thought of a morrow,
And staunch amid seas of doom a dream sets the ultimate isles.

He whom a dream hath possessed treads the impalpable marches.
From the dust of the day's long road he leaps to a laughing star,
And the ruin of worlds that fall he views from eternal arches,
And rides God's battlefield in a flashing and golden star.

Shaemas O'Sheel
(1886—   )

MY LADY

FAST and faster the dancers fly.
Gaily my lady flashes by,
Bright on her bosom the jewels gleam;
While in the depths, 'mid heat and steam,
Where gasses creep and stones fly thick,
The diamond digger swings his pick—
But who wants to know
Of the depths below
Where Labor is weaving
Its shroud of woe?

Bravely my lady sweeps along,
Greedily viewed by the envious throng;
The wealth of a world on her shoulders lies,
While over the way, with weary eyes,
Stitch by stitch, through an endless day,
Her seamstress toils and receives as pay—
    But a lady so fair
    One should always spare
    The tedious tale
    Of a life of care.

The wine glows red in my lady's glass;
Many and merry the jests that pass;
Loving laughter and winning smile
Circle from lip to lip, the while,
Clothed in rags, at the very gates,
Gaunt-eyed hunger in silence waits—
    But sights like these
    Would little please
    My lady in her
    Hours of ease.

Sweetly humble my lady's face
As she bends her knee at the throne of grace;
She thinks of the sin, the sorrow and shame;
Thinks of the story of Him who came
From the starry regions of infinite space
With a message of love to the human race—
    So my lady will give a charity fete,
    And wear a gown of the latest date.

William C. Owen
(1854—   )

THE LOST STRIKE

THE STRIKE is lost? We laugh at you, you conquerors of a day!
Our unfed bellies shake with laughter at you!
So seriously you puff and strut and prate of victory!
Your little policemen with their tiny clubs,
Your pretty jingling Cossacks, neat and trim, like nursery toys,
Your spitting Maxims on their polished motor cars,
Your panderers, hired in a brothel, decked with sheriff's star—licensed
    to bathe their hands in workers' blood.

Your comical injunctions, writs and ordinances,
Your mimic courts, your doll's-house jails,

Your clockwork press ticking off clockwork lies,
Your tricky stick of dynamite, your planted bombs!
These are your gods! To whom you turn in time of need; to whom
    you pray, whom you adore!
Fit gods are they for YOU!

The strike is lost? A lie! No strike is lost, nor ever shall be!
We don our chains again—uncowed, and wait—and laugh.
You and your little gods have done some ill—broken some heads,
    blasted some woman's ears with foul abuse;
But in the hands of that which guides the universe—your little ill
    has wrought a mighty good.
We struck—a thousand mutinous slaves;
We lose—a thousand warriors, pledged to the social war—rapt in a
    social faith—brothers and sisters compact in holy solidarity.

The strike is lost? We laugh at you, you conquerors of a day!
Our unfed bellies shake with laughter at you!
So seriously you puff and strut and prate of victory!
Look forward five—ten years! Your hour has come!
Call at your gods—and bid them roll the tide of evolution back,
Call at your gods—and bid their tiny bludgeons batter the heart from
    Labor's mighty breast!

Your hour has come!
Great Labor laughs—and with one careless jovial sweep of his broad
    shoulders hurls you and your dear gods—your little gods—
    into the noisome vat of Nature's excrement.

Edgcomb Pinchon

COMMISSION

Go, MY SONGS, to the lonely and the unsatisfied,
Go also to the nerve-wracked, go to the enslaved-by-convention,
Bear to them my contempt for their oppressors.
Go as a great wave of cool water,
Bear my contempt of oppressors.

Speak against unconscious oppression,
Speak against the tyranny of the unimaginative,
Speak against bonds.
Go to the bourgeoisie who is dying of her ennuis,
Go to the women in suburbs.
Go to the hideously wedded,
Go to them whose failure is concealed,
Go to the unluckily mated,
Go to the bought wife,
Go to the woman entailed.

Go to those who have delicate lust,
Go to those whose delicate desires are thwarted.
Go like a blight upon the dulness of the world;
Go with your edge against this,
Strengthen the subtle cords,
Bring confidence upon the algæ and the tentacles of the soul.

Go in a friendly manner,
Go with an open speech.
Be eager to find new evils and new good,
Be against all forms of oppression.
Go to those who are thickened with middle age,
To those who have lost their interest.

Go to the adolescents who are smothered in family—
Oh, how hideous it is
To see three generations of one house gathered together!
It is like an old tree with shoots,
And with some branches rotted and falling.

Go out, defy opinion,
Go against this vegetable bondage of the blood.
Speak for the free kinship of the wind and spirit,
Go against all forms of oppression.

Ezra Pound
(1885—   )

THE RED MAN IN THE SETTLEMENTS

FROM wilderness remote he breaks
    With stealthy springing tread;
The little town a moment takes
    A glimpse of times long dead.

He scorns to see the things we own,
    But sullen stares beyond,
Alone, impassive, cold, unknown;
    With us he feels no bond.

One moment flocking with a stare
    To see the red man pass
The townsfolk feel the street's hot glare
    And dream of springs and grass.

They see a breathless, dusty town
    They had not known before;
The red man in his robes is gone,
    The townsfolk toil once more.

And whence he came, and whither fled,
  And why, is all unknown;
His ways are strange, his skin is red,
  Our ways and skins our own.

Frank Prewett
(1882—   )

SUBWAY

Sons of the city slums
With tired hands, pasty faces, battered souls
Will help fashion a new world.

Worlds are not fashioned lightly
And much blood will flow under bridges.

Arms grow so tired that they become arms and not annexes to machine
Arms become so tired and bellies so empty
That a nine-pound rifle weighs nothing.

See you, masters of the earth,
Pasty faces can quicken with life,
And tired hands will some day quicken with life, pull triggers,
  Build new worlds.

John Ramburg
(1906—   )

A CHRISTMAS CAROL

Hark, the Herald Angels sing,
Glory to our Golden king;
Peace on earth and mercy mild,
While we rob the starving child.

God of Mammon, hear us cry!
Hark! Our praises strike the sky;
While the joy-bells proudly ring,
Flesh and bones to thee we bring.

Mammon! God, by men adored.
Mammon; Everlasting Lord,
Veiled in "Fat" our Godhead see,
Hail, Incarnate Deity.

Hail, thou heavenly prince of cash,
Hail, thou lord of sword and lash;
Human blood to thee we bring;
Hark, the jangling joy-bells ring.

Ragnar Redbeard

SKYSCRAPERS

So STRAIGHT and lean above the city's squalor,
  Like phallic symbols thrusting to the sky,
The buildings rise, each one a shoulder taller,
  To dwarf the tiny structure that is I.

Aloft they mount in granite and in marble,
  The citadels and temples of our day,
Rising like larks that used to soar and warble
  Above green fields where children were at play.

O mighty monuments to gain and greed,
  How high shall your unbending columns run
Ere time shall tear you down and all your breed
  Shall lie in fallow meadows 'neath the sun!

Henry Reich, Jr.
(1892—   )

REVEILLE

COME FORTH, you workers!
Let the fires go cold—
Let the iron spill out, out of the troughs—
Let the iron run wild
Like a red bramble on the floors—
Leave the mill and the foundry and the mine
And the shrapnel lying on the wharves—
Leave the desk and the shuttle and the loom—
Come,
With your ashen lives,
Your lives like dust in your hands.

I call upon you, workers,
It is not yet light
But I beat upon your doors.
You say you await the Dawn
But I say you are the Dawn.
Come, in your irresistible unspent force
And make new light upon the mountains.

You have turned deaf ears to others—
Me you shall hear.
Out of the mouths of turbines,
Out of the turgid throats of engines,
Over the whistling steam,
You shall hear me shrilly piping.
Your mills I shall enter like the wind,
And blow upon your hearts,
Kindling the slow fire.

They think they have tamed you, workers
Beaten you to a tool
To scoop up hot honor
Till it be cool—
But out of the passion of the red frontiers
A great flower trembles and burns and glows
And each of its petals is a people.

Come forth, you workers—
Clinging to your stable
And your wisp of warm straw—
Let the fires grow cold,
Let the iron spill out of the troughs,
Let the iron run wild
Like a red bramble on the floors. . . .

As our forefathers stood on the prairies
So let us stand in a ring,
Let us tear up their prisons like grass
And beat them to barricades—
Let us meet the fire of their guns
With a greater fire,
Till the birds shall fly to the mountains
For one safe bough.

Lola Ridge

VISION

I CAME to the mountains for beauty
  And I find here the toiling folk,
On sparse little farms in the valleys,
  Wearing their days like a yoke.

White clouds fill the valleys at morning,
  They are round as great billows at sea,
And roll themselves up to the hill-tops
  Still round as great billows can be.

The mists fill the valleys at evening,
  They are blue as the smoke in the fall,
And spread all the hills with a tenuous scarf
  That touches the hills not at all.

These lone folk have looked on them daily,
  Yet I see in their faces no light.
Oh, how can I show them the mountains
  That are round them by day and by night?

Jessie B. Rittenhouse
(1869—   )

THE BURIED GOLD DIGGERS

NONE thought them brave
When they lived and toiled;
When they silently slid to a gruesome grave
Each day at sunlit morning hours.
When day by day into bondage sold,
They gave their manly strength for gold.

They died
The pawns of a monstrous greed.
What silence and despair were theirs,
As life ebbed low in that golden doom!
What thoughts as death blew out the light
In that terrible, helpless, hopeless night!

They were dead—
(And they called them brave!)
The men who dug the yellow gold;
The glittering, sinister, deadly gold.
Gold! That makes men cheat and lie
And thousands of nameless workers die.

Gold! Glittering, sinister, deadly gold!
When will mankind YOUR death behold?

Matilda Robbins.

BECAUSE*

BECAUSE the weight of our humility,
Wherefrom we gain
A little wisdom and much pain,
Falls here too sore and there too tedious,
Are we in anguish or complacency,
Not looking far ahead
To see by what mad couriers we are led
Along the roads of the ridiculous,
To pity ourselves and laugh at faith
And while we curse life bear it?
And if we see the soul's dead end in death,
Are we to fear it?

What folly is here that has not yet a name
Unless we say outright that we are liars?
What have we seen beyond our sunset fires
That lights again the way by which we came?

*From The Man Against the Sky

Why pay we such a price, and one we give
So clamoringly, for each racked empty day
That leads one more last human hope away,
As quiet fiends would lead past our crazed eyes
Our children to an unseen sacrifice?

Edwin Arlington Robinson
(1869—   )

FLAMES

PRISONERS in the dark of wood,
Fast in fibred solitude,
Passionate scarlet-silken things—
Dancing daggered folk with wings—
Fettered children of the sun
Who would storm the sky and run
Flame-armed, uniformed with light,
Burning death and spurning night,
Exiled and disarmed must lie
Locked in wood until they die .. .. ..
Or until the blazing key
Of a match shall set them free;
Then in a wild flash and maze,
Fiercer for their dungeon days,
Up they quiver integral,
While their cells and fetters fall
Ashes . . . and they leap and run
Upward to their Lord, the sun. . . .

(Pity, pity us who lie
Wooden flames until we die!)

E. Merrill Root
(1895—   )

I SHALL SHOUT THAT DAY

ONE day—
Not now, for earth encloses me and I
Am native to the dung;
One day—
Out of the dark cellars of my grief
I shall mount, I shall climb to laughter;
I shall send the white tendrils of my sick desire
Up from the cold and sounding darkness of my space in Time
And blindly search and find out at last
A path to day and laughter.

My roots are firm in ordure—I am strong;
Yes, I shall struggle, I shall climb
Until the mould is broken and the light
Shines through, and mirth
Possesses me, and I possess
The wild, great heart of mirth;
I shall shout that day
As morning glories shout;
I shall stand with the trees and wave
In strong contention with the wind, and blow
Across the wheat, and flow
With rivers;
With the cattle I shall rove
And crops, and gaze upon the plain.

One day—
I shall be free.

James Rorty
(1890—   )

WARNING

ON THE dry leaves,
In letters of white fire,
The frost has written:
M'ne, M'ne, Tekel Upharsin.
And all night long
I heard the oaks
Tearing their beards in lamentation,
And the maples
Bending their garments
Stained in the feast days:
While some Daniel of the wind
Arose among them
And spoke in ghost of prophecy:
"The torch-carriers in the armies of the snow
Shall burn your days
Like wooden houses.
The idol-makers of the hail
Shall come with chisel and hammers
And beat upon you,
Till you stand like carved silences;
And nothing shall live in you,
Save death,—
And nothing shall stir the land
Save the wings of the black angel!"

David Rosenthal

THE DAY MUST COME

THE song of whirring spindles,
The song of plying shuttles,
The song of ascending smoke
Is dumb and will not sound
Till the girls who whirr the spindles,
The men who make the smoke
Master the purpose of work,
And gather the fruits of work
For nourishing the joy of work.

Martin Russak
(1906—   )

HOMO RAPIENS

WHAT mocking elf, on impish mischief bent,
Called Man, this barbarous Man, the Sapient;
Man, who, disdainful of the nobler way,
Still lives by rapine, a dull beast of prey,
Nor spares, if so a savage gust he win,
To rob his fellows or devour his kin?
Yet nearer than he knew that jester came
To give rapacious Man the fitting name;
For change one single letter, and behold—
In "Homo Rapiens" the true tale is told.

Henry S. Salt
(1851—   )

SKYSCRAPER

BY DAY the skyscraper looms in the smoke and sun and has a soul.
Prairie and valley, streets of the city, pour people into it and they
mingle among its twenty floors and are poured out again back
to the streets, prairies and valleys.
It is the men and women, boys and girls so poured in and out all day
that give the building a soul of dreams and thoughts and
memories.
(Dumped in the sea or fixed in a desert, who would care for the
building or speak its name or ask a policeman the way to it?)

Elevators slide on their cables and tubes catch letters and parcels and
iron pipes carry gas and water and sewage in and out.
Wires climb with secrets, carry light and carry words, and tell terrors
and profits and loves—curses of men grappling plans of business and questions of women in plots of love.

Hour by hour the caissons reach down to the rock of the earth and
hold the building to a turning planet.
Hour by hour the girders play as ribs and reach out and hold together
the stone walls and floors.
Hour by hour the hand of the mason and the stuff of the mortar
clinch the pieces and parts to the shape an architect voted.
Hour by hour the sun and the rain, the air and the rust, and the
press of time running into centuries, play on the building
inside and out and use it.

Men who sunk the pilings and mixed the mortar are laid in graves
where the wind whistles a wild song without words.
And so are men who strung the wires and fixed the pipes and tubes
and those who saw it rise floor by floor.
Souls of them all are here, even the hod-carrier begging at back doors
hundreds of miles away and the bricklayer who went to state's
prison for shooting another man while drunk.
(One man fell from a girder and broke his neck at the head of a
straight plunge—he is here—his soul has gone into the stones
of the building.)

On the office doors from tier to tier—hundreds of names standing
for a face written across with a dead child, a passionate lover,
a driving ambition for a million dollar business or a lobster's
ease of life.

Behind the signs on the doors they work and the walls tell nothing
from room to room.
Ten-dollar-a-week stenographers take letters from corporation officers,
lawyers, efficiency engineers, and tons of letters go bundled
from the building to all ends of the earth.
Smiles and tears of each office girl go into the soul of the building just
the same as the master-men who rule the building.

Hands of clocks turn to noon hours and each floor empties its men
and women, who go away and eat and come back to work.
Toward the end of the afternoon all work slackens and all jobs go
slower as the people feel day closing on them.
One by one the floors are emptied. . . . The uniformed elevator men
are gone. Pails clang. . . . Scrubbers work, talking in foreign
tongues. Broom and water and mop clean from the floors
human dust and spit, and machine grime of the day.
Spelled in electric fire on the roof are words telling miles of houses
and people where to buy a thing for money. The sign speaks
till midnight.

Darkness on the hallways. Voices echo. Silence holds. . . . Watchmen walk slow from floor to floor and try the doors. Revolvers bulge from their hip pockets. . . . Steel safes stand in corners. Money is stacked in them.

A young watchman leans at a window and sees the lights of barges butting their way across a harbor, nets of red and white lanterns in a railroad yard, and a span of white and blurs of crosses and clusters over the sleeping city.

By night the skyscraper looms in the smoke and the stars and has a soul.

Carl Sandburg

GOVERNMENT

THE Government—I heard about the Government and I went out to find it. I said I would look closely at it when I saw it.

Then I saw a policeman dragging a drunken man to the calaboose. It was Government in action.

I saw a ward alderman slip into an office one morning and talk with a judge. Later in the day the judge dismissed a case against a pickpocket who was a live ward worker for the alderman. Again I saw this was the Government, doing things.

I saw militia men level their rifles at a crowd of workingmen to stay away from a shop where there was a strike on. Government in action.

Everywhere I saw that Government is a thing made of men, that Government has blood and bones, it is many mouths whispering into many ears, sending telegrams, aiming rifles, writing orders, saying "yes" and "no."

Government dies as the men who form it die and are laid away in their graves and the new Government that comes after is human, made of heartbeats, of blood, ambition, lust, and money running through it all, money paid and money taken, and money covered up and spoken of with hushed voices.

A Government is just as secret and mysterious and sensitive as any human sinner carrying a load of germs, traditions and corpuscles handed down from fathers and mothers away back.

Carl Sandburg

From SMOKE AND STEEL

SMOKE of the fields in spring is one,
Smoke of the leaves in autumn another.
Smoke of a steel-mill roof or a battleship funnel,
They all go up in a line with a smokestack,
Or they twist . . . in the slow twist . . . of the wind.

If the north wind comes they run to the south.
If the west wind comes they run to the east.
    By this sign
    all smokes
    know each other.
Smoke of the fields in spring and leaves in autumn,
Smoke of the finished steel, chilled and blue,
By the oath of work they swear: "I know you."

Hunted and hissed from the center
Deep down long ago when God made us over,
Deep down are the cinders we came from—
You and I and our heads of smoke.

                *   *   *   *   *   *

Some of the smokes God dropped on the job
Cross on the sky and count our years
And sing in the secrets of our numbers;
Sing their dawns and sing their evenings,
Sing an old log-fire song:
        You may put the damper up,
        You may put the damper down,
        The smoke goes up the chimney just the same.

Smoke of a city sunset skyline,
Smoke of a country dusk horizon—
        They cross on the sky and count our years.

                *   *   *   *   *   *

Smoke of a brick-red dust
        Winds on a spiral
        Out of the stacks
For a hidden and glimpsing moon.
This, said the bar-iron shed to the blooming mill,
This is the slang of coal and steel.
The day-gang hands it to the night-gang,
The night-gang hands it back.

Stammer at the slang of this—
Let us understand half of it.
        In the rolling mills and sheet mills,
        In the harr and boom of blast fires,
        The smoke changes its shadow
        And men change their shadow;
        A nigger, a wop, a bohunk changes.

A bar of steel—it is only
Smoke at the heart of it, smoke and the blood of a man.

A runner of fire ran in, ran out, ran somewhere else
And left—smoke and the blood of a man
And the finished steel, chilled and blue.

So fire runs in, runs out, runs somewhere else again,
And the bar of steel is a gun, a wheel, a nail, a shovel,
A rudder under the sea, a steering-gear in the sky;
And always dark in the heart and through it,
      Smoke and the blood of a man.
Pittsburg, Youngstown, Gary—they make their steel with men.
In the blood of men and the ink of chimneys
The smoke nights write their oaths:
Smoke into steel and blood into steel;
Homestead, Braddock, Birmingham, they make their steel with men.
Smoke and blood is the mix of steel.

      The birdmen drone
      in the blue; it is steel
      a motor sings and zooms.

     *   *   *   *   *   *

Steel barb-wire around The Works.
Steel guns in the holsters of the guards at the gates of The Works.
Steel ore-boats bring the loads clawed from the earth by steel, lifted
    and lugged by arms of steel, sung on its way by the clanking
    clam-shells.
The runners now, the handlers now, are steel; they dig and clutch
    and haul; they hoist their automatic knuckles from job to job;
    they are steel making steel.
Fire and dust and air fight in the furnaces; the pour is timed, the
    billets wriggle; the clinkers are dumped:
Liners on the sea, skyscrapers on the land; diving steel in the sea,
    climbing steel in the sky.

     *   *   *   *   *   *

Luck moons come and go.
Five men swim in a pot of red steel.
Their bones are kneaded into the bread of steel:
Their bones are knocked into coils and anvils
And the sucking plungers of sea-fighting turbines.
Look for them in a wooden frame of a wireless station.
So ghosts hide in steel like heavy-armed men in mirrors.
Peepers, skulkers—they shadow-dance in laughing tombs.
They are always there and they never answer.

In the subway plugs and drums,
In the slow hydraulic drills, in gumbo or gravel,
Under dynamo shafts in the webs of armature spiders,
They shadow-dance and laugh at the cost.

     *   *   *   *   . *   *

The ovens light a red dome.
Spools of fire wind and wind.
Quadrangles of crimson sputter.
The lashes of dying maroon let down.
Fire and wind wash out the slag.
Forever the slag gets washed in fire and wind
The anthem learned by the steel is:
    Do this or go hungry.
Look for our rust on a plow,
Listen to us in a threshing-engine razz.
Look at our job in the running wagon wheat.

        *   *   *   *   *   *

Fire and wind wash at the slag.
Box-cars, clocks, steam-shovels, churns; pistons; boilers, scissors—
Oh, the sleeping slag from the mountains, the slag-heavy pig-iron
    will go down many roads.
Men will stab and shoot with it, and make butter and tunnel rivers,
    and mow hay in swaths, and slit hogs and skin beeves, and steer
    airplanes across North America, Europe, Asia, round the world.
                                            Carl Sandburg

THE LIARS*

A LIAR goes in fine clothes.
A liar goes in rags.
A liar is a liar, clothes or no clothes.
A liar is a liar and lives on the lies he tells.
And dies in a life of lies.
And the stonecutters earn a living —with lies—on the tombs of liars.

A liar looks 'em in the eye
And lies to a woman,
Lies to a man, a pal, a child, a fool.
And he is an old liar; we know him many years back.

    A liar lies to nations.
    A liar lies to the people.
A liar takes the blood of the people
And drinks this blood with a laugh and a lie,
    A laugh in his neck,
    A lie in his mouth.
And this liar is an old one; we know him many years back.
    He is straight as a dog's hind leg.
    He is straight as a corkscrew.
He is white as a black cat's foot at midnight.

The tongue of man is tied on this,
On the liar who lies to nations,
    *March, 1919.

The liar who lies to the people.
The tongue of man is tied on this
And ends: To hell with 'em all.
　　　　　　To hell with 'em all.
It's a song hard as a riveter's hammer,
　　Hard as the sleep of a crummy hobo,
　　Hard as the sleep of a lousy doughboy,
Twisted as a shell-shock idiot's gibber.

The liars met where the doors were locked.
They said to each other: Now for war.
The liars fixed it and told 'em: Go.

Across their tables they fixed it up,
Behind their doors away from the mob.
And the guns did a job that nicked off millions.
The guns blew seven million off the map,
The guns sent seven million west.
Seven million shoving up daisies.
Across their tables they fixed it up,
　　The liars who lie to nations.

　　And now
　　Out of the butcher's job
　　And the boneyard junk the maggots have cleaned,
　　Where the jaws of the skulls tell the jokes of war ghosts,
Out of this they are calling now: Let's go back where we were.
　　　　Let us run the world again, us, us.
Where the doors are locked the liars say: Wait, and we'll cash in again.

So I hear The People talk.
So I hear them tell each other:
　　Let the strong men be ready.
　　Let the strong men watch.
　　Let your wrists be cool and your head clear.
　　Let the liars get their finish,
　　The liars and their waiting game, waiting a day again
　　To open the doors and tell us: War! get out to your war again.

So I hear the people tell each other:
　　Look at to-day and to-morrow.
　　Fix this clock that nicks off millions.
　　When The Liars say it's time
　　Take things in your own hands
　　　　To hell with them all,
The liars who lie to nations,
The liars who lie to The People.

Carl Sandburg
(1878—   )

FIGHT TO A FINISH

THE boys came back. Bands played and flags were flying:
　　And crowds of Yellow-Pressmen thronged the street
To cheer the soldiers who'd refrained from dying,
　　And hear the music of returning feet.
"Of all the thrills and ardors war has brought,
This moment is the finest" (so they thought).

Snapping their bayonets on to charge the mob,
　　Grim Fusiliers broke ranks with glint of steel.
At last the boys had found a cushy job.

　　　　　*　　*　　*　　*　　*

I heard the Yellow-Pressmen grunt and squeal;
And with my trusty bombers turned and went
To clear the butchers out of Parliament.

　　　　　　　　　Sigfried Sassoon
　　　　　　　　　　(1886—　　)

TRUTH
I.

I HAVE all appearances, and yet one form.
You shall never know me, if you know not to see unafraid.
From your house you see heaven through windows;
Come into the open; how now can you see the sky, without looking
　　　　through glass?
Tear down your houses to find me;
I am under the cornerstone,
I am deep in the subsoil.
Build up your towers to find me;
I am where the spires point,
I am beyond their power of direction.
Seek, and you shall not find me,
For I come unannounced, unsuspected—
I am with you now;
Do you behold me?

Is there grass at your feet? I am in it;
I am in pavements of crowded streets.
I hide in shop windows
And sail across meadows and woods, flaunting.
I give shape to the people you brush in your living,
I give power to your enemies and love to your friends,
I animate you—do you behold me?
I have all appearances, and yet one form.

II.

Cover me with bruises, pelt me with stones, flay me;
Drive me from your dwellings, spit upon me in your streets,
Name me with loathing.
I am among you; do you behold me?
Crowd by me, bustling; you have important affairs.
Wait, here's a lark!   They are leading me captive;
Join with the mob that revile.
Meet me with force and with cunning, sweep to my friends with
     bribes,
Find my betrayer, make me bear my cross
To mine own burial.
Thus I shall know I am worthy,
Thus I shall win to survive.

Joseph T. Shipley
(1893—   )

"THIS I SHALL HOLD"

This I shall hold against the intruding years:
That here within the hollow of this cup of hills
I have touched deep, immutable springs of livingness;
That here the jangled pattern of the days was blown,
A negligible wraith, across the easement of the hills,
Here, like immortal trumpeters, the winds rang out
And at their convocation memories came
Flooding the shadowy rim of trees with living light
While time and space like rusty bands fell off
From all the pulsing world, and once again
I was aware of immanences bright
That melted even the granite of the hills
Like very flakes of snow.
And all the dreams and loves of men were woven
Into a palpable tissue of delight
Wherefrom there rose a temple with its base
Spanning all nations and its spires
Joining all skies. . . .
And I glimpsed then what little children know;
That life and death are one to him who goes
Gallantly on;
That all the bitter creeds are a miasma blown
Before one living breath.
That he who hastens on love-quickened ways
Helps build the temple of becoming man;
Who sends his shaft of dream across the ache of time
Shall lighten travelers on the path of gods;
Yes, he shall quicken even the sullen stones

And ease the birth of every groping thing.
And he shall know beyond the cramping knowledges
Of many books;
And he shall contact tides of light that ran
When Plato was a boy;
And he shall eat of bread that shall be sweet
As that a Poet broke on Olivet.
Easily he shall come to know
The "Open Secret" hidden through the years,
For his awakening eyes
All races and all nations shall be one
With, in their midst, a temple.

*　　*　　*　　*　　*

This I shall hold against the intruding years.

Mary Siegrist

THE BLIND PEDLAR

I STAND alone through each long day
Upon these pavers; cannot see
The wares spread out upon this tray
—For God has taken sight from me.

Many a time I've cursed the night
When I was born. My peering eyes
Have sought for but one ray of light
To pierce the darkness. When the skies

Rain down their first sweet April shower
On budding branches; when the morn
Is sweet with breath of spring and flowers,
I've cursed the night when I was born.

But now I thank God, and am glad
For what I cannot see this day
—The young men cripples, old, and sad,
With faces burnt and torn away.

Or those who, growing rich and old,
Have battened on the slaughter,
Whose faces, gorged with blood and gold,
Are creased in purple laughter!

Osbert Sitwell
(1892—   )

CARNEGIE'S LIBRARIES*

THERE is a scent on the books of dead men's bones,
  And a spatter of blood over all;
There's a rough, ragged hole in each leaf you turn,
  Like the wound from a rifleman's ball.

There's the last gasp of men shot down at command
  Of this gracious and generous man;
There's the blood and groan, the grief and the sham—
  You picture it, any who can.

There's a picture of Homestead—will we ever forget
  How those brave ragged men were defenselessly slain—
Were slaughtered like beasts, like poor hunted beasts,
  By Carnegie's will and for Carnegie's gain?

Will we ever forget how their mothers and wives
  In their rags and their woe knelt down in the dust,
And clasped their dear dead then, just as they fell
  By riflemen's ball and bayonet's thrust?

Will we ever forget how the press of the land
  Made light of the slaughter by saying: The dead
Were foreign-born men, who, in impudence, asked
  For the right to living and earning their bread?

Will we ever forget how, in sweatshop and mine,
  The fathers and mothers and children are slain?
How virtue is bartered and childhood is crushed
  By Carnegie's will and for Carnegie's gain?

How the skeleton babes, the milkless breast
  Give their poor little lives to his greed?
How the girls on the street and the mothers in rags
  Are reflecting his generous deed?

And this is his gift, all shining with blood,
  The gift that he proffers with arrogant hand;
This is the penance for murder and lust;
  This is his jest to the slaves of the land.

But the books are not dumb; they have eloquent tongues
  To tell you their pitiful story—
How the bodies and souls of women and men
  Have built him his temple of glory.

*Andrew Carnegie is now deceased. Yet the system that brought him forward, and particularly his *dole*-libraries, is still the disgraceful monument of our own shame.
—M. G.

How the walls are of bones cemented with blood,
 And wet the dropping of tears;
Of hearts that have broken for wrongs unwritten
 These hundreds and hundreds of years.

For these wrongs to our comrades we'll never forget,
 Nor this master of bread, with his cunning and greed.
And the gift that he proffers—we spurn it and scorn him,
 For we hold it in keeping with his class and deed.

Alice T. Sorenson

BILLIARD ACADEMY

GREEN tables spaced, alight
under yellowlow lights.
shirtsleeved young fellows pose
themselves in special attitudes
about them, stickinhand
or cigarette deftly
held, then slide cues
sharply through taut fingers. the balls
shine round and clear, quick blobs
of color on faultless fields,
where rapid vengeance rolls
and clicks, returns
or poorly judged, deflects
to pass and spend itself in motion
rebounding gingerly from cushions . . .
this play of pallid youths
reflects, in poolroom atmosphere,
psychology of waste.
grimly they twist
time into tangled skeins.
and pool-school students, lucubrate
the minutiae of nullities.

Herman Spector
(1905—   )

From ANARCHY

MEN coveting, fighting and dying, an endless strife
In ignorant fever for power and pride and life:
The destined prey of the lusts of desire and disease.

Yet sighs the absurd unreasoning voice of our blood
For a world, alas!—and there is no bitter cold there,
No scorching heat, nor blossom with worm in the bud,
And babes do not die, nor blindness comes to the old there,

But the sun shines fair, and the rain falls soft, and the clime
Conspires with the soil for the loveliest fruits of time,
And the young are strong, and the old go green to the grave
Without pain, and none is master and none is slave.
And music sounds from the boats, and garlands are woven
By maids at noon, and great calm statues are cloven
Out of the cliffs, by the shrines of sunnier gods,

Divine, magnificent spirit of man that will face
Invincible ever the battle with hopeless odds
And cannot but dream ere he falls of a time and a race,
Of a day when the world of men maturer grown
Will live without law in perfect wisdom and grace
Like the solar system hanging in awful space,
Its parts sustained serenely by love alone!

J. C. Squire
(1884—   )

THE ROAD

BECAUSE our lives are cowardly and sly,
    Because we do not dare to take or give,
Because we scowl and pass each other by,
    We do not live; we do not dare to live.

We dive, each man, into his secret house,
    And bolt the door, and listen in affright,
Each timid man beside a timid spouse,
    With timid children huddled out of sight.

Kissing in secret, fighting secretly!
    We crave and hide like vermin in a hole,
Under the bravery of the sun and sky
    We flash our meannesses of face and soul.

Let us go out and walk upon the road,
    And quit for evermore the brick-built den,
The lock and key, hidden, shy abode
    That separates us from our fellow-men.

And by contagion of the sun we may
    Catch at a spark from that primeval fire,
And learn that we are better than our clay,
    And equal to the peaks of our desire.

James Stephens
(1882—   )

THE ALARM CLOCK

THE brazen loud alarm clock beats my brain;
A hammer strikes the raw thought; I wake, and rise,
And drag my bleeding thought through bogs of pain
To where the gray mills loom as darkness flies.

We stand before the gates, my thought and I,
And hoarse cries the mill-throat, (A vampire song!)
Till we are drawn . . . and lost! Hell's Lorelei
Then breathes her sated sigh upon the wrong.

It's evening: evening: Vomited from the maw
Of Greed's gray disgorging beast, I go my way
A sucked-out, broken thing, again to draw
In sleep a mending breath before the day.

It's night now: night now: night: I wind the clock:
A thought sweeps the dull brain, red wave on wave.
This tyrant bawd and I! (Myself I mock.)
I! master! make me to this thing a slave!

By God, some night this monster I will take
And hack its iron heart, and wreck! And then a span
I'll sleep. I'll sleep. And when again I wake
'Twill be to work in joy and live, a man!

Rose Pastor Stokes
(1879—   )

CITY COMRADESHIP

FACE on face in the city, and when will the faces end?
Face on face in the city, but never the face of a friend;
Till my heart grows sick with longing and dazed with the din of the
    street,
As I rush with the thronging thousands in a loneliness complete.

Shall I not know my brothers! Their toil is one with mine.
We offer the fruits of our labor on the same great city's shrine.
They are weary as I am weary; they are happy and sad with me;
And all of us laugh together when evening sets us free.

Face on face in the city, and where shall our fortunes fall?
Face on face in the city,—my heart goes out to you all.
See, we labor together; is not the bond divine?
Lo, the strength of the city is built of your life and mine.

Anna Louise Strong
(1885—   )

"SAFE FOR DEMOCRACY"

SAFE for Democracy, they said.
True; for our noblest youth are dead.

Let but another world-war kill
The rest, it will be safer still!

L. A. G. Strong
(1896—   )

IN A WAR MUSEUM

HERE are trophies of the war,
  Relics of the battlefields;
Tattered banners, flags galore,
  Bayonets and battered shields.
Pistols, lances, shot and shell,
  Dirks and daggers. Who can tell—
    That bent sabre red with rust,
      Might have chopped off some wise head?

Does man profit by this show?
  Is there naught that he can glean
From these trophies? Does he know
  What these blood-stained relics mean?
Does he cherish them with pride,
  Knowing youths have bled and died?
    Homes destroyed and laws transgressed?
      Men transformed to maddened beasts
        By our ministers and priests?

Here are trophies of the fray,
  Twisted swords with gleaming blades;
Medals hung in neat array,
  Cannons, rifles and grenades.
These mementos of Hell's fire,
  Are they objects to admire?
    Are the weapons hanging here
      Relics that the wise should prize,
        When the dull, beribboned spear
          Robbed an artist of his eyes?

Norman Stuckey

REVOLUTION

WHAT husks of last year's winter close you in,
Tomorrow's world—what dead, what wrinkled skin
Of ancient parchments, laws, beliefs! what dried,
Worn, tattered layers keep the life inside,

Where slender as a sword, and tender green
It trembles, pushes, patient and unseen:
Vibrating atom, fronded silken thread,
Some day to shake, to sunder back the dead
Two halves of hemispheres—to pierce the crust
Of ages' rubbish, crowns and cults and dust!

See, iron arms, that clutter all the wide
Plateau of liberty—see, fortified
Dull spikey towns—you cannot hold your own
Against one seed a fecund earth has grown!
Alarmed you stand, alert to meet your foe,
Ready to battle blow for thundering blow;
Nor do you see this sprout of common wheat,
The blade, between your firm implanted feet.

Genevieve Taggard
(1894—   )

LABOR

Brick walls built by Labor
   Keep the sun away;
Towers wrought by Labor
   Set cold winds at play;
Fires stoked by Labor
   Make the sky dark gray;
So what is the good of
   Labor anyway?

Elizabeth Thomas

GOVERNMENT—THE LIVING GOD

I make the right,
I make the wrong,
I make the truth and error.
I am the State,
I am the Law,
I am the living terror.

I own the earth,
I own the sea,
I own the treasure hoards.
In every land,
In every clime,
I am the "Lord of Lords."

I suck the strength
From out the veins
Of mad laborious hordes.
I rule and reign
Behind a wall
Of fifty million swords.

Richard Thorland

From THE SINGERS IN A CLOUD

ON THE earth the battles war against light,
Heavy lies the harrow, bitter the field.
Beauty, like a river running through the night,
Streams past the stricken one whom it would have healed,
But the darkened faces turn away from sight.
Blind, bewildered nations sow, reap, and fall.
Shadows gather all.

Far above the birdsong bright shines gold.
Through the starry orchard earth's paths are hung;
As she moves among them glowing fruits unfold,
Such that the heavens there reawaken young.
Overhead is beauty, healing for the old.
Overhead is morning, nothing but youth,
Only lovely youth.

Ridgley Torrence
(1875—   )

From THE TIME-CLOCK

"TICK-TOCK! Tick-tock!"
Sings the great time-clock.
And the pale men hurry
And flurry and scurry
To punch their time
Ere the hour shall chime.
"Tick-tock! Tick-tock!"
Sings the stern time-clock.

"It-is-time-you-were-come!"
Says the pendulum.
"Tick-tock! Tick-tock!"
Moans the great time-clock.
They must leave the heaven
Of their beds. . . . It is seven,
And the sharp whistles blow
In the city below.

They can never delay—
If they're late, they must pay.
"God help them!" I say.
But the great time-clock
Only says, "Tick-tock!"

They are chained, they are slaves
From their birth to their graves!
And the clock
Seems to mock
With its awful "Tick-tock!"
There it stands at the door
Like a brute as they pour
Through the dark little way
Where they toil, night and day.
They are goaded along
By the terrible song
Of whistle and gong,
And the endless "Tick-tock!"
Of the great time-clock.
"Tick-tock! Tick-tock!"
Runs the voice of the clock.

Charles Hanson Towne
(1877—   )

BREED, WOMEN, BREED!

BREED, little mothers
With the tired backs and the tired hands,
Breed for the owners of mills and the owners of mines!
Breed a race of danger-haunted men,
A race of toiling, straining, miserable men,
Breed for the owners of mills and the owners of mines.
Breed, breed, breed!

Breed, little mothers
With the sunken eyes and the sagging cheeks,
Breed for the bankers, the crafty and terrible masters of men!
Breed a race of machines,

A race of anemic, round-shouldered, subway herded machines.
Breed, little mothers,
With a faith patient and stupid as cattle,
Breed for the war-lords!
Offer your woman-flesh for incredible torment,
Rack your frail bodies with the pangs of birth
For the war-lords who strangle your sons!

Breed, little mothers,
Breed for the owners of mills and the owners of mines,
Breed for the bankers, the crafty and terrible masters of men,
Breed for the war-lords, the devouring war-lords,
Breed, women breed!

Lucia Trent
(1897—   )

THE SACRIFICE

LIKE the sheep in the shambles that bleed,
  Like rubbish that roars in the draft,
We are slain on the altar of Greed
  And burned to the image of Graft.

By wreck, and explosion, and fire,
  By swindling, and thieving, and traps,
We are robbed—that a stock may go higher;
  We die—lest a dividend lapse.

A wink, and a jest, and a fee,
  And the State's whole duty is met.
Created for slaughter were we;
  How dare we ask more than we get?

So we scream for an agonized hour
  In the smoke and the steam and the flame;
And the State drops a tear, and a flower;
  "God willed it—who, who was to blame?"

But the sleek, idle money-lord thieves;
  And the vampire broods fat in his den;
So the dollars pour in, what are lives?
  So the gold gathers fast, what are men?

Irwin St. John Tucker
(1886—   )

DISTINGUO

FREEDOM, yes, but a Freedom combed and curled,
A safe, tame Freedom, eating from the hand,
A Freedom which will lie down at command.
Not this wild wench whose scarlet flag unfurled
Threatens our cozy, comfortable world
With voice like thunder echoing through the land,
Who tramps the highway with her ragged band
Of va-nu-pieds from the depths upwhirled.
God save us from her—We've no use for kings,

Crowns are obnoxious, sceptres are taboo,
But lawyers, plutocrats, are sacred things.
Touch not the Black Coat, lest you should undo
The very woof of life and fling destroyed,
Our spinning earth to chaos and the void.

Lizinka Campbell Turner

CLAY HILLS

It is easy to mould the yielding clay.
And many shapes grow into beauty
Under the facile hand.
But forms of clay are lightly broken;
They will be shattered and forgotten in a dingy corner.

But underneath the slipping clay
Is rock. . . .
I would rather work in a stubborn rock
All the years of my life,
And make one strong thing
And set it in a high, clean place,
To recall the granite strength of my desire.

Jean Starr Untermeyer
(1886—   )

CALIBAN IN THE COAL MINES

God, we don't like to complain—
    We know that the mine is no lark—
But—there's the pools from the rain;
    But—there's the cold and the dark.

God, You don't know what it is—
    You, in Your well-lighted sky,
Watching the meteors whizz;
    Warm, with the sun always by.

God, if You had but the moon
    Stuck in Your cap for a lamp,
Even You'd tire of it soon,
    Down in the dark and the damp.

Nothing but blackness above,
    And nothing that moves but the cars—
God, if You wish for our love,
    Fling us a handful of stars!

Louis Untermeyer

SUNDAY

IT WAS Sunday—
Eleven in the morning; people were at church—
Prayers were in the making; God was near at hand—
Down the cramped and narrow streets of quiet Lawrence*
Came the tramp of workers marching in their hundreds;
Marching in the morning, marching to the grave-yard,
Where, no longer fiery, underneath the grasses,
Callous and uncaring, lay their friend and sister.
In their hands they carried wreaths and drooping flowers,
Overhead their banners dipped and soared like eagles—
Aye, but eagles bleeding, stained with their own heart's blood—
Red, but not for glory——red, with wounds and travail,
Red, the buoyant symbol of the blood of all the world . . .
So they bore their banners, singing toward the grave-yard,
So they marched and chanted, mingling tears and tributes,
So, with flowers, the dying went to deck the dead.

Within the churches the people heard
   The sound, and much concern was theirs—
God might not hear the Sacred Word—
God might not hear their prayers!

Should such things be allowed these slaves—
   To vex the Sabbath peace wih Song,
To come with chants, like marching waves,
   That proudly swept along . . .

Suppose God turned to these—and heard!
   Suppose He listened unawares—
God might forget the Sacred Word,
   God might forget their prayers!

And so (oh, tragic irony)
   The blue-clad Guardians of the Peace
Were sent to sweep them back—to see
   The ribald song should cease;

To scatter those who came and vexed
   God with their troubled cries and cares.
Quiet—so God might hear the text;
   The sleek and unctuous prayers!

Up the rapt and singing streets of little Lawrence,
Came the stolid soldiers; and, behind the bluecoats,
Grinning and invisible, bearing unseen torches,

*Lawrence (Mass.), is one of the largest mill industrial centers in U. S., and has witnessed some of the bloodiest strikes in the country's history.—M. G.

Rode red hordes of anger, sweeping all before them.
Lust and Evil joined them—Terror rode among them;
Fury fired its pistols; Madness stabbed and yelled . . .
Through the wild and bleeding streets of shuddering Lawrence
Raged the heedless panic, hour-long and bitter.
Passion tore and trampled; men once mild and peaceful
Fought with savage hatred in the name of Law and Order.
And, below the outcry, like the sea beneath the breakers,
Mingling with the anguish, rolled the solemn organ . . .

Eleven in the morning—people were at church—
Prayers were in the making—God was near at hand—
It was Sunday!

Louis Untermeyer
(1885—   )

THE WINNERS

NEVER on the winning side,
　Always on the right—
Vanquished, this shall be our pride
　In the world's despite.

Let the oily Pharisees
　Purse their lips and rant,
Calm we face the Destinies:
　Better "can't" than Cant.

Bravely drain, then fling away,
　Break the cup of sorrow!
Courage! He who lost the day
　May have won the morrow.

George Sylvester Viereck
(1884—   )

INCARCERATED

OH, I COULD weep sometimes to go to the public schools
And see little children sitting in long rows
On hard board seats!

So many hours a day away from the green lanes and butterflies,
So many hours away from the faces of mothers, the ministries of
　　　home;
Sitting, sitting, oh so patiently, expectantly—
Sitting in long rows on hard bench seats!

The smug, pleased face of the school-mistress!
The sour, lined face, the peaked, petulant neurotic face,
The doll-like, painted face of the school-mistress!
But once in a hundred times the face of a true teacher—pedagogue,
    leader of children.
What is it all for, this wholesale incarceration of childhood?
I demand of you to show cause why it should be.
And I come to you with Nature's writ of habeas corpus,
That you release these children, sitting so patiently, pathetically—
Sitting in long rows on hard board seats.

Elizabeth Waddell

ATAVISM

IT WILL come about eventually . . .
I cannot be this ordered self forever.

Like the rumble of guns
From afar . . .

I am tired of mating and meandering.
I want the yellow canyons of desire.

I will be no docile thing—
But a restless eagle in space.

Threshing is better than sowing.
I have spread seeds too long!

Now there is rich harvest of the unknown—
Riot and strange thoroughfares.

There is din of thunder
And storm on the air.

Like the rumble of guns from afar . . .
I cannot be this ordered self forever!

Blanche Shoemaker Wagstaff
(1888—   )

REITERATION*

DAWN—
And the steel-voiced trumpets of industry
Stab the sleeping workers to consciousness.

Breakfast—
Gulping of indigestible foods and liquids
In the stolid atmosphere of hasty words.

*From *Poems of a Toiler*

Factories—
Gates and the ting-ting-ting of time clocks,
Interspersed with sharp contentions of timekeepers.

Work—
The avaricious jaws of machinery, growling, cursing;
Masticating raw materials, souls, flesh,
With the avidity of starved monsters.

Dusk—
Trumpets! and the sudden realization of identity,
The weary drag of heavy muscles homeward.

Night—
The frugal meal, the monotony of responsibilities,
The unread newspaper, the heavy sleep of death.

Dawn—
     *   *   *   *   *   *
     *   *   *   *   *   *

Jim Waters

HEADS HIGH

STONE, steel, and dungeon,
  Thus the workers paid.
You who build for the ages
  Face them unafraid.
Cross, rope and fagot,
  Water, rack, and wheel,
Well the heroes faced them—
  Let your strength be steel.
Now the day is nearing,
  The workers' kingdom nigh,
Who strikes a blow for freedom?
  Who lives though he may die?
The rebels from the circus,
  The prophets old and grey,
Arena victims bleeding
  Are tramping on today.
Look, Socrates is marching,
  The hemlock in his hand,
And Spartacus beside him
  With all his doughty band.
Now the day is nearing,
  The workers' kingdom nigh.
Who stands with them for freedom?
  Who lives with them that die?

Hate, death, and prison,
These the rebels knew.
You, the heirs of rebels,
Must be rebels too!

Henry George Weiss
(1898—   )

THE STRIKER

MANY have sung the soldier
From the rude, red days of old,
To this madder hour of more murderous power
And death schemes manifold.
But no one has sung the striker,
Tho a better fighter he
For the living cause and the larger laws
Of the empire that is to be.

Many have sung the statesman
Of nation and state and clan;
Tho he served himself from the purse of pelf
And lorded it over man.
Yet greater than he, the striker,
Lacking both fame and fee,
At the cost of all he has built the wall
Of the city that is to be.

Many have sung the scholar,
Maker of book and school,
Tho his ease was earned by the throng unlearned
Who slaved that the few might rule.
But the lore and the law of the striker
Setteth the whole world free;
Neither ease nor toil shall the spirit spoil
In the knowledge that is to be.

Many have sung the saintly,
The pure of all times and creeds;
But, alas, the good have denied the food
For even the children's needs;
Kinder by far the striker,
And truly more righteous he,
For he stakes his meal on the common weal
And the justice that is to be.

Some day, when all are toilers,
    And nobody toils for naught,
When the worker rules over kirks and schools,
    And shapes all the realm of thought:
They shall sing the song of the striker,
    No longer an outcast he,
But with arms abreast he shall stand confessed
    In the triumph that is to be.

                  Robert Whitaker
                    (1863—   )

TO A REBEL

O DAUNTLESS soul, I too have scorned all censure
    And fought the fight and shot my arrow true;
Though sorely hurt I've sought Truth's high adventure,
    Nor do I now seek peace nor pardon sue.

                  Hinton White
                    (1866—   )

THE BEGGARS

THE LITTLE pitiful, worn, laughing faces,
Begging of Life for Joy!

I saw the little daughters of the poor,
Tense from the long day's working, strident, gay,
Hurrying to the picture-place. There curled
A hideous flushed beggar at the door,
Trading upon his horror, eyeless, maimed,
Complacent in his profitable mask.
They mocked his horror, but they gave to him
From the brief wealth of pay-night, and went in
To the cheap laughter and the tawdry thoughts
Thrown on the screen; into the seeking hand
Covered by darkness, to the luring voice
Of Horror, boy-masked, whispering of rings,
Of silks, of feathers, bought—so cheap!—With just
Their slender starved child-bodies palpitant
For Beauty, Laughter, Passion—that are Life:
(A frock of satin for an hour's shame,
A coat of fur for two days' servitude;
"And the clothes last," the thought runs on, within
The poor warped girl-minds drugged with changeless days;
"Who cares or knows after the hour is done?")
Poor little beggars at Life's door for Joy!

       *   *   *   *   *   *

The old man crouched there, eyeless, horrible,
Complacent in the marketable mask
That earned his comforts—and they gave to him!

But ah, the little painted, wistful faces
Questioning Life for Joy!

Margaret Widdemer

THE TOILERS*

TINSEL-MAKERS in factory gloom,
Miners in ethylene pits,
Divers and druggists mixing poisonous bloom;

Huge hunters, men of brawn,
Half-naked creatures of the tropics,
Furred trappers stealing forth of Labrador dawn;

Catchers of beetles, sheep-men in bleak sheds,
Pearl-fishers perched on Indian coasts,
Children in stifling towers pulling threads;

Dark bunchy women pricking intricate laces,
Myopic jewelers' apprentices,
Arabs who chase the long-legged birds in sandy places:

They are invisible slaves,
The genii of her costly wishes,
Climbing, descending, running under waves.

They strip earth's dimmest cell,
They burn and drown and stifle
To build her inconceivable and fragile shell.

Florence Wilkinson

*From *Our Lady of Idleness*

TO A HARNESSED THOROUGHBRED

SLEEK-LIMBED, glossy, rippling hide,
Where those supple muscles slide,
Rhythmic shock on shock, in time
To the hoof-beats' clicking rhyme:

Strength like fine elastic steel,
Nerved so taut that head and heel
Shift together in swift response
To the veriest feather, once
Let a finger's grip come light
On these lines, drawn tight.

Bitted—bridled. . . . Can no fire
Light your limbs with quick desire,
Flicker down that silken skin,
Shake in tawny flames the mane,
Like a wild horse long ago
Shook it in the blinding snow,
Shook it at the burning sun,
Screamed and splashed where rivers run!

Kick the silly shafts apart:
Tinderwood and flimsy cart
Shattered, for a soul ablaze
With the whinnying prairie days!

Untamed, radiant, proud and high—
Thunderous hoofs, a blue-bright sky,
Billowed grass, and fleeing wind
Miles before you and behind. . . .

Robert Wolf
(1895—   )

CONTEMPT

I SPIT upon the laws that thieves have made
to give the crooked strength to rob the weak.

I spit upon a country full of wealth
where millions live in squalor and in want.

I spit upon the flag that waves above
a nation made of masters and of slaves.

I spit upon religions that defend
a hell on earth and preach a heaven beyond.

I spit upon all morals that contend
that the joy of life is not life's highest end.

I spit upon the education that
turns into Babbitts what might have been men.

Upon this whole damned system do I spit,
and while I spit—I weep.

Adolf Wolff
(1889—   )

THIS—OUR WORLD*

AN IRON world without a soul;
The patient sky above waiting;
The patient men below waiting;
The blue sky above forever listening, inviting, expectant;
The tired men below forever listening, hopeful, expectant;
The flaming sun above ordering abundance;
The flaming hell below denying enough;
Forever clamoring; forever devouring;
Devouring the men who are mates for mothers;
Fathers, steel-muscled, broad-chested, dominant;
The women, mothers of children:
The innocent children with white bodies, fluent,
Morning glories bearing the
Seeds of the unknowable Future.
Mothers, undulant, flexible; crypts of the ages; alabaster vessels of life.
In the dim dawn, before the whistles command,
I see an army, ever hungry, never full;
They bend gray faces above their pauper bowls,
And suck up eagerly Starvation's dole.

    *   *   *   *   *   *

They go down into the dripping corridors,
Into the dark womb of the Earth, their mother;
The mother who devours her children;
Nay not the Earth, their mother, devours them,
But they are devoured of men, their brethren.
They go down into the caverns of the Earth,
And sitting on the shoulders of each,
Crouching close at his ear, is Death.
They rain gold into the laps of their owners
Who bask in the sun and breathe the bright air
Sifted by the leaves:
But unto these toilers is tossed only enough
Of the spoil of their combat to keep Life's poor, gray smoke ascending.

    *   *   *   *   *   *

I see a monster.
His feet are of gold; his hands are of gold;
Golden is his head; his legs are golden;
But his heart is of clay.
His eyes are red as rubies,
And his golden hands are folded upon his swollen belly, which is of
    gold;
Into his open maw flows an endless procession:
Men with gray faces, women with sunken eyes,
And the little children who have never laughed.

    *   *   *   *   *   *

*From *The Poet in the Desert*

Can a machine conceive beauty,
Or has a machine imagination?
The inventions of Man have enslaved him,
He thinks not for himself; he works not for himself;
He dreams not at all; his hoping is only against hunger.
The monsters he has harnessed
Have become the obedient dragons of the masters,
And have snatched him into slavery,
The end of his toil is profit for the Oppressors.
Accursed is labor for another, without justice,
Contemptible is the labor of a slave.
Blessed is leisure, the miraculous gateway.
The ponderous machines should have unlocked the gates of the mirac-
ulous gardens, but they are ogres before the gates.

* * * * * *

Only Man has enforced his brother;
Only Man has compelled servitude.
Only Man has dwarfed his own godhood, cherished Poverty and
exalted Ugliness.
Only Man has defied Nature and set up the idols of his ignorance.
He has denied Freedom and Beauty.

* * * * * *

Shall I sing of Liberty when there is no Liberty?
Shall I sing of Freedom when there is none?
Shall I sing love-songs to young lovers who are slaves?
My soul thrills even as I think the laburnum
In Spring-time thrills to link her chains of gold.
I am lost in the great miracle which Nature
Has endlessly wrought out of freedom.
But Man sits amid his own ruins, eating husks.
Do the slavish ones perceive the mysterious cycles,
Or the coming of new leaves?
Do they know that life may be glad for all
And love glad for all?
For them the Earth is only a grave.
Do the men and women cheated of their own souls
Know the unwearied freedom of the great Nurser?
They love by law and they unlove by law.

* * * * * *

The State! Force! Authority!
Hater of freedom; oppressor of the poor; creator of poverty;
Foster-mother of crime.
The unsated monster which devours
The men with despairful eyes; the

Women with tired faces,
And the little children whose fingers are so soft;
Rose-petals, delicately pink.
It feeds upon babes, blinking innocently ere they have waked to the
morning.
It gluts upon the breasts of mothers, which are so white,
And upon the hearts of resolute men, which are so red.
Its wings are death; its eyes are graves;
Destroyer of the Soul.

* * * * * *

And if the State should die, whore of
Force and prostitute of privilege?

Then peace in freedom, and in freedom, peace.
The law of Self made beautiful.
Man shaking out his plumes into the sun.
Poets whose songs shall hold the ages listening;
Painters of visions,
Sculptors of gods, for men shall be as gods
In temples of grandeur;
Where happily the people shall worship Beauty.
Brotherhood shall be one with selfishness,
The *Golden Rule* the wisest selfishness.
Gone war; gone violence; gone brutal brows;
Gone poverty, oppression, crime and degradation.
Across the earth shall gleam Freedom,
As welcome unto men of weary souls as waking of a summer day
Unto the dawn-mad anarchy of birds.

* * * * * *

Onward, ever onward, it comes resistless as the Tide of Time; men
with pale faces;
Women with despairful eyes,
And little children who have never laughed.
Dancing with the glee of demons are their fluttering banners; the
rags of their poverty;
From mines, mills and factories;
From the slimy slums of cities;
From the dark caverns of the earth;
From the narrow and dripping tunnels of darkness, come the rats of
Civilization;
From the clamorous and devouring penitentiaries of Industry;
From the white-hot, roaring hells of furnaces;
From the mind-madding laughter of the machines
And the devouring cruelty of the pest-houses of Greed.

* * * * * *

They are not going down into the pits.
They are not marching to the factories.
They are not going to the furnaces;
Nearer, more near; stronger; louder; more strong;
They come, and the mutter of their lips is
Revolution, Revolution, Revolution.

         *   *   *   *   *   *

Oh, Revolution, dread angel of the Awful Presence,
Warder of the gate of tears,
Open and set the captive free.
Dark, silent, loving, cruel and merciful one,
Hold yourself not aloof.
Is there not enough?
You are our only hope, our only redeemer.
Come with thunder and with lightning,
That the air may be clear.
Come with deluge and tempest, that the earth may be purified.
Come with agony and bloody rain, that Life may be born anew,
The glad life of a perfect place, and songs stirring the air.
Pitch head-long from the cloudy battlements
And, with heavenly-fire, utterly destroy
This distorted and mis-shapen world.

Charles Erskine Scott **Wood**
(1852—   )

THE ROAD TO HELL

As CHUM and pal I have been hailed
By the fallen and the failed:
As comrade I have halved my crust
With dust-stained children of the dust;
As brother I have lipped the drink
Of sunken ones too low to sink.
I find them cronies good enough,
Their souls still filled with finer stuff
Than all the solemn, righteous folk
Who never stoop to crack a joke.
Aye, the elect ones of the Lord
Quite frankly make me sick and bored.
If yonder sleek, round-bellied priest
Is on the list for Heaven's feast,
If Jesus died to help the rich
Relieve their endless money itch,
I don't need Feast or kingdom Come;
I'm for the Hobo and the Bum,

The soul "that's mildewed to the core,"
For brother thief and sister whore;
And if theirs is the road to hell,
I like the journey very well.

Clement Wood
(1888—   )

TO A FRIEND WHOSE WORK HAS COME TO NOTHING

Now ALL the truth is out,
Be secret and take defeat
From any brazen throat,
For how can you compete,
Being honor bred, with one
Who, were it proved he lies
Were neither shamed in his own
Nor in his neighbors' eyes?
Bred to a harder thing
Than Triumph, turn away
And like a laughing string
Whereon mad fingers play
Amid a place of stone,
Be secret and exult,
Because of all things known
That is most difficult.

William Butler Yeats
(1865—   )

A PORTRAIT

WHEN John's horse has worked
his days,
then John will loose him out
to graze.
When John is old and wasted—
well—
he'll work until he swaps
his hell.

Gremin Zorn
(1903—   )

INITIALED
AND ANONYMOUS

DIVES

You go to church clad in your Sunday best,
And pray for all the needy and oppressed;
And who the needy are, you best should know.
For you, and such as you, do keep them so.

You praise the Lord and rise refreshed from prayer,
To kick the hungry beggar down the stair;
And fondly think you'll enter Heaven's gate
Because you have put a penny in the plate.

Your daughters, too, to sing their (dress) maker's praise,
In church assemble on the Sabbath days;
While half the gaudy flimmery they wear
Would keep a poor man's family for a year.

You leave the house of God resigned and meek,
To rob and cheat your neighbors all the week;
You tell the poor of mansions in the sky,
And draw your rack-nets from the slum close by.

Though indigence and want are everywhere,
You will not see—your eyes are closed—in prayer.

Freedom, London—Cynicus

THE LAST WORD

THERE shall come a time like thunder;
  There shall dawn a red, red day,
When the worker meets the master,
  And the worker comes to say:

I have carried you for ages
  On my broad, submissive back;
I have fought in all your battles
  With the buzzards on my track.

I have given blood and muscle
  To your temple and your throne,
While your greedy eyes have glistened,
  And at last you asked for bone.

I have built your giant cities;
  I have dug your myriad mines,
I have made your mighty engines
  And your leagues of railroad lines.

I have toiled in sweat and sorrow
    While your priests have whispered "Wait!"
And your politicians howled,
    "Let us vote to change the State."

I have dressed in shabby garments;
    I have eaten fearful stuff;
And I simply come to tell you
    That I think I've had enough.

Yes, enough of sham and flubdub
    From your slimy parliaments,
And enough of Hell and Heaven
    From your cross-hung innocents.
        Solidarity—G. G. F.

TWO MEN ARE LEAVING THE PRISON TODAY

Two men are leaving the prison today—
    Two thousand watch them go.
Two men smile as they walk away—
Two thousand caged-in men must stay!

Two men are leaving the pit of hell;
    But they leave two thousand there,
Who rush like mad at the ring of a bell
And crawl off to sleep in a dirty cell
    And breathe in prison-filthy air.

Two men are leaving the prison walls
    With a five dollar bill to spend—
Two thousand men in the cells and halls
Turn back again to the bugle call,
    Like galley slaves to the end.

Two men shall see their homes again—
    Two thousand men shall not!
A few shall go who die self-slain,
A few shall break and go insane;
    But all, all of the men shall rot!
        One Big Union Monthly—C. O. G.

TO THE FOES OF FREEDOM

SEEK US with gifts, but the gifts shall not charm us,
Woo us with smiles, and the smiles shall be vain;
Crush in your madness, and yet it won't harm us,
How can the cause that is deathless be slain?

* * * * * *

Gather your hirelings and traitors around you,
Strengthen your ranks with liars and slaves,
The spirit of freedom shall rise to confound you,   .
The armies of progress shall trample your graves.

* * * * * *

Bribe you our weaklings, it shall not avail you;
Load us with chains, yet our souls shall be free;
Kill, yet the weapons of murder shall foil you,
And blood shall make perfect the harvest to be.

* * * * * *

You have mocked at our cries in the night of our sorrow,
You laughed at our dreams, but our dreams shall come true,
In our eyes is the light of a shining To-morrow,
And we leave, in our triumph, the darkness and you.

Labour Leader, London—M.

HAVE YOU PAID THE BOY?

You have paid the boy for the toil you bought;
He has had the price of his weary days
When he crushed the dreams that would come unsought,
When he heard the call of the woodland ways,
And the endless drone of the whirring wheels
Held the subtle surge of the blurred refrain
Of the mumbling bees in the grass that steals
Thru the meadow fence and along the lane.

And the eyes that strained as he did his task
Felt the weight of the dreams till mirage came
And the dust-grimed walls were a sullen mask
Of the far fair hills where the flowers flame,
And the cluttered floor was a thing to fade
To sweep for land with its velvet sod
And a laughing brook where a boy can wade
By the banks where the drowsy blossoms nod.

You have paid the boy. Have you paid for all?
You have paid him fair for the work he gave.
But the pictures hid by the gloomy wall,
And the coaxing hands that the tree tops wave,

And the country road where the wreathing dust
Marks the flying feet of a happy lad—
You have paid the boy—and your course is just;
Can you pay for the fun he never had?

For his ways today are the ways of men
And his face is set with the lines of age;
Tho' the years of his life are a little span,
Was he paid for this when he got his wage?
You have paid the boy—but he paid you more
Than the days of toil he gave to you,
For he wasted all the untold store
Of the wonder dreams that he never knew.

Chicago Tribune—W. D. N.

AS IT IS

A FARMER once was husking corn,
    And the stalk contained four ears;
He'd hoed it hard both night and morn;
    'Twas the best he'd had for years.

He husked the first ear, and he eyed it
    With joy and complacent content;
But the landlord was there and spied it
    And said: "I'll take that for RENT."

Then he husked the second in pleasure,
    And smiled in his simple glee;
"That's the INTEREST on the mortgage,"
    Said another; "give that to me."

The railroad director stood near him
    (Here the farmer began to whine);
"That's my PROFIT on transportation,
    And that ear is mine."

"All right," said the farmer bland—
    He was no great reflector—
As he plucked the fourth ear, from his hand
    It was snatched by the TAX COLLECTOR.

Then he shouldered his share—to a neighbor
    Said he: "I'll take a walk—
Since me and my wife for our labor,
    B'gosh!—we've got the STALK."

Solidarity—P. 5 P.

TO A FACTORY WHISTLE

O GRIM-VOICED Demon, soulless Monster, why
Must I your summons heed, nor fail to come
When you would call me back to toil, while some
Loiter along the way? Is your hoarse cry
For me alone? May these stand idly by,
Yet take the loaf and leave me but the crumb?
Surely, justice is dead, or else turned dumb:
Why does my brother loiter and not I?
Or why, with bended back and pain-wracked frame,
Must I, for these long, weary hours each day,
Stifle both sense and soul? Is it that he
May live and labor not? Justice? A name!
I toil that both may live and he may play.
Why are these things so? Grim Monster, answer me!

Industrial Pioneer—S. P.

A SONG OF BROTHERHOOD

I DREAMED of a broad brotherhood and the high march hand in hand;
I dreamed of a sweet sisterhood, Love reigning o'er the land.
I woke before the dawning and cast my eyes around,
And there, where Hell was yawning, lay Love upon the ground.

Fell fiends were clustered round her, black Hate and Passion red,
Green-eyed Suspicion bound her, and Mammon held her head;
Upon her heart was pressing pale Tyranny's cold hand;
With arms aloft in blessing old Faiths and Customs stand.

Hope leaves her to Despair, who stands with drooping eyes;
Eld shakes his snowy hair, Death reaches for the prize;
When o'er the mountain height is shot a ruddy glow,
And the fierce Lord of Light is fastly striking at the foe.

They shake, they sway and shiver, they scatter and they flee!
While like a mighty river flow forward all the free;
Their scarlet flag floats higher, as with the birds they sing,
Love shall be our Messiah, and Freedom be our King.

Labour Leader, London—B. S.

ARISE!

Ho! TILLERS of the rugged soil!
Ho! toilers for your bread!
Why should you, LANDLESS, toil and starve
While landlord drones are fed?

Why should this fair and fruitful earth—
The right of every man—
Be wrenched from you, who toil to feed
A bloated robber clan?
Awake! ye men of ceaseless toil—
The land belongs to you;
'Tis God's free gift to each and all—
Then rise and claim your due!
God never made you for machines,
Nor merchandise, nor brutes,
To toil and starve, while bloated drones
Are feasting on your fruits.
Then up! ye plundered, landless slaves!
Arise, be freemen all,
And claim your birthright to the air,
The sun-light and the soil!
And then will bounty crown your toils,
The landless hosts be free,
And earth's glad millions join the songs
Of Freedom's Jubilee.

Pleasure Boat (1847)—*Anonymous*

FRANCISCO FERRER *

HE STROVE to spread the light in darkened Spain,
To teach the child to love and seek the Truth,
To liberate the unfolding mind of Youth,
That Church and State by crafty lies enchain.
Lest their dominion o'er the toiler wane,
Lest Tyranny be foiled by Spirits freed,
The vile oppressors planned this bloody deed—
And by their licensed murderers he was slain.

Another victim of the tyrant's laws;
Another crime by soldier, priest and king;
Another blow at human liberty!
Comrades in Spain, in Freedom's deathless cause!
From every land your brother's protest rings:
What shall YOUR answer to this outrage be?

Freedom, London—Anonymous

*Francisco Ferrer, murdered October 13, 1909, was the first great forerunner of libertarian education in Spain. His pioneer activity the State and Church could only put an end to by killing the man, in the vain hope of likewise killing his ideas.

—M. G.

HOLD THE FORT*

WE MEET today in Freedom's cause
    And raise our voices high;
We'll join our hands in union strong,
    To battle or to die.

Chorus:
    Hold the fort for we are coming—
    Union men, be strong   .
    Side by side we battle onward,
    Victory will come.

Look my Comrades, see the union
    Banners waving high.
Reinforcements now appearing,
    Victory is nigh.

See our numbers still increasing;
    Hear the bugles blow.
By our union we shall triumph
    Over every foe.

Fierce and long the battle rages,
    But we will not fear,
Help will come whene'er it's needed,
    Cheer, my Comrades, cheer.

*English Transport Workers' Strike Song.

HUNGER

I COME among the peoples like a shadow.
I sit down by each man's side.

None sees me, but they look on one another.
And know that I am there.

My silence is like the silence of the tide
That buries the playground of children;

Like the deepening frost in the slow night,
When birds are dead in the morning.

Armies trample, invade, destroy,
With guns roaring from earth and air.

I am more terrible than armies,
I am more feared than a cannon.

Kings and chancellors give commands;
I give no command to any;

But I am listened to more than kings,
And more than passionate orators.

I unswear words, and undo deeds,
Naked things know me.   .
I am Hunger.   .

Pearson's Magazine—Anonymous

LABOR *

WE HAVE fed you all for a thousand years,
   And you hail us still unfed,
Tho' there's never a dollar of all your wealth
   But marks the workers dead.
We have yielded the best to give you rest,
   And you lie on crimson wool;
For if blood be the price of all your wealth
   Good God, we have paid in full!

There's never a mine blown skyward now
   But we're buried alive for you;
There's never a wreck drifts shoreward now
   But we are its ghastly crew;
If blood be the price of your cursed wealth
   Good God, we have paid it in full!
Go, reckon our dead by the forges red,
   And the factories where we spin.

We have fed you all for a thousand years,
   For that was our doom, you know,
From the days that you chained us in your fields
   To the strike of a week ago.
You ha' eaten our lives and our babies and wives,
   And we're told it's your legal share:
But if blood be the price of your lawful wealth,
   Good God, we ha' bought it fair!

Anonymous

*A parody upon Rudyard Kipling's poem in praise of present society.—M.G.

TRANSLATIONS

Armenian

THUS SPAKE MAN

DEEP sunk in thought I wandered in a city dead—by fire,
Where walls, like blackened skeletons, in ruin rose on high.
Enshrouded by the shadow of Destruction all things seemed,
Smothered beneath the sun that shone within a tomb-like sky.

Destruction with its breath of flame in triumph boasted high:
"Thus in one day, one moment, I destroy the pride and grace
Of works that Man has taken years to build upon the earth;
And low he lies before me when I show him my stern face!"

But Man, of mighty will power, when he heard this haughty boast,
Raised up his sorrow-laden head, and like a giant cried:
"Destruction, you are longing for my downfall and defeat,
But you are all in error, you are blinded by your pride!

"Creating, still creating, I shall combat you for aye.
You may destroy, but I shall build for evermore with joy,
Till Godhood shall awake in me, and when that day shall dawn
Then even grim Destruction itself I shall destroy!"

Arshag D. Mahdesian

Belgian

THE SONG OF THE FORGES

O FRENZIED forges with your noise and blaring,
　　Red, reeking fires that comb dishevelled skies,
Your hollow rumbling is like stifled swearing,
　　And the grassed earth about you burns and dies.

What blind man, mad man, intent on gain and plunder,
　　Thinks he is matter's master, in your maw
Lugubriously rolls a hollow thunder
　　That says: We forge, and forge, without a flaw.

The chains from which thou hast not wit to save thee,
　　O foolish man! we rivet link by link
The shackles which forever shall enslave thee.
　　Sweat, pant, and fill the furnace to the brink.

Throw in the coal, and pour the crackling casting
　　Through the cut sand, beat, crush the pig to shape,
Temper the sword, sheet, deck, and rig with masting
　　The tyrant ships that sweep the sea with grape.

303

Crowd the machines, the hamlet and the haven,
  To prison thee more deep than dungeons hold
In durance making thee a pauper craven . . .
  Stupid humanity! we weld and weld

With the vile toil disease beyond reclaiming,
  And imbecility, and discontent,
Murder, and hate that sets the mansion flaming,
  Bloody revolt and heavy punishment.

We forge the fate of every generation;
  We crush the father and the child as well,
Spitting at heavens that shake with consternation
  The soot and coal of our relentless hell.

See! To the stainless blue of skies upcurling
  Our towering chimneys belch polluted breath,
Above the waste and ravaged lands unfurling
  Their sable flags of slavery and death.

Ivan Gilkin
(1858—1924)

BURNING GLASS

ANCIENT hours I behold
  Under regrets ripening,
  And fairer flora spring
From their secret's azure mould.

Desires blow through my spirit.
  O glass upon my desires!
  And the withered grass my soul fires,
When breathing memories stir it.

It grows with my thoughts for mould,
  And in the blue fleeing fast
  I see the grief of the past
Their flower-petals unfold.

My soul through memories gropes
  Feels the touch of their
  Curtaining dead mohair;
And greens with other hopes.

Maurice Maeterlinck
(1862—   )

From *Contemporary Belgian Poetry, by Jethro Bithell*

From THE BUTCHER'S STALL*

HARD by the docks, soon as the shadows fall
The dizzy mansion-fronts that soar aloft,
When eyes of lamps are burning soft,
The shy, dark quarter lights again its old
Allurement of red vice and gold.

Women, blocks of heaped, blown meat,
Stand on low thresholds down the narrow street,
Calling to every man that passes;
Behind them, at the end of corridors,
Shine fires, a curtain stirs
And gives a glimpse of masses
Of mad and naked flesh in looking-glasses.
Hard by the docks.
The street upon the left is ended by
A tangle of high masts and shrouds that blocks
A sheet of sky;
Upon the right a net of grovelling alleys
Falls from the town—and here the black crowd rallies
And reels to rotten revelry.

It is the flabby, fulsome butcher's stall of luxury,
Time out of mind erected on the frontiers
Of the city and the sea.

Far-sailing melancholy mariners
Who, wet with spray, through grey mists peer,
Cradled among the rigging cabin-boys, and they who steer
Hallucinated by the blue eyes of the vast sea-spaces,
All dream of it, evoke it when the evening falls;
Their raw desire to madness galls;
The wind's soft kisses hover on their faces;
The wave awakens rolling images of soft embraces;
And their two arms implore
Stretched in a frantic cry towards the shore.

And they of offices and shops, the city tribes,
Merchants precise, keen reckoners, haggard scribes,
Who sell their brains for hire, and tame their brows,
When the keys of desks are hanging on the wall,
Feel the same galling rut at even-fall,
And run like hunted dogs to the carouse.

*From *The Octopus Cities*

Out of the depths of dusk come their dark flocks,
And in their hearts debauch so rudely shocks
Their ingrained greed and old accustomed care,
That they are racked and ruined by despair.

It is the flabby, fulsome butcher's stall of luxury,
Time out of mind erected on the frontiers
Of the city and the sea.

Come from what far sea-isles or pestilent parts?
Come from what feverish or methodic marts?
Their eyes are filled with bitter, cunning hate,
There fight their instincts that they cannot sate;
Around red females who befool them, they
Herd frenzied till the dawn of sober day.
The panelling is fiery with lewd art;
Out of the wall nitescent knick-knacks dart;
Fat Bacchus and leaping satyrs in
Wan mirrors freeze an unremitting grin.

And women with spent loins and sleeping croups
Are piled on sofas and arm-chairs in groups,
With sodden flesh grown vague, and black and blue
With the first trampling of the evening's crew.
One of them slides a gold coin in her stocking;
Others by bacchanalia worn out,
Feeling old age, and, sniffing them, Death's snout,
Stare with wide-open eyes, torches extinct,
And smooth their legs with hands together linked.

It is the flabby, fulsome butcher's stall of luxury,
Wherein Crime plants his knives that bleed,
Where lightning madness stains
Foreheads with rotting pains,
Time out of mind erected on frontiers that feed
The city and the sea.

Èmile Verhaeren
(1855—1916)

From *Contemporary Belgian Poetry, by Jethro Bithell*

Chinese

BATTLE HYMN OF THE CHINESE REVOLUTION (1912)

FREEDOM, one of the greatest blessings of Heaven,
United in Peace, thou wilt work on this earth ten thousand wonderful new things.

Grave as a spirit, great as a giant rising to the very skies,
With the clouds for a chariot and the wind for a steed,
Come, come to reign over the earth!

For the sake of the black hell of our slavery,
Come, enlighten us with a ray of the sun! . . .

In this century we are working to open a new age.
In this century, with one voice, all virile men
Are calling for a new making of heaven and earth.

Hin-Yun, our ancestor, guide us!
Spirit of Freedom, come and protect us!

Anonymous

French

THE MARSEILLAISE

Ye sons of toil, awake to glory!
  Hark, hark! what myriads bid you rise!
Your children, wives and grandsires hoary:
  Behold their tears and hear their cries.
Shall hateful tyrants, mischief breeding,
  With hireling hosts, a ruffian band,—
  Affright and desolate the land,
While peace and liberty lie bleeding?

Chorus:

  To arms, to arms, ye brave!
  Th' avenging sword unsheathe!
  March on, march on,
  All hearts resolved
  On Victory or Death!

With luxury and pride surrounded,
  The vile, insatiate despots dare,
Their thirst for gold and power unbounded,
  To mete and vend the light and air;
Like beasts of burden would they load us,
  Like gods would bid their slaves adore;
But Man is Man, and who is more?
  Then shall they longer lash and goad us?

Chorus:

Oh, Liberty! can man resign thee,
  Once having felt thy generous flame!

Can dungeons' bolts and bars confine thee!
Or whips thy noble spirit tame?
Too long the world has wept, bewailing
That Falsehood's dagger tyrants wield;
But Freedom is our sword and shield
And all their arts are unavailing.

Chorus:

Claude Joseph Rouget de Lisle
(1760—1836)

English version *by Charles H. Kerr*

INSCRIPTION FOR A CITY'S GATE OF WARRIORS

FEAR not the shadow! Open, lofty gate,
Thy door of bronze, thy door of iron straight.
Deep in a well men have cast down the key,
Accursèd thou if terror closes thee;
Sever with keen and double-edgèd blade
Hands that have shut thee and that have betrayed.
For under thy dark vault rank forth the feet
Of marching men who never saw retreat,
And in their midst, poised nobly and old,
Went naked Victory with wings of gold,
And with calm wave of sword their banners led.
Upon their lips her ardent kisses bled,
And at their crimson mouths the trumpets rang
With murmurs of fierce bees and copper clang!
Wild swarms of war, from hives of armor go,
Pluck from ripe flesh the flowers of death that glow,
And if ye to these native walls return,
See that upon thy marble threshold burn,
When beneath Victory's wings has passed your tread,
Stains of clear blood from sandals steeped in red.

Henri de Règnier
(1864—   )

English version *by Ludwig Lewisohn*

STRIKE!

WHOE'ER you are who suffer, who endure,
You whom I love, whom I have sought to cure,
Have pitied, warned, defended many a time—
You who struck root in evil, sown by crime,
Brothers of mine, down-trodden, outcast, lost—
Spurn you the man who profits by your cost!
Follow the soaring, not the halting sprite;

Mount upwards to the future, to the light!
No longer let yourselves be swayed; resist;
Ay, though he call him by what name he lists,
Resist the man, whoever he may be,
Who counsels you against humanity.
Strike! against famine, against miseries;
Oh that you knew how near your triumph is!

Victor Hugo
(1802—1885)

English version *by Sir George Young*

ONE FLAG

. So BE it! Our globe is but a hell
Of torments, crimes and sins abhorred,
Where Force by dint of fire and sword
Subdues his victims all too well. . . .

A god whom patriots adore,
I scorn thee, for in thee I see
The symbol of barbarity;
Therefore I hate thee, god of war.

As mothers curse thee so curse I—
Mothers whose sons were racked with pain—
Whose mutilated bodies slain
Are heaped in vain beneath the sky.

With pick and hammer let us rise
And break this idol's shape of stone
Breathing forth slaughter from its throne
Hid in the inmost shrine of lies.

Down with the temple that from above
Set up a blood-bespattered rag,
And let us with a world-wide flag
Find freedom in the work of love!

Theodore Jean

English version *by Ernest Crosby*

THE INTERNATIONAL

ARISE, ye pris'ners of starvation!
Arise, ye wretched of the earth,
For Justice thunders condemnation,
A better world's in birth.

No more tradition's chain shall bind us.
　Arise, ye slaves; No more in thrall!
The earth shall rise on new foundations,
　We have been naught, we shall be all.

Refrain:
'Tis the final conflict,
　Let each stand in his place,
The International Party
　Shall be the human race.

We want no condescending saviours,
　To rule us from a judgment hall;
We workers ask not for their favors,
　Let us consult for all.
To make the thief disgorge his booty
　To free the spirit from its cell,
We must ourselves decide our duty,
　We must decide and do it well.

The law oppresses us and tricks us.
　Taxation drains the victim's blood;
The rich are free from obligations,
　The laws the poor delude.
Too long we've languished in subjection,
　Equality has other laws:
"No rights," says she, "without their duties,
　No claim on equals without cause."

Behold them seated in their glory,
　The kings of mine and rail and soil!
What have you read in all their story,
　But how they plundered toil?
Fruits of the people's toil are buried
　In the strong coffers of a few;
In voting for their restitution,
　The men will only ask their due.

Toilers from shops and fields united,
　The party we of all who work;
The earth belongs to us, the people,
　No room here for the shirk!
How many on our flesh have fattened!
　But if the noisome birds of prey
Shall vanish from the sky some morning,
　The blessed sunlight still will stay.

Eugene Potter

English version *by Charles H. Kerr*

German

THE LOCOMOTIVE

How dear you are to me,
Black giant racers, throbbing hearts of steel
That rhythmically Earth vibrates to feel!
I shout in ecstasy,
For all your deep unrest flows through my blood
When in the mist and night wind I have stood
Swung by your speed,
A roaring axle that unceasing turns,
A molten morsel of a world that burns,
A part of you, indeed—And we have flown
In your vertiginous rush to the unknown,
On! like the planets seven.
I am flesh and blood, and steel and fire too,
And plumed with smoke-wreaths gold and white and blue,
Banners of dreams flung in the face of Heaven.

Max Barthel
(1893—   )

English version *by F. W. Stella Brown*

BLACKSMITH PAIN

PAIN is a blacksmith,
Hard is his hammer;
With flying flames
His hearth is hot;
A straining storm
Of forces ferocious
Blows his bellows.
He hammers hearts
And tinkers them,
With blows tremendous,
Till hard they hold.—
Well, well forges Pain.—
No storm destroys,
No frost consumes,
No rust corrodes,
What pain has forged.

Otto Julius Bierbaum
(1865-1910)

English version *by Jethro Bithell*

THE WORKINGMAN

WE HAVE a bed, we have a child,
my wife!
We have work to do, you and I too,
we have wind and rain and a sun that's mild,
and all that we lack is a little thing,
to be as free as the birds of the wing—
Just time.

When we go through the fields on a Sabbath day,
my child,
and over the meadows everywhere
we see the swallows, gleaming and gay,
we can look as bright as birds of the air,
it is not raiment for which we pray:
Just time.
Just time! we scent stormwinds, wrathful and wild,
we folk.
Only a small eternity;
all that we lack, my wife, my child,
is what we make blossom and bear and be,
to feel as bold as the birds in the tree—
Just time!

Richard Dehmel
(1863—   )

English version *by Babette Deutsch and Avrahm Yarmolinsky*

REVOLUTION

AND tho' ye caught your noble prey within your hangman's sordid
thrall,
And tho' your captive was led forth beneath your city's rampart wall;
And tho' the grass lies o'er her green, where at the morning's early red
The peasant girl brings funeral wreaths—I tell you still, she is not
dead!

And tho' from off the lofty brow ye cut the ringlets flowing long,
And tho' ye've mated her amid the thieves' and murderers' hideous
throng,
And tho' ye gave her felon fare—bade felon garb her livery be,
And tho' ye set the hokum-task—I tell you, she still is free!

And tho' compelled to banishment, ye hunt her down thru endless
lands,
And tho' she seeks a foreign hearth, and silent 'mid its ashes stands;

And tho' she bathes her wounded feet where foreign streams seek
    foreign seas,
Yet—yet—she never more will hang her harp on 'Babel's willow trees.

Ah, no! she strikes it very strong, and bids their loud defiance swell,
And as she mocked your scaffold erst, she mocks your banishment as
    well.
She sings a song that starts you up astounded from your slumberous
    seats,
Until your heart—your craven heart—your traitor heart—with terror
    beats!

No song of plaint, no song of sighs for those who perished unsubdued.
Nor yet a song of irony at wrong's fantastic interlude—
The beggar's opera that ye try to drag out thru its lingering scenes,
Tho' moth-eaten the purple be that decks your tinsel kings and queens.

Oh, no! the song those waters hear is not of sorrow, nor dismay—
'Tis triumph song—victorious song—the pæans of the future's day—
The future—distant now no more—her prophet voice is sounding free.
As well at once your Godhead spake: I was, I am, and I will be!

Will be—and lead the nation off to the last of all your hosts to meet,
And on your necks, your heads, your crowns, I'll plant my strong,
    resistless feet!
Avenger, Liberator, Judge—red battles on my pathway hurled,
I stretch forth my almighty arm, till it revivifies the world.

Ye see me only in your cells; ye see me only in the grave;
Ye see me only wandering lone, beside the exile's sullen wave—
Ye fools! Do I not live where ye have tried to pierce in vain?
Rests not a nook for me to dwell in every heart and every brain?

In every brow that boldly thinks, erect with manhood's honest pride—
Does not each bosom shelter me that beats, with honor's generous tide—
Not every workshop, brooding woe—not every heart that harbors
    grief?
Ha! Am I not the Breath of Life, that pants the struggles for relief?

'Tis therefore I will be—and lead the people yet your hosts to meet,
And on your necks, your heads, your crowns, will plant my strong,
    resistless feet!
It is no boast—it is no threat—thus history's iron law decrees—
The day grows hot, O Babylon! 'Tis cool beneath the willow trees!

Ferdinand Freiligrath
(1810—1876)

English version *by Ernest Jones*

BEGIN—ANEW*

Thou hast destroyed it,
The beautiful world,
With powerful fist.
It sinks, it sunders!
A demigod had shivered it.
We carry the ruins
Over into the Naught,
And wail
Over the lost beauty.
Mighty (one)
Of the sons of Earth,
More glorious
Build it again;
In thy bosom build it up!
New life-carrier,
Begin
With sense undimmed
And may new songs
Sound over it!

Johann Wolfgang von Goethe
(1749—1832)

*From *Faust*

English version *by Charles M. Bakewell*

THE WEAVERS

Their eyelids are drooping, no tears lie beneath;
They stand at the loom, and grind their teeth;
"We are weaving a shroud for the double dead,
And a threefold curse in its every thread—
   We are weaving, still weaving.

"A curse to the Godhead to whom we have bowed,
In our cold and hunger, we weave in the shroud;
For in vain have we hoped and in vain have we prayed;
He has mocked us and scoffed at us, sold and betrayed—
   We are weaving, still weaving.

"A curse for the king of the wealthy and proud,
Who has for us no pity, we weave in the shroud;
Who takes our last penny to swell out his purse,
While we die the death of a dog—yea, a curse—
   We are weaving, still weaving.

"A curse for our country, whose cowardly crowd
Hold her shame in high honor, we weave in the shroud;
Whose blossoms are blighted and slain in the germ,
Whose filth and corruption engender the worm—
    We are weaving, still weaving.

"To and fro flies our shuttle—no pause in its flight—
'Tis a shroud we are weaving by day and by night;
We are weaving a shroud for the worse than dead,
And a threefold curse in its every thread—
    We are weaving, still weaving."

Heinrich Heine
(1799—1856)

English version *by J. L. Joynes*

THE COMRADE'S SONG

Work and pray, so you are told,
Briefly pray, for time means gold.
Poverty grins over your bed—
Briefly pray, for time means bread.

And you dig and plow and mow,
And you saw and drill and sow,
And you hammer and you spin—
What do you, O workers, win?

At the loom you toil and weave,
For their ore the rock you cleave,
And the horn of plenty still
To its very brim you fill.

Where tho, is prepared your meal?
Where do you a warm heart feel?
Where's for you a festive garb?
Where for you a sword so sharp?

Everything by you is wrought,
But of all for you there's naught!
And of all things but alone
Is the chain you forge your own—

Chain that round your body clings,
That has bent your spirit wings,
That enthralls your children, too—
That is the reward for you.

Gems, you raise from darkest mine,
Are but made for rogues to shine;
Cloth you weave, but curse and fear
Bears for you in soldiers' gear.

Houses that your hands erect
Have no roof you to protect.
Those whom you with all provide
Tread on you in haughty pride.

Human bees, did nature true
Give but honey unto you?
See the drones about you soar!
Have you lost the sting you bore?

Waken, workers, to your right!
Learn at last to know your might!
All the wheels will cease to go
If your strong arm wants it so.

Pale will your oppressors turn
When your burden you will spurn,
When aside the plough you lay,
When "It is enough" you say.

Break the yoke in twain!
Break the dread of slavery's pain!
Break the pain of slavery's dread!
Bread means freedom, freedom bread!

George Herwegh
(1817—1875)

CHALLENGE TO STRIKE

LET the hammers rest.
Let the wheels stop.
Let the fires burn down.
Put out the light.
Disturb the idler's comfort.
Shut off the supplies of their larders.
Harvest which doesn't nourish you, may rot.
Coal, which doesn't warm you, may vanish underground.
Chimney that doesn't smoke for you, may collapse.
Look here.
The burgeoisie builds upon your labor's ground.
His house is rich. His bed is soft.
By your labor's favor he feeds his belly.

By your labor's favor his wife dresses.
Industrious, brought up to master you,
By your labor's favor.
And you? Prolets?—Labor-creatures?
And your hired barracks? Hunger towers?
And your children?—Misery-brats?
Curse upon every slag for burgeoisie-pack.
Curse upon every step into their slavery.
Curse upon their thanks. Curse upon their traitor's wages.
Yours is the Earth.
Out of the workshops!
On the street!

Oskar Kanehl
(1888—   )

English version *by Paul Acel*

IN A LARGE CITY

To AND FRO in the great sea of the city,
   Drifts this one and that one, hither and thither—
One glance in passing, and past and gone:
   The organ-grinder plays his song!

Drops that fall into the great sea of the void,
   This one and that one, hither and thither—
One glance at a hearse, and past and gone:
   The organ-grinder plays his song!

Swims a funeral procession in the sea of the city,
   This one and that one, hither and thither—
One glance at my coffin, and past and gone:
   The organ-grinder plays his song!

Detlev von Liliencron
(1844—1909)

English version *by Sasha Best*

WORLD CITIZENSHIP

YEA, greater is the heart, the soul is freer,
   The wind is nobler and the world profounder,
That, girt by ruffian jubilee's frippery gear,
   Stands forth, the highest freedom's bold expounder!

Love the whole earth! Love not a single land
   Because by chance "thy country" it is called!
A land is never free. Dost kiss the hand
   Which into fetters thrust thee, and enthralled?

Oh! break the bonds of narrowness and night!
A scoundrel he that spake: This land for me!
Curse him that scanted thee and me the right
Men and citizens of the world to be!

John Henry Mackay

English version *by H. L. Koopman*

AMONG ENEMIES

THERE the gallows, rope and hooks;
And the hangman's beard is red.
People round and poisoned looks—
Nothing new and nothing dread!

Know it well, from fifty sources,
Laughing in your face I cry:
Would you hang me? Save your forces!
Why kill me who cannot die?

Beggars ye! who hate the tougher
Man who holds the envied lot.
True I suffer, true I suffer—
As to you—ye rot, ye rot!

I am breath, dew, all resources,
After fifty hangings; why!
Would you hang me? Save your forces!
Why kill me who cannot die?

Friedrich Nietzsche
(1844—1900)

HOPE

WE SPEAK with the lip, and we dream in the soul,
Of some better and fairer day;
And our days, the meanwhile, to that golden goal
Are gliding and sliding away.
Now the world becomes old, now it is young,
But *"The Better"* is ever the word on the tongue.

And it is not a dream of a fancy proud,
With a fool for its dull begetter;
There's a voice at the heart that proclaims aloud—
"We are born for a something Better!"
And that Voice of the Heart, oh, ye may believe,
Will never the Hope of the Soul deceive!

Johann Christoph Friedrich Von Schiller
(1759—1805)

English version *by Lord Edward Lyton*

FROM THE IMPRISONED

NIGHTS of mine, you good sisters of the imprisoned,
The stillness becomes filled with your trembling sounds.
Lying on the hard bench I listen attentively—
I hear your heart-throbs, brothers, you
From here and there . . . from there and here . . .
Imprisoned in the jails of all continents,
In Atlanta and in Memphis, in Calumet and Barcelona, in Calcutta—
     and in Mayland—
You, brothers, we in the struggle and rebellion, in strikes and revolts—
Accept my greeting, you brothers, we.

They wish to forbid you the world and the world is your wishing!

And to you my greeting:
You brothers in the prisons of Africa and Asia,
In the jails of Australia:
You dark, yellow, brown protectors of your own piece of land,
That is devoured and oppressed by Europe's tender fist.
To you my greeting, you brothers in the jails,
In the prisons of the whole world.
To you,
Who in your homes' dire need brought you up,
Whom in your own house the longing has broken down,
And who from sleep have drawn forgetfulness—
You, who were made thieves, robbers, sluggers, murderers
Made—made!
You, who are brothers of mine by the same fate—accept my greeting.

I listen and I think:
Who could say about himself that he isn't imprisoned—
Though no jail has forestalled his heaven,
And no building has robbed him of earth?
And I hear your heart-throbs, brother, you
From here and there . . . from there and here . . .

Oh, would that I could hear
With the eternal great love of a dreamed-about God—
The heart I would hear—
The united great heart
Of both human sexes,
Of all stars, all animals,
Of fields, flowers and stones—
The throbbing of the great heart
Of everything, everything
That lives.

Ernest Toller
(1895—   )

English version *by Marcus Graham*

PEOPLE—WHOSE FAULT?

IF THEY have sought to smite you low,
Yourselves have crouched before the blow;
Befooled, to the commands of knaves
Yourselves have turned the ears of slaves.

Have they despoiled you at their will?
You bowed your heads, submissive still,
While they, for plenty, bitterest need—
For freedom, slavery decreed.

Their lordship, with your slavery bent,
Is but their right, if you consent;
Have but the will, then you shall see
You own the welfare of the free!

Anonymous

Greek

CAPTIVE GOOD ATTENDING CAPTAIN ILL

DOTH some one say that there be gods above?
There are not; no, there are not. Let no fool,
By the old false fable, thus deceive you.
Look at the facts themselves, yielding my words
No undue credence; for I say that kings
Kill, rob, break oaths, lay cities waste by fraud,
And doing thus are happier than those
Who live calm, pious lives day after day.
How many little States that serve the gods
Are subject to the godless but more strong,
Made slaves by might of a superior army!

Euripides
(406—480 B.C.)

English version *by John Addington Symonds*

Hungarian

THE SONG OF THE STREET

'TIS but a perfumed myth, the parlor song;
Wild is the street song, wild and new and strong.
The old song is of myth and victory;
The new is bloody, and rings mournfully.
In parlors all is false, e'en to the tear;
Even the street's mad laughter is sincere.
What in the parlor is deemed holiest

Is in the street an outworn tune, a jest.
Affected weeping, crafty laughter low—
The street is bold in joyance and in woe.
The parlor song is morbid, sickly, pale—
The street displays its heart, and does not quail.
There for the old gods they shed tears of woe;
Here the sun set upon them long ago.
There skilful, splendid chorals greet the ear;
Simple but stormy songs are sounding here.
The myth tomorrow may to heaven have flown;
The street song to an earthquake will have grown!

Andrew Ady

English version *by Alice Stone Blackwell*

WAR AND PEACE

PEACE, peace be unto all the world,
But ne'er by tyrants' will!
Only from Freedom's holy hands
Let peace the broad earth fill.

If universal peace on earth
In this wise there may be,
Then let us cast our arms away,
And sink them in the sea.

But, if not so, arms, arms till death,
A never-ending fray!
Yes, even if the war shall last
Until the Judgment Day!

Alexander Petöfi

English version *by Alice Stone Blackwell*

Indian

DAWN

CHILDREN, my children, the daylight is breaking,
The cymbals of moon sound the hour of your waking.
The long night is o'er, and our labor is ended.
Fair blow the fields that we tilled and we tended.
Weak were our hands, but our service was tender,
In darkness we dreamed of the dawn of yon splendor;
In silence we strove for the joy of the morrow,
And watered the seeds from the wells of our sorrow.
We toiled to enrich the glad hour of your waking,
Our vigil is done,—lo, the daylight is breaking.

Serajinni Naidu
(1879—   )

NATIONALISM

THE sun of the century sets amidst the blood-red clouds of the
    West and the whirlwind of hatred.
The naked passion of self-love of Nations, in its drunken delirium
    of greed, is dancing to the clash of steel and the
    howling verses of vengeance.
The hungry self of the Nation shall burst in a violence of fury
    from its own shameless feeding.
For it has made the world its food,
And licking it, crunching it, and swallowing it in big morsels,
It swells and swells
Till in the midst of its unholy feast descends the sudden shaft
    of heaven piercing its heart of grossness.
The crimson glow of light on the horizon is not the light of the
    dawn of peace, my Motherland.
It is the glimmer of the funeral pyre burning to ashes the
    vast flash—the self-love of the Nation—dead under
    its own excess.
The morning waits behind the patient lark of the East,
Meek and silent.

Rabindranath Tagore
(1861—   )

Italian

THE PHILOSOPHIC FLIGHT

Now THAT these wings to speed my wish ascend,
    The more I feel vast air beneath my feet,
    The more toward boundless air on pinions fleet,
    Spurning the earth, soaring the heaven, I tend:
Nor makes them stoop their flight the direful end
    Of Dædal's son; but upward still they beat.
    What life the while with this death could compete.
    If death to earth at last I must descend?
My own heart's voice in the void air I hear.
    Where wilt thou bear me, O rash man! Recall
    Thy daring will! This boldness waits on fear!
Dread not, I answer, that tremendous fall:
    Strike through the clouds, and smile when death is near,
    If death so glorious be our doom at all!

Giordano Bruno
(1548—1600)

English version *by John Addington Symonds*

FROM THE BROTHELS*

WE CANNOT tell if this life be beautiful or sad.
Yesterday my fate brought me abundant delight and champagne—
To-morrow you perhaps will rot with infernal disease.
By day we hold ourselves pure like the pupils of some sacred convent;
We embroider in patterns of lilies, and we write to our parents at
    home.
To one who comes when we may love we bestow the love of calm
    virgins.
By night we walk naked in the midst among men;
But we wear our veils of lace.
We cannot tell why they should scorn us, those who dwell outside.
But there still are some poets who honor us now, as before,
And declare we are priestesses still of the temple and vestals of Time.
They, we believe, would hang bells on our houses
Of gold and of silver that should peal through the air, giving voice
    forever, forever at large across the whole city.

Paolo Buzzi
(1878—   )

*From *Songs of the Imprisoned*
English version *by Harold Monro*

FREEDOM'S DEAD

IN AUTUMN sad, the priest chants to the dead—
The dead below the ground, their saints in heaven.
The bells are mute, and draperies, bright today,
Tomorrow dark, are to the altar given.

We, with one heart and with one sacred rite,
Unto thy saints, thy dead, O Liberty!
Now quaff the red wine of the funeral feast,
As did the Greeks in ancient days gone by.

Alas! when drinking to the glorious dead,
The youth of Greece, in happy days long flown,
Recalled the monarchs slain, the conquered foes,
And thou in Athens then didst reign alone.

O'er grass-grown trenches where our dead are laid,
The shepherd brings his flock to browse at morn;
Your blood, O heroes, feeds red roses now,
The wanton conqueror's pillows to adorn!

Above the graves the white crowd gazing stands—
Stands waiting, from the mountains to the sea.
Upon the day of vengeance they will rest,
The day of justice and of liberty!

Giosué Carducci
(1836—1907)

English version *by Alice Stone Blackwell*

Japanese

THE BEGGAR'S COMPLAINT

THE heaven and earth they call so great,
    For me are very small;
The sun and moon they call so bright,
    For me ne'er shine at all.

Are all men sad, or only I?
    And what have I obtained—
What good the gift of mortal life,
    That prize so rarely gained—

If naught my chilly back protects
    But one thin grass-cloth coat,
In tatters hanging like the weeds
    That on the billows float?

If here in smoke-stained, darksome hut,
    Upon the bare cold ground,
I make my wretched bed of straw,
    And hear the mournful sound—

Hear how mine aged parents groan,
    And wife and children cry,
Father and mother, children, wife,
    Huddling in misery—

If in the rice-pan, nigh forgot,
    The spider hangs its nest,
And from the hearth no smoke goes up
    Where all is so unblest?

Shame and despair are mine from day to day,
But, being no bird, I cannot fly away.

                    —Anonymous

Ancient Japanese Classic

Jewish

REVOLUTION

I COME like a comet ablaze, like the sun when the dawn is awaking.
I come like tumultuous tempest, when thunder and lightning are
    breaking;
I come like the lava that rushes from the mighty volcanoes in motion;

I come like the storm from the north that arouses and angers the
ocean.

I come because tyrants have put up their thrones in place of the
nations;
I come because rulers are foddering peace with their war preparations;
I come because ties that bound people together are now disconnected;
I come because fools think that progress will stay in the bounds they
erected.

I come because out in the wastes made by rulers I arose to existence;
I come because despots have roused me to anger and armed resistance;
I come because life is too real to be murdered by foolish endeavor;
I come because freedom can nowhere be chained and enshackled
forever.

I led the downtrodden and tyrannized peoples of past generations;
I helped them to throw off enslavement, and gain their complete
liberations;
I marched with the spirit of progress, and aided its every endeavor;
And I shall march on with the peoples, until I shall free them forever.

You money-bag saints, you crowned cut-throats, anointed with strife
and contentions;
I come to destroy you, your laws, and your lies and your foolish
conventions;
Your hearts that are thirsting for blood, I shall pierce till the life in
them ceases;
Your crown and your sceptres, your little gold toys I shall break into
pieces.

And pluck off your purples and tear them to rags, and then hurl to
damnation;
The baubles which people bow down to like fools with their loud
jubilation;
The glittering pride of your false frozen world I shall melt till it
vanish,
Like snow when the sun breathes upon it, like night that the day
comes to banish.

And I shall destroy all your spider-web morals, the lies you determine;
Your priests with their darkness and falsehoods I come to root out like
the vermin;
Your heavens and hells, and your saviors and prophets, your gods
and your devils,
I come to destroy them, to free all the earth and air from their evils.

So hang me or shoot me, your efforts are futile—a waste of endeavor;
I fear neither prisons nor tortures, nor scaffolds nor awe whatsoever.
Anew I shall rise from the earth, and its surface with weapons shall
    cover,
Until you sink down in your graves, till your power for evil is over.

Basil Dahl (Joseph Bovshover)
(1872—1916)

English version *by J. Leftvich*

A SUMMONS

How long, oh, how long will ye slave for a master?
  How long bear the chains? How long bow your head?
How long pile up wealth and brave all disaster,
  For him who denies you mere bread?
How long will the night last? How long will your eyes
  Be closed to the evil and harm? Look, at length
The day is beginning to dawn! 'Tis time to arise!
  And show to the world your marvelous strength!

Preach truth to your brethren. Preach to the mass;
  Preach freedom through slavery's foul doors;
Preach them to live and to die for their class—
  Teach courage—the battle is yours.

And master and slave shall both disappear
  When humanity's flag is unfurled;
And the fragrance of flowers shall waft through the air
  When Freedom shines over the world.

David Edelstadt
(1866—1892)

English version *by Bella Robbins*

THE BANNER

Not of silk or cloth of gold
  Is it made, our banner fair.
On a wild and awful night,
  When the tempest filled the air,

Roared the ancient spinning-wheel;
  By it, pale Necessity,
In a cellar corner damp,
  By a candle dim to see,

Spun the gray threads for our flag,
  Wove them firm, with care and pains,

Dyed them with the last red drops
From her own exhausted veins.

Every fresh and bleeding wound,
  Every grief and every woe,
From the dungeons underground,
  From the black abyss below;

From the starving villages,
  From the towns where people teem;
Where, deceptive and confused,
  Life is like a nightmare dream;

All the sufferings and pangs
  That for long years void of truth
Had been poisoning her soul
  Like the wicked serpent's tooth;

All things with which Tyranny
  Had opposed her from the start—
Gall he poured into her soul,
  Lead he poured into her heart—

All these things the people's Need
  With the red threads interwove.
Lo, the banner fluttered, waved,
  And toward heaven upward strove!

And the shadows paler grow,
  And the cock's crow sounds afar,
And upon the banner red
  Glimmers now the morning star!

Sh. Frug
(1860—1916)

English version *by Alice Stone Blackwell*

WALL STREET AT NIGHT

THE NARROW street, where only a moment ago life has tossled and
  seethed, is silent now; only dead stillness hovers and waits
  till life will return here.

Here men have sought fortune . . . The petty, the insignificant has
  boomed itself here; here the human beast has bared itself,
  has bargained away peace of soul for silver coins.

Here blood is reeking, from here revenge shouts aloft, here Mammon
　　has horribly sucked out the soul from human beings.

Why has all this noise been? The night is silent, has made an end
　　silently and blackly to the noise, will blot out the noise makers
　　too—and that the end.

M. L. Herbert

English version *by Samuel J. Imber*

From PRISON POEMS

I

THE windows are barred,
And frozen the walls;
Feebly the light
Of the doorlamp falls.

Under a cover
Of gray I lie;
A point on the wall
Has fastened my eye.

I am far from myself,
Forget all I know;
Who knows? perhaps I
Was freed long ago.

And maybe I died,
And dutifully
The doorlamp was lit
In my memory.

II

Dry are the tears,
And laughter is bleak;
The good and the bad
Are equally weak.

Our bodies are beaten
With iron bands,
And he who is fearful
Licks the guard's hands.

We all are shadows
In the house of dead pains.
Does the silence scare you?
Then rattle your chains!

H. Leivick
(1888—　　)

English version *by A. B. Magil*

REVEL, REVEL, ANGRY TEMPESTS!

REVEL, revel, angry tempests,
Sweep across the earth—
Break the branches from the tree-tops,
Ruin is your mirth!

Drive the songsters from the woodland,
Chase them from the sky—
Those that cannot fly your fury
Let them fall and die!

Tear the shutters from the windows,
Smash the panes in glee—
Burn a candle in the darkness,
Quench it angrily!

Revel, revel, tempests, revel,
Break and bend and mar—
Long will last the dreary winter,
Summer is yet far! . . .

Abraham Raisen
(1875—   )

English version *by Alter Brody*

IN THE FACTORY

ALL day in the shop the machines roar so wildly
That often I sink and am lost in the din;
Sunken and lost in the terrible tumult,
The soul in me ceases. . . . I am a machine.
I work and I work and I work without reckoning,
Making, creating—endless the task!
For what? And for whom? I know not, I ask not;
Machine cannot answer, machine cannot ask.

No, here is no feeling, no judgment, no reason;
This labor, the bloody, the endless, suppressed
The noblest and finest, the truest and richest,
The highest, the purest, the humanly best.
The minutes, the hours, the days and the seasons,
They vanish, swift-fleeting like straws in a gale.
I drive the wheel madly as though to overtake them,
I chase without wisdom, or wit, or avail.

The clock in the workshop, it rests not a moment;
It points on, and ticks on: Eternity—Time.

And once someone told me the clock has a meaning—
Its pointing and ticking has reason and rhyme.
And this too he told me—or had I been dreaming?—
The clock wakens life in us, forces unseen;
And something besides. . . . I forget what; oh, ask not!
I know not, I know not, I am a machine.

At times, when I listen, I hear the clock plainly;
The reason of old—the old meaning—is gone.
The maddening pendulum urges me forward
To labor and labor and still labor on.
The tick of the clock is the voice of my master;
The face of the clock is the face of my foe.
The clock—I can hear, I can hear, how it drives me!
It calls me "Machine!" and it cries to me "Sew!"

At noon, when about me the wild tumult ceases,
And gone is the master, and I sit apart,
And dawn in my brain is beginning to glimmer,
The wound comes agape at the core of my heart;
And tears, bitter tears flow; tears that are scalding;
They moisten my dry, meagre dinner—my bread;
They choke me—I cannot! my bread lies uneaten;
Oh, heavy the labor! Oh, bitter the need!

The workshop at mid-day—it is not a workshop:
A battlefield—bloody; a lull on the plain.
Around and about me the corpses are lying,
And out of the earth cries the blood of the slain.
A moment—and listen! The signal is sounded:
The dead rise again, and renewed is the fight.
They struggle, these corpses; for strangers, for strangers!
They struggle, they fall, and they sink into night.

I gaze on the battlefield; wrath flames within me,
And Vengeance and Pain stir their fires in me.
The clock—now I hear it aright!—it is crying:
"An end to the bondage! Arise, and be free!"
It quickens my feeling, it quickens my reason;
It points to the moments, the precious, that fly.
Oh, worthless am I if I longer am silent,
And lost am I, lost! if in silence I die.

The man in me sleeping begins to awaken;
The thing that was slave into slumber has passed:
Now, up with the man in me! Up and be doing!
No misery more! Here is freedom at last!

When sudden: A whistle!—the boss—an alarum!—
I sink in the slime of the stagnant routine;
There's tumult . . . they struggle. . . . Oh, lost is my ego—
I know not, I care not, I am a machine! . . .

Morris Rosenfeld
(1862—1923)

English version *by Rose Pastor Stokes*

From THE PROPHET

I AM the plough, I am the sod,
The tempest, and the lightning's dart.

I am the flood-swell none may pass,
The hurricane that wrecks, pursues.
And I am rain that glad bedews
A desert for one blade of grass.

I am the cloud-mist distant seen,
The echo from a mountain height,
I am a high deed's high delight
And quickening sorrow that makes green.

I am the threshold and the key,
I am the gate and gate-way long.
I am a promise, and a song
With singing woodlands back of me.

Yeoash (Solomon Bloomgarden)
(1870—1927)

English version *by Marie Syrkin*

WORKERS

TORTURED beings who go into subjection
For vast flung-about years. . . .
I am with you, brothers, following you
And carrying your anger within my breast!

Giants in chains of gold and of want
With heads and shoulders bent,
Prophets silenced, mutely you carry
The sentence in your eyes.

And whosoever shall win—you are the victors,
For you are the builders of life!
Your proudness grows and surges within me
More than your lamentations burn me.

Nahum Yood
(1889—   )

English version *by Marcus Graham*

Norwegian

THE MINER

BEETLING rock, with roar and smoke
Break before my hammer-stroke!
Deeper I must thrust and lower
Till I hear the ring of ore.

From the mountain's unplumbed night,
Deep among the gold-veins bright
Diamonds lure me, rubies beckon,
Treasure-hoard that none may reckon.

There is peace within the deep—
Peace and immemorial sleep;
Heavy hammer, burst, as bidden,
To the heart-nook of the hidden.

Once I, too, a careless lad,
Under starry heavens was glad,
Trod the primrose paths of summer,
Child-like knew not care nor cummer.

But I lost the sense of light
In the poring womb of night;
Woodland songs, when earth rejoiced her,
Breathed not down my hollow cloister.

Fondly did I cry, when first
Into the dark place I burst:
"Answer, spirits of the middle
Earth, my life's unending riddle!—"

Still the spirits of the deep
Unrevealed their answer keep;
Still no beam from out the gloomy
Cavern rises to illume me.

Have I erred? Does this way lead
Not to clarity indeed?
If above I seek to find it,
By the glare my eyes are blinded.

Downward then! the depths are best;
There is immemorial rest.
Heavy hammer burst, as bidden,
To the heart-nook of the hidden!—

Hammer-blow on hammer-blow
Till the lamp of life is low.
Not a ray of hope's fore-warning;
Not a glimmer of the morning.

Henrik Ibsen
(1828—1906)

English version *by F. E. Garrett*

Roumanian

WE WANT LAND

(FRAGMENT)

HUNGRY and naked and without a home am I.
My shoulders, you have charged them with loads,
And you spit at me, and you have beaten me,
And I have been to you a dog.
Wandering landowner, brought by the wind,
If you have an understanding with Hell
That we shall be gods to you, beat us more;
We will endure loads, so we will endure want,
Bridle of horses, yoke of cattle:
      But we want land.

A piece of corn left from yesterday,
If you see it in our home, you take it away.
Away you take our boys to the war,
And our girls, you take them too.
You curse our dearest and our holiest things—
No pity have you, nor faith!
Hungry, our children are dying on the road;
And we submit our pity for them—
Our lives would not be such dreadful things
      If we had land.

You have put seed of wheat in the field,
But we have buried here our forefathers and fathers,
Mothers, sisters, and brothers.
Away, you heretics!
Our land is dear and holy to us,
Because it is our cradle and our grave.
With hot blood always we have defended it,
And all the waters that moistened it,
Are but the tears we have shed.
      We want land.

*   *   *   *   *   *

We have no strength and we can't go on
To live always a life of beggary
And of tortures put upon us
By the bosses brought by winds—
Oh, beware, you God Almighty,
That we ask not for land but for blood!
When the time shall come when we can endure no more,
When hunger shall arouse us all, beware of us!
Even were you all Christs, beware!
                    Even in your graves!

George Cosbuc
(1866—1923)

English version *by Maurice Aisen*

Russian

From THE TWELVE

2

THE wind is a whirl, the snow is a dance.
In the night twelve men advance.

Black, narrow rifle-straps,
Cigarettes, tilted caps.

A convict's stripes would fit their backs.
Fire marks their nightly tracks.

Freedom, ekh, freedom—
Unhallowed, unblessed!
Trah-tah-tah! . . .

Fire blazes upon their track.
Their rifle-straps are gleaming black.

March to the revolution's pace,
We've a fierce enemy to face.

More daring, friends, take aim, the lot!
At Holy Russia let's fire a shot.

At hutted Russia,
Fat-rumped and solid,
Russia, the stolid!

Ekh, ekh, unhallowed, unblessed. . . .

9

The city's roar is far away,
Black silence broods on Neva's brink.
No more police! We can be gay,
Comrades, without a drop to drink.

A bourgeois, a lonely mourner,
His nose tucked in his ragged fur,
Stands lost and idle at the corner,
Tagged by a cringing, mangy cur.

The bourgeois like a hungry mongrel,—
A silent question,—stands and begs;
The old world like a kinless mongrel
Stands there, its tail between its legs. . . .

11

And the twelve, unblessed, uncaring,
Still go marching on,
Ripe for death and daring,
Pitying none.

On, with rifles lifted,
At the hidden enemy.
Through deaf alleys where the snow is sifted,
Where the lonely tempest tosses free.
Onward, where the snow has drifted
Clutching at the marcher's knee.

The red flag
Flaunts in their faces.

Steady beat
Their sounding paces.

Grimly followed
Are their traces.

Ruthlessly the storm-wind smites
Days and nights.

Forward, forward, the thundering beat
Of the workers' marching feet.

Alexander Blok
(1880—1921)

English version *by Babette Deutsch and Avrahm Yarmolinsky*

From THE CITY

UNDER a brooding, coal-black pall
  (Its depths lit up by the furnace-glare)
Thou liest fenced with a gateless wall;
  A chimneyed cordon rings thy lair.

A spider of stone and steel and glass,
  Thou swayest thy tangled web of wires:
Thou settest snares which none may pass
  With a subtle skill that never tires.

A dragon, wingless, gorged with food,
  Thou crouchest o'er thy ravined gains,
With gas and water for the blood
  Which courses through thy iron veins.

Thou who at once art fair and foul,
  Hast built thee palaces wrought of gold,
And jewelled brothels, cheek by jowl
  With the hoary monuments of old.

Yet art thou sure thou wilt not list
  To tocsin rung amid those halls
Where now thy courtesans hold tryst
  With those who batten on thy thralls?

Hark, thy taverns ring again
  With the mirthless laughter of debauch—
Of those who seek to drown their pain
  In fiery depths which sear and scorch.

*   *   *   *   *

O wondrous city, 'spite thy glance
  Of snake-like fascination, thou
Hast forged weapons which perchance
  Are poison to strike thee even now.

Valery Bryusov
(1873—1924)

English version *by C. J. Haggarth*

VISION*

FORGOTTEN by the world,
Near the dark sea
I saw a valley
Of deepest grief.

*St. Petersburg Prison, 1907

Under the gloomy sky
In great sadness
Ancient forests
Their branches swayed;
And burning tears
Down dark wrinkles
Of aged trunks
Morosely ran. . . .
The sky lamented;
The waves groaned;
Scowling pines
Longingly moaned.

In that unescapable anguish
Shadows roamed;
Wrung their hands;
Fell on their knees,
Forgotten by the world,—
Their Creator begged . . .
And their song re-echoed
In the sorrowful valley
By the sea and forest,
Like a burial sigh. . . .

No one listened.
Sans sun, *sans* light,
Under everlasting cold,
Without a welcome greeting,
Bound by the sea
And the dreamy forest—
They drank
Burning desperation.

He who had not known in life
Suffering for mankind,
Who in holiday joyousness
Had not heard sobbing,
And had not seen sorrow,
Nor noticed tears,
Him, in the valley,
Sobbing, I met.

V. Eichenbaum
(1882—   )

English version *by Nora Bojarzky*

THE SONG OF THE STORM-FINCH

THE STRONG wind is gathering the storm-clouds together
Above the gray plain of the ocean so wide.
The storm-finch, the bird that resembles dark lightning,
Between clouds and ocean is soaring in pride.

Now skimming the waves with his wings, and now shooting,
Swift, arrow-like, into the dark clouds on high,
The storm-finch is clamoring loudly and shrilly;
The clouds can hear joy in the bird's fearless cry.

In that cry is the yearning, the thirst for the tempest,
And anger's hot might in its wild notes is heard;
The keen fire of passion, the faith in sure triumph—
All these the clouds hear in the voice of the bird.

The sea-gulls lament when a storm is impending,
They flit o'er the waves with a wail in their cry;
They are ready to hide in the depths of the ocean
Their dread of the tempest that threatens on high.

The cargeese and grebes, too, shriek hoarsely in terror,
They mourn and complain when the tempest is near;
They know not the joy of a life-and-death struggle;
The crash of the thunderbolt fills them with fear.

The fat, foolish penguin hides, timid and craven,
In nooks of the cliffs, where it finds a safe home;
Alone the proud storm-finch soars freely and boldly
Above the rough ocean, all hoary with foam.

Still nearer and darker the storm-clouds are lowering
Above the broad ocean; the waves as they beat
Are singing and dancing; they lift themselves upward
As if they were longing the thunder to meet.

The thunder is crashing, the billows are roaring,
And foaming with rage, and they shriek and they gasp
As they strive with the gale. Now the storm-wind clasps fiercely
A bevy of waves in his powerful grasp,

And hurls them, with all his mad strength, in grim fury,
Against the precipitous cliffs of the rock.
The emerald masses of water are shattered
To spray and fine mist by the force of the shock.

The storm-finch, the bird that resembles dark lightning,
Is soaring with cries 'mid the tempest's fierce breath;
Like an arrow he pierces the clouds; with his pinions
He dashes the foam from the billows beneath.

He darts like a haughty black demon of tempest,
In wild exultation that knows no alloy.
'Twixt the sea and the sky he is laughing and sobbing;
He laughs to the clouds, he is sobbing for joy!

In the wrath of the thunder, the keen, quick-eared demon
Has long since detected a note of fatigue.
He is firm in his faith that the clouds will not cover
The bright sun for aye, though they stretch league on league.

The storm-wind is howling, the thunder is roaring;
With flame blue and lambent the cloud-masses glow
O'er the fathomless ocean; it catches the lightnings,
And quenches them deep in its whirlpool below.

Like serpents of fire in the dark ocean writhing,
The lightnings reflected there quiver and shake,
As into the blackness they vanish forever.
The tempest! Now quickly the tempest will break!

The storm-finch soars fearless and proud 'mid the lightnings,
Above the wild waves that the roaring winds fret;
And what is the prophet of victory saying?
"Oh, let the storm burst! Fiercer yet—fiercer yet!"

Maxim Gorky
(1868—   )

English version *by Alice Stone Blackwell*

LION AND GNAT

BE GENTLE with the small,
And think it shame to do the feeble wrong!
The vengeance of the weak is very often strong.
Then be not arrogant, nor think that strength is all.
I have a tale to tell you that,—
Of how the lion's pride was humbled by a gnat.
Well, here, as I've been told, is how the story went:
The lion with the gnat put on a cold contempt.
The gnat was filled with rage; he could not stand the slight.
The gnat he rose in arms and sallied forth to fight.
He's knight and bugler, too; he trumps with all his breath
And challenges his foe to fight him to the Death.
The lion laughs; but gnat's not jesting.
On back, or eyes, or ears, our trumpeter comes pesting;

And picking out his spot, and waiting for his chance,
With eagle's swoop he lunges
And in the back his sting he plunges.
The lion quivers; at the foe his tail he flaunts.
But nimble is our gnat; besides, he knows no fear.
Full on the forehead perched, he is sucking near the brain;
The lion twists his head, the lion shakes his mane;
Our hero strikes and strikes again,
Gets home upon the nose, or pricks behind the ear.
How lion swore!
How terrible his roar!
He grinds his teeth with foaming jaws;
He tears the earth up with his claws.
The forest shakes all round, those awful tones to hear;
The beasts are terror-struck, they hide, they fly in fear,
The best foot first, and quick at that,
As if the flood had come, or some great conflagration.
And who? A gnat
Has thrown them into this consternation.
The lion's rage is spent; his frantic efforts cease;
He falls upon the ground and sues the gnat for peace.
The gnat has slaked his ire; his ardor he restrains.
Achilles' part is played; 'tis Homer's now remains;
His own
The trump that to the woods shall make his triumph known.

Ivan Krylov
(1768—1844)

English version *by Bernard Pares*

A THOUGHT

I GAZE with grief upon our generation.
Its future black or vacant—and to-day,
Bent with a load of doubt and understanding,
In sloth and cold stagnation it grows old.
When scarcely from the cradle we were rich
In follies, in our father's tardy wits.
Life wearied us—a road without a goal,
A feast upon a foreign holiday.
Toward good and evil shamefully impassive,
In mid-career we fade without a fight.
Before a danger pusillanimous,
Before a power that scorns us we are slaves.
Precocious fruit, untimely ripe, we hang,
Rejoicing neither sight nor touch nor tongue,
A wrinkled orphan runt among the blossoms,
Their beauty's hour the hour of our decay.

The hues of poetry, the shapes of art,
Wake in our minds no lovely ecstasy.
We hoard the dregs of feelings that are dead,
Misers, we dig and hide a debased coin.
We hate by chance, we love by accident;
We make no sacrifice to hate or love.
Within our minds presides a secret chill
Even while the flame is burning in our blood.
A bore to us our fathers' gorgeous sporting,
Their conscientious childish vast debauch.
We hasten tomb-wards without joy or glory,
With but a glance of ridicule thrown back.
A surly-hearted crowd and soon forgotten,
We pass in silence, trackless from the world,
Tossing no fruit of dreaming to the ages,
No deed of genius even half begun.
Our dust the justice of the citizen
In future time will judge in songs of scorn. . . .
Will celebrate the weak and squandering father
In bitter mockery the cheated son.

Mikhail Yuryevich Lermontov
(1814—1841)

English version *by Max Eastman*

SONG OF THE OLD "REBBLE"*

ME HAVE ye gaoled and chained and burned,
I have writhed in bitter agony;
I have wasted to death for liberty;—
But how to slay me ye never learned.

I have gnawed my fingers lacking food;
I have rotted in dungeons dank, forlorn;
My flesh in shreds vultures have torn
And feasted in the martyr's blood.

And I have been one running sore
Under the lash, my life's blood lost.
And oft my carcass, ocean-tossed,
From ocean-deeps was washed ashore.

But from my ashes to new birth
I rise again, I rise from death;
My soul, returning home to earth,
Builds a new body for its breath.

*From *Faust and the City*

I went, I come, I shall not rest;
I will eat through the whole world's chains;
I will dry the tears of all oppressed,—
The last of tears for the last of pains.

How shall I dry the tears of woe,
Tears of oppressed and humbled slaves!
Down with the tyrant's purple show!
To your graves, princes! Down to your graves!

Down! And be ancient wrongs forgot,
And cleansed be all hearts of pride,
When, in their blood-stained graves to rot,
Your heads and crowns fall side by side!

A. V. Lunacharsky
(1876—   )

OCTOBER

WE TRAMPLE filial obedience,
We have gone and sat down saucily,
Keeping our hats on,
Our feet on the table.

You don't like us, since we guffaw with blood,
Since we don't wash rags washed millions of times,
Since we suddenly dared
Ear-splittingly to bark: Wow!

Yes, sir, the spine
Is as straight as a telephone pole,
Not my spine only, but the spine of all Russians,
For centuries hunched.

Who makes a louder noise on earth now than we?
You say: Bedlam—
No milestones—no stakes—
Straight to the devil—On the church porch our red cancan is glorious.

What, you don't believe? Here are hordes,
Droves of clouds at men's beck and call,
And the sky like a woman's cloak,
And no eyelash of sun.

Jesus is on the cross again, and Barabbas
We escort, mealy-mouthed, down the Tverskoi Prospect. . . .
Who will interrupt, who? The gallop of Scythian horses?
Violins bowing the Marseillaise?

Has it ever before been heard of, that the forger
Of steel bracelets for the globe
Should smoke his rotten tobacco as importantly
As the officer used to clink his stirrups?

You ask—And then?
And then dancing centuries.
We shall knock at all doors
And no one will say: Goddamyou, get out!

We! We! We are everywhere:
Before the footlights, in the center of the stage,
Not softy lyricists,
But flaming buffoons.

Pile rubbish, all the rubbish in a heap,
And like Savonarola, to the sound of hymns,
Into the fire with it. . . . Whom should we fear?
When the mundiculi of puny souls have become worlds?

Every day of ours is a new chapter in the Bible.
Every page will be great to thousands of generations.
We are those about whom they will say:
The lucky ones lived in 1917.
And you are still shouting: They perish!

You are still whimpering lavishly.
Dunderheads!
Isn't yesterday crushed, like a dove
By a motor
Emerging madly from the garage?

Anatoly Marienhof
(1897—   )

English version *by Babette Deutsch and Avrahm Yarmolinsky*

OUR MARCH

SLOG BRUTE streets with rebel tramping!
Higher, the crags of haughty heads!
We will wash all the planets' cities
In the surge of a second flood.

Pied days, these.
Slow drags the dray of years.
Our god's Speed.
Our hearts are drums.

Who can match the glow of our gods?
Will the waspy bullets bite?
We strike back with songs for weapons.
Massive gold—our thundering voices.

Lacquer the lawn, green,
Carpet the days, grass;
Harness the quick years, sky,
Under a rainbow yoke.

Look at heaven, gaping with boredom:
We have shut it out from our songs.
Hey, Great Dipper, demand
That they hoist us to heaven alive.

Drink to joy! Shout!
Spring has flooded our blood.
Heart, exult, beat!
Our hearts are as crashing brass.

Vladimir Mayakovsky
(1894—   )

English version *by Babette Deutsch and Avrahm Yarmolinsky*

IN THE CROWD

Score not the crowd, though true at times she be
Shallow and petty, soulless and blind.
For there are moments when the crowd you see
Not as a wretched slave and venal soul,
But a kingdom—the crowd, a titan; the crowd!
You are not just with her: for in her suffering
You did not go to suffer with her—you her bard, her son!
You shunned her cursing, shunned her wailing,
You loved her from afar, suffered with her alone!
Come and blend with her, let not the moment pass by
When in her weakness she is responsive,
When from deeds evil and evil in intention,
With grievous losses she is shaken!

Semion Yakovlevitch Nadson

FORWARD

LEAVE your sorrows for a while
Yield not when a storm's in sight,
Struggle for the distant smile
Of the bright dawn through the night.
Strive, meanwhile your life-bread earning,
In the name of light and learning
Place your honest torch on high!
Though they stamp you with disdain,
Though the crowd in its vexation
Hurls at you, perhaps in vain,
Over-hasty condemnation,
Go! Nor let your courage fail!
Go that trodden path of strife,
Never let your bosom quail
At the storm of struggling life!
To the fallen lend your hand,
Waken those in darkness dreaming,
And as in the crowd you stand,
Hurl the Truth-torch brightly gleaming!

Semion Yakovlevitch Nadson
(1862—1889)

English version *by Helen J. Harwitt*

YE SONGS OF MINE

YE SONGS of mine! Of universal sorrows
  A living witness ye;
Born of the passion of the soul, bewailing,
  Tempestuous and free,
The hard heart of humanity assailing
  As doth her cliffs the sea.

N. A. Nekrassov
(1821—1877)

English version *by Marta Gilbert Dickinson*

IN ALEXIS RAVELIN*

ALWAYS the same dim, cheerless, dusty vaults,
  The same bars darkening all the window space!
Long ranks of years, that seem like evil dreams
  In broken sleep, stretch out before my face.

*P. Polivanov was a revolutionist who attempted the rescue of some friends from prison. Being caught, he was sentenced to twenty years imprisonment in the fortress of Schlüsselburg. At the end of his term, after being released, shattered in nerves, he committed suicide.

If but one distant sound could here be heard
   Of life, broad, free, and seething like the main,
It would have stirred me with its mighty strength
   And eased the burden of this torturing pain.

No, all around me reigns a deathly hush,
   Heart-crushing, grave-like; in it nothing stirs
Save now and then the buzzing of a fly,
   Or in the corridor the clash of spurs.

Bright burden of emotions and of strife,
   Time of impassioned hope and fancy high,
Of faith in glad days for posterity—
   Where are you now? Vanished as dreams go by!

A mist has settled over all the past,
   Enwrapping it forever in its shroud;
And it has thickened to a winding sheet—
   And hangs above me like a boding cloud.

That leaden cloud depresses heavily;
   It chills the brain, with long confinement worn,
And pierces deep my soul with poison hot
   Of black and heavy thoughts, in prison born.

P. Polivanov

English version *by Alice Stone Blackwell*

MESSAGE TO SIBERIA

DEEP in the Siberian mine,
Keep your patience proud;
The bitter toil shall not be lost,
The rebel thought unbowed.

The sister of Misfortune, Hope,
In the under-darkness dumb,
Speaks joyful courage to your heart:
The day desired will come.

And love and friendship pour to you
Across the darkened doors,
Even as round your galley-beds
My free music pours.

The heavy-hanging chains will fall,
The walls will crumble at a word;
And freedom greet you in the light,
And brothers give you back the sword.

Alexander Sergeyevitch Pushkin
(1799—1837)

English version *by Max Eastman*

THE REVOLUTIONIST

I saw a spacious house. O'erhung with pall,
A narrow doorway pierced the sombre wall.
Within was chill, impenetrable shade;
Without there stood a maid—a Russian maid,
To whom the icy dark sent forth a slow
And hollow-sounding Voice:

"And dost thou know,
When thou hast entered, what awaits thee here?"
"I know," she said, "and knowing do not fear."
"Cold, hunger, hatred, Slander's blighting breath."
The Voice still chanted, "suffering—and Death?"
"I know," she said.

"Undaunted, wilt thou dare
The sneers of kindred? Art thou steeled to bear
From those whom most thou lovest, spite and scorn?"
"Though love be paid with hate, that shall be borne,"
She answered.

"Think! Thy doom may be to die
By thine own hand, with none to fathom why,
Unthanked, unhonored, desolate, alone,
Thy grave unmarked, thy toil, thy love unknown,

And none in days to come shall speak thy name."
She said: "I ask no pity, thanks, or fame."
"Art thou prepared for crime?"
She bowed her head:
"Yes, crime, if that shall need," the maiden said.

Now paused the Voice before it asked anew:
"But knowest thou that all thou holdest true
Thy soul may yet deny in bitter pain,
So thou shalt deem thy sacrifice in vain?"
"E'en this I know," she said, "and yet again
I pray thee, let me enter."

"Enter then!"
That hollow Voice replied. She passed the door.
A sable curtain fell—and nothing more.
"A fool!" snarled some one, gnashing. Like a prayer,
"A saint!" the whispered answer thrilled the air.

Ivan Turgeniev
(1818—1883)

English version from the prose-poem *by Arthur Guiterman*

AS OCEAN'S STREAM

As OCEAN's stream girdles the ball of earth,
From circling seas of dream man's life emerges,
And as night moves in silence up the firth
The secret tide around our mainland surges.

The voice of urgent waters softly sounds;
The magic skiff uplifts white wings of wonder.
The tide swells swiftly and the white sail rounds,
Where the blind waves in shoreless darkness thunder.

And the wide heavens, starred and luminous,
Out of the deep in mystery aspire.
The strange abyss is burning under us;
And we sail onward, and our wake is fire.

Fyodor Tyutchev
(1803—1873)

English version *by Babette Deutsch and Avrahm Yarmolinsky*

TRANSFIGURATION

EY, RUSSIANS!
Fishermen of the universe,
You who have scooped sky with the net of dawn,
Blow your trumpets!

The earth is roaring
Beneath the plow of the storm;
The golden-tusked plow
Is crushing the rocks.

A new sower wanders
Across the fields.
He throws new seeds
Into the furrows.

A radiant guest is riding
Toward you in a chariot.
Across the clouds
A wild mare races.

The breeching of the mare:
The blue.
The bells on the breeching;
—The stars.

Sergey Yesenin
(1895—1925)

English version *by Alexander Kann and Roberta Holloway*

THE ANARCHIST MARCH

LET's sing a song under sounding blows,
Under explosions and bullets, under blazing flames,
Under the Black Banner of gigantic battle,
Under alarming sounds of the calling bugle.

Tear down, brothers, palaces and temples,
Let's break the chains, tear down the crowns;
Enough submission and slavish love—
We'll drown the sufferings of the people in blood!

Awaken, arouse, the will of the masses
At the Commune's groans and Ravaschol's call,
At the clamoring of revenge for the perished masses,
Under the bourgeoisie oppression and hangman's knotting toll.

They are many, countless, suffering victims,
Murdered on the headsman's block, perished in prisons;
It's true, they are many, serving you
Who have fallen in the heroic class struggle.

Their moans call from under the skies of Russia,
Their groans call, like whispering voices,
Echoing over Paris, Siberia's dullness,
As they call to valiant battle. . . .

Anonymous

English version *by Marcus Graham*

Sanskrit

POVERTY*

A BEGGAR to the graveyard hied
And there "Friend corpse, arise," he cried;
"One moment lift my heavy weight
Of poverty; for I of late
Grow weary and desire instead
Your comfort; you are good and dead."
The corpse was silent. He was sure
'Twas better to be dead than poor.

*From *The Panchatantra*
English version *by Arthur W. Ryder*

Spanish

MY CLARION CALL

COME to me, O ye sorrowful and hungry!
Come to me, ye who here are cursed and naked!
All the helpless mothers, mad to see your children
Suffer agonies that cleave the heart asunder!
Come to me, ye weak and pallid children,
Ye who sacrifice your blood for all the lusty!
Aye, to me, starving mob, bring your sorrows!
Come to me, O ye prostitutes and lepers!
All ye thieves, all ye dirty, crawling beggars
Weeping for the bread ye are deprived of!
Come to me, ye who cross the field and cities,
Gnawing at your wrists, and with fits of anger,
Heaping up your breasts with bitter feelings
For the frowning men in coming generations!
Come, yes, come, O eternally forsaken!
Come, and haughty stand with me before the tyrant,
And like iron, facing him with our rebellion,
Steel and iron, yes, and so to be the harder!
I, O mob, am the minstrel of your grievings!
And this voice—roaring like a mad rebellion—
Is your voice—rising from your slimy caverns—
Light and pain—which, uprising to the heavens,
Seem the clamor of your voices in your ragings,
Calling forth all human souls to struggle,
And redeeming all the world from the barbarians!

Alberto Giraldo

From "ANARCHS"

THE MUTE gapings of the mine
Swallowed phalanxes of workers
Who, suspended over hideous gulfs,
Seem swallows
Poised at fantastic heights;
Phosphorescent as glow-worms,
Yellowish, tremulous,
Along dizzy edges their torches prick the dark;
And, blackened with coal,
They cling down the cold tunnels
Like a wretched colony of beetles
Boring a rotten tree.

* * * * *

Miserable artists, your vain dream
Flies lonely amid the shadows

As fireflies threading a summer night.
The murderous light of the lamps,
Gilding the arrogant columns,
Will scorch your immortal brows
And your sapphire wings, O madmen!
Without bread or love or a cave
Where sleep might ease your fever,
You succumb to the barbarous chain
Dragging you toward the Seine-mud:
Dogs, miners, artists,
The arid enclosures that shut you in
Consume your livid flesh;
And in the world's Sahara
You find the water of tears only.

Valencia Guillermo

English version *by Muna Lee*

FAREWELL! *

WE CANNOT break our chains with weak desire,
With whines and supplicating cries.
'Tis not by crawling meekly in the mire
The free-winged eagle learns to mount the skies.

The gladiator, victor in the fight,
On whom the hard-contested laurels fall,
Goes not in the arena pale with fright
But steps forth fearlessly, defying all.

O victory, O victory, dear and fair,
Thou crownest him who does his best,
Who, perishing, still unafraid to bear,
Goes down to dust, thy image in his breast.

Farewell, O comrades, I scorn life as a slave!
I begged no tyrant for my life, though sweet it was;
Though chained, I go unconquered to my grave,
Dying for my own birth-right—and the world's.

Ricardo Flores Magón

---

*Written just before his death (1923) while incarcerated in the Federal prison, Leavenworth, Kansas. Magon was an active Mexican rebel, and at the behest of the Mexican Government the U. S. Government seized him, its agents beat him up fiercely and afterwards held him for years in jail, until his death.—M.G.

THE CLOUD

WHY dost thou grieve, as rises from the sea
The cloud, black-hooded, climbing silently
Towards heaven's height?
From it fresh coolness through the sky shall flow,
And pure the air and green the ground shall grow,
And fair the light.
Then tremble not! Let storm-winds rage with might,
Let deafening thunders roll, fierce lightning smite
Wide, far and free.
These dread convulsions do not come in vain;
The people, with strong hands of ruddy stain,
Win Liberty!

Salvador Diaz Miron
(Mexico)

English version *by Alice Stone Blackwell*

MY SHIELD

PROTECTION beg I none from men of might,
Nor adulate the lofty with a smile;
Alone, and with my shield resplendent, I'll
Withstand the harsh clash of the fearful fight.
My breast by manly fury is made light;
And breathes no truce nor rest for any while.
I do not fear the prison dark and vile,
Let retrogrades and traitors great and small
Avenge their rancor and their wrath on me,
A noble heart feels slander not at all;
And my stark hand forever-more shall wield
Not the unworthy knife of tyranny
But Right's good sword: by this I keep the field.

Alfonzo Zepedo

English version *by Steven F. Byington*

Ukrainian

THE HAIDAMAKY—"KNIGHTS OF VENGEANCE"

"HAIDAMAKY" they call us, unrelenting and stern,
With the wrongs of our nation for vengeance we burn.

Our forebears were tortured; our grandsons will be
Unless we shall show them how men may be free.

Haidamaky they call us, forever the same,
And we lay down our lives, caring nothing for fame.

For the time long has passed when the yoke pressed us sore:
If a hundred shall fall there are yet thousands more.

Out of misery's chains the trampled shall rise,
And to Freedom's bright flag they will lift dazzled eyes.

Truth and courage for oath, and our vengeance for breath—
Haidamaky they call us, men who fear not their death.

Taras Sewchenko
(1814—1861)

English version *by Florence Randal Livesay*

TO THE POETS

"ART—that's a bourgeois invention!" . . .
"Art—for enjoyment only!" . . .
"Counter-revolution—art!" . . .
Thus are yelling cripples on the highway,—
Like reptiles. . .

Cry of a slave—'tis enjoyment his?
Creative pain—bourgeoisie's relish?
Counter-revolution—to aspire to freedom? . . .
Ay, foolish, trice foolish—whoever thinks so!

How then—cannot suffering and pain
      be embraced by art?
Cannot aspiration of a down-trodden class
      be introduced in a work of art?
And who's he that hates such art?
      —Beast!

Oh, ye bards of a down-trodden class!
Oh, ye poets, sensitive troubadours,—
Awake! . . . Into masses! . . .
Tear away the blind—background for whimsical ego—
And strike thunder like Eolian strings
And call out the life, and call out tornadoes . . .
Be like wind that disperses clouds,—
Let the strings rebound, let the trumpets thunder!

Nicholas Tarnowsky
(1895—   )

INDEX

LaVergne, TN USA
03 January 2009
168733LV00014B/110/A